PROSPERO'S RETURN?

Historical Essays on Race, Culture and British Society

Paul B Rich

Publication

To Andrew and Diana Larman

.

First published in 1994 by Hansib Publishing Limited.
Tower House, 141-149 Fonthill Road, London N4 3HF,
England

Typeset and produced by Hansib Publishing Ltd, London
Printed by Bracken Press, Hatfield, Hertfordshire

Cover design by Kash Ali and Stefan Brazzo
Cover illustration by Shareef Ali

British Library Cataloguing in Publication Data
Rich, Paul B., *1950 –*
Prospero's Return? Historical essays on race, culture and
British society.

1. Great Britain. Race relations.
I. Title
305.8'00941

ISBN 1–870518–40–3

We shall not cease from exploration
And the end of all our exploring
Will be to arrive where we started
And know the place for the first time.

T S Eliot.

Acknowledgements

I would like to thank the editors of the following journals for allowing me to republish the articles which make up the chapters of this book: Introduction partly formed from "The Quest For Englishness", *History Today*, 37 (June 1987), pp. 24-30; Chapter One reprinted from *History of European Ideas*, 9, 4 (1988); Chapter Two reprinted from *Patterns of Prejudice*, 18, 3 (July 1984), pp. 3-17; Chapter Three reprinted from *Ethnic and Racial Studies*, 7, 4 (October 1984), pp. 536-52; Chapter Four reprinted from *New Community*, XII, 1 (winter 1984-85), pp. 75-88; Chapter Five reprinted from *New Community*, XIII, I (spring-summer 1986), pp. 1-17; Chapter Six reprinted from *Immigrants and Minorities*, 6, 2 (July 1987), pp. 151-73; Chapter Seven reprinted from *History Today*, 36 (January 1986), pp. 14-20; Chapter Nine reprinted from *Ethnic and Racial Studies*, 10, 2 (April 1987), pp. 149-68.

Also by Paul B Rich

White Power and the Liberal Conscience:
Racial Segregation and South African Liberalism, 1921-60

Race and Empire in British Politics

Race, Government and Politics in Britain (with Zig Layton Henry)

The Dynamics of Change in Southern Africa (editor)

Hope and Despair: English Speaking Intellectuals and
South African Politics, 1896-1976

Contents

Abbreviations

ANC	African National Congress
APS	Anti-Slavery and Aborigines Protection Society
APU	African Progress Union
CARD	Campaign Against Racial Discrimination
CO	Colonial Office
CRO	Commonwealth Relations Office
ILO	International Labour Organisation
ILP	Independent Labour Party
LCP	League of Coloured Peoples
MCF	Movement for Colonial Freedom
NAACP	National Association for the Advancement of Coloured People
NCCL	National Council for Civil Liberties
PAC	Pan-Africanist Congress
RRG	Race Relations Group of the Institute of Sociology
SCM	Student Christian Movement
UNESCO	United Nations Economic Social and Cultural Organisation
WASU	West African Students Union
WISC	West Indian Standing Conference
YMCA	Young Men's Christian Association

Introduction

Race, Immigration and the Question of "Englishness"

The settlement in the post war period of black ethnic minority communities in British society raises fundamental questions about Britain's history and cultural identity. The presence of black communities within Britain represents a challenge not only at the political and economic level, as cumulative evidence has revealed extensive racial discrimination and interracial hostility by the middle to late 1960s, but also to British society's conception of its identity and values. In one sense, many of the dilemmas within British imperial history have been brought home to indigenous British society after a long period in which empire and imperialism were treated as marginal phenomena of limited significance or interest. The ghost of Prospero, Shakespeare's prototypical empire builder in *The Tempest*, can perhaps be seen to have returned to the land of his birth. The theme of empire and its resulting impact on British institutions and values has thus become of considerable significance for scholars and analysts trying to explain the reluctance of British society to adapt to an emergent multiracial society.

It is clear that the imperial experience bit deep into British society and culture, and was of considerable importance in helping to forge a mythology of homogeneous British national identity that overlaid internal class divisions in the middle to late nineteenth century.[1]

The awareness of this process, and indeed of its scope, even now has not fully dawned in a broad range of British historiography. In part, this can be explained by the compartmentalisation of imperial history into a separate subdiscipline. The study of imperial intrusion into overseas territories and the resulting colonial annexation is treated in isolation from internal British society and culture. "Empire" and its wide-ranging economic, ideological and political ramifications appeared to be a separate phenomenon from British society itself, which some hoped would resurface phoenix-like in the wake of the empire's demise in the 1950s and 1960s.

The hope that British society could in some manner engage in a collective return to the status quo which existed before the advent of imperialism in the last quarter of the nineteenth century has been undermined by the presence of people whose migration to Britain had occurred through the imperial link. Communities of Afro-Caribbean and South Asian settlers in Britain are a powerful reminder that empire has connoted not only a complex mosaic of differing patterns of rule and government over alien territories, but also a system of economic, ideological and cultural linkages forged over a period of some four centuries from the time of the Elizabethan merchant adventurers of the sixteenth century. It has not been easy to disconnect quickly from such a long imperial past. The imperial legacy rested on the growth and expansion of the slave trade in the seventeenth and eighteenth centuries, the advent of "free trade imperialism" in the middle nineteenth century and on the final burst of imperial expansion from the end of the 1870s with the "Scramble for Africa" and the acquisition of a number of colonies in Africa, the Pacific and the Middle East. It really only finished with the end of the Second World War and the beginnings of decolonisation with Indian and Pakistani independence in 1947.

The retreat from empire was a carefully orchestrated one, with only a few hiccups such as Rhodesia and the Falklands. The nature of the imperial purpose became redefined away from the Victorian ideal of *mission civilisatrice* and uplifting "backward races" to that of a beneficent "Commonwealth of Nations". The Commonwealth ideal took over in imperial discourse from the end of the First World War onwards and served, in the vital decolonisation period after the Second World War, as a slogan to mask from British public opinion the full impact of the retreat from "great power" status. Even as late as the 1930s, Britain, as the centre of a worldwide imperial system, had many of the trappings of a superpower,[2] so that the rapid decline to a minor island off the west coast of Europe was an enormous political and cultural shock. The continuing notion, though, that Britain and its monarch remained the hub of the Commonwealth was able in part to compensate for this massive loss of international prestige. But it was not understood that the wider imperial heritage within British society had generated deep resistance to the attempts to make the British imperial mission an apparently benign one.

These strains form the substance of a number of chapters in this volume which is concerned with exploring the ideological debates that accompanied the rise of nineteenth-century imperialism and then pursuing them into the twentieth century and the era of decolonisation and black New Commonwealth immigration. These chapters have been written as a continuation of the work behind the volume *Race and Empire in British Politics*[3] which sought to trace the theme of racist ideas and imperial expansion into the twentieth century and the era of formal abandonment of colonies in the 1940s and 1950s. However, they are also concerned with the emergence of a distinct notion of British nationalism in the course of the late nineteenth and early twentieth centuries as a number of writers and intellectuals engaged in a return to their "roots" as the imperial ideal failed.

The Problem of Nationalism

Nationalism in English society has not been a subject that has especially interested historians and social analysts until comparatively recently. This is perhaps a legacy of the Whig domination of English historiography and its emphasis on parliament and good government to the exclusion of political doctrine, which has often been seen as more of a problem confronting central European political history. The attainment of political stability by the mid-Victorian era has usually been perceived as a result of both the insulation of English politics from the turbulence of European nationalism and a preoccupation with issues surrounding the moral responses to industrialisation and urbanisation.

Even in its heyday in the nineteenth century, the "condition of England" question assumed a unique cultural and political entity entitled "England". There was, in a considerable body of Victorian thought, a conscious idea of England that, not although reaching the ideological precision of European nationalist visionaries such as Mazzini, nevertheless exerted a hold over both educated opinion and more popular sentiments.

Unlike many of its European neighbours, England lacked a nationalist intelligentsia and by the 1880s much of the energy of intellectual opinion passed into a wider imperial enthusiasm that came to be termed (after a book by Sir Charles Dilke published in 1867) *Greater Britain*.[4] Many historians of the latter part of the century chose to emphasise the growth in imperial sentiment in England's mission and to show how more parochial and inward-looking versions of English patriotism tended to become eclipsed by a more expansionist jingoism that culminated in the "mafficking" mobs of the Anglo-Boer War of 1899-1902.

If imperialism came to define a considerable variety of English national ideals from the 1880s onwards, it was hardly a complete or all-embracing phenomenon. Carried to its logical conclusion, empire would have superseded any sense of English nationalism through the attainment of some wider imperial entity. This was the theme of much imperialist historiography in the tradition of J R Seeley's *The Expansion of England* (1883) which emphasised an historical process which absorbed English development into a transcontinental and imperial one. It was an ideal which by no means commanded universal assent. As the historian Edward A Freeman warned his colleagues in *Macmillan's Magazine* in 1885, 'the soberest of us will be driven to turn Jingoes and sing "Rule Britannia" if we are asked that Great Britain shall sink to become one canton or three cantons of Greater Britain.'[5] Imperial federation seemed to threaten English national identity at a time when economic and industrial changes increasingly divorced the population from its rural roots. Thus, while the imperial idea and the pursuit of some form of "Anglo-Saxon" alliance with fellow white English-speaking societies in Australia, America and South Africa appealed to some imperial enthusiasts in the years up to the Boer War, there were already signs of an important cultural and intellectual movement towards an indentification with the native English landscape and culture.

Some recent cultural historians such as Herbert Sussman and Martin Weiner have begun to look more closely at the indigenous cultural forces within nineteenth-century English society which resisted a ready identification with economic expansion and urban industrialisation. In contrast to the emphasis in imperial historiography on the 1880s, the "scramble for Africa" and the mobilisation of pro-imperial opinion by the yellow press, this "economic backwardness" school has sought to explain contemporary problems of British economic decline by looking to the progressive failure of nineteenth-century capitalism in a society which was the first to undergo an industrial revolution. For this school, the decade of the 1850s was crucial to the emergence of an intellectual climate increasingly critical of the ravages of industrialisation and the brutalisation of an urban working class. While earlier writers like Carlyle had been willing to accept both city life and the disciplines of the Protestant work ethic, from the middle of the century onwards there began to surface a moral crusade against industrialism in such novels as Dicken's *Hard Times* (1854), Ruskin's *Unto This Last* and in the radical attacks on capitalism from such figures as William Morris, H M Hyndman and Edward Carpenter.[6]

More recently, though, Alun Hawkins has argued (in an essay "The Discovery of Rural England" in the collection edited by Robert Colls and Philip Dodd, *Englishness: Politics and Culture*) that the formation of the

English cultural myth accompanied the incorporation of the industrial middle class into the commercial bourgeoisie of the south and London. [7] The earlier Gothic ideal in architecture was displaced by a more self-conscious moral pastoralism and a search for the life and culture of villages. In many respects, this was a retreat to the ideal of "merrie England" and a pre-industrial and medieval culture in which human relationships had not yet been complicated by the cash nexus or the demands of profit. It was, also, the assertion of a sense of English cultural and national identity at a time when this appeared to be threatened by more cosmopolitan forces within industry or empire building. It is to this movement in the late nineteenth century, especially after 1880, that we should look for the roots of the English national ideal.

The moral reaction to the Victorian industrialism was significant for its identification with an English national ideal rooted in a mythical past. As Mark Girouard has shown in an important analysis of Victorian culture, there was a general cult of medieval and courtly romance in nineteenth-century England following the romantic historical novels of Sir Walter Scott. [8] It was possible for such ideals to be fitted into a mission of building an imperial "Greater Britain" overseas, and indeed many imperial novels emphasised the chivalric aspects of colonial adventurers and the need to protect white womanhood from the dangers of black savages. The chivalric theme related even more directly to the visible symbols of Britain's (or more especially England's) past, especially with the growing interest in Tudor history and the exploits of the Elizabethan merchant adventurers such as Raleigh, Drake and Hawkins.

The "merrie England" myth embraced both a moral critique of capitalist industrialism and a search into England's distant past.[9] This to a considerable degree led to a conservative appropriation of a radical patriotic discourse and the blunting of any potential radical populism. The movement was exemplified by the publication in 1885 of the novel by the naturalist Richard Jefferies, *After London*, in which the capital city and urban civilisation in general are swept away and a return made to a medieval social order in close harmony with nature. London has disappeared into a black, poisonous lake, and the hero of the story ends up marrying and planning to settle down in a fortified castle. The book had a considerable impact and William Morris read it aloud to his friends in his Oxford rooms. Morris' own *News from Nowhere* (1890) was written in a similar idiom; the hero dreams of a future golden age in which a medieval society has returned to England and where human sensibilities, especially sexual ones, are allowed free play in a communist-like society liberated from the restrictions of urban capitalist living. Here was an alternative kind of adventure which sought to avoid the rapacious exploits of Victorian imperialism.

The mythical nature of this medievalism was undoubtedly significant for a generation whose religious uncertainties had been undermined by the advent of Darwinism, and who felt insecure in a rapidly urbanising world. Between 1801 and 1901 the population of England and Wales grew by 24 million, 80 per cent of whom lived in towns. Furthermore, the development of capitalist agriculture produced rapid mechanical and technological changes causing the old rural population to be increasingly divided along class lines. By the 1880s it became apparent that much of the older rural way of life was disappearing. It seemed especially important to many writers to anchor what was happening within some kind of historical tradition. Jefferies, for all the power of *After London*, was out of tune with this historical consciousness, preferring to pursue a more mystical nature religion which tried to deny the dominant evolutionist faith of the age. His autobiography, *The Story of My Heart* (1883), which was taken seriously by a number of his contemporaries, urged that there was 'no evolution any more than there is design in nature. By standing face to face with nature, and not from books, I have convinced myself that there is no design and no evolution. What there is, what was the course, how and why, is yet not known.'[10]

Such mysticism had its attractions for a minority in British society and filtered down into movements like theosophy in the early years of the twentieth century. But for an age attracted by science, more concrete explanations were demanded and the search for English roots became bound up with attempts at producing a "science" of race. In many cases, theories of the racial origins of the English people tended to reinforce views concerning their "Saxon" or "Teutonic" origin.[11]

This obsession with historical continuity and the notion of the English as the racial "survivors" of earlier demographic migrations were confirmed by the biologist and Darwinian anthropologist, Thomas Henry Huxley. In a paper entitled "On Some Fixed Points in British Ethnology" in 1871, Huxley saw Britain as made up of only two main races, the dark-skinned 'Melanochroi' and the light-skinned 'Xanthochroi'. These he saw as continuous from the time of Tacitus' observations during the Roman occupation. This distinction broadly resembled the traditional "Celtic" and "Teutonic" classification of racial types in British society, with the Celts resident mainly in the north and the west and the Teutons scattered over other parts of the British Isles.[12]

The interest in race in the 1860s and 1870s reflected a wider European interest in national identities at a time when Italy and Germany obtained national unification. The pseudoscience of anthropometry became increasingly popular as the measurement of skulls and the heads of the living people seemed to provide a method of establishing patterns of "racial" continuity on scientific grounds. In 1884 the mathematician and founder of the pseudoscience of eugenics, Sir Francis Galton (a cousin of Charles Darwin), measured some 9,000 people at an International Health Exhibition in South Kensington. Although fierce disputes remained among physical anthropologists as to the exact criteria by which anthropometric "types" might be established, the notion that there were scientific and biological entities called "races" pervaded a considerable proportion of the literature in England and English national identity.

The effect of this Darwinian anthropology lay especially in its reinforcing the idea of the distinctiveness of races. Earlier writers, like Ralph Waldo Emerson in *English Traits* (1854), had emphasised English racial ancestry, but had also written of the intermixture of such elements as "Celt" and "Saxon". Emerson had seen English nationality as a southern English phenomenon, based mainly on the character of the English governing class:

> It excludes Ireland, and Scotland, and Wales, and reduces itself at last to London, that is, to those who come and go thither. The portraits that hang on the walls in the Academy Exhibition at London, the figures in Punch's drawings of the public men, or of the club houses, the prints in the shop windows, are distinctive English, not American, no, nor Scotch, nor Irish: but 'tis a very restricted nationality. As you go north into the manufacturing and agricultural districts, and go to the population that never travels, as you go into Yorkshire, as you enter Scotland, the world's Englishman is no longer found.[13] (emphasis mine)

By the 1870s and 1880s, there was a growing recognition of both the urbanisation and mobility of a population who had hitherto 'never travelled'. The emphasis shifted towards the significance of old racial types as survivors from a rural past and landscape that were under growing threat. The naturalist and novelist W H Hudson was an acute observer of supposed racial types in his travels through southern England in the latter part of the century. Like Jefferies, Hudson hated the 'strangeness' of cities; coming from a childhood in Argentina, his observations were goaded in some degree by a search by the colonial outsider for roots and identity in British society. Hudson sought to apply Huxley's classification to the English people, seeing those in Berkshire, Oxfordshire and the Midlands as the 'common modified Saxon type'. In Hampshire, however, the presence of 'small, narrow headed men of black hair' indicated a race of 'Iberian' descent who stretched back to the neolithic period. 'Like the small existing herds of indigenous white cattle,' he concluded, 'they have preserved their peculiar physical character down to the present time by remaining mixed with the blue-eyed people.'[14]

This was a mode of race classification that had become absorbed into a wider pastoral movement in English nature writing by an essentially urban-based group writing about the countryside and its people without actually being part of it. The rural English racial survivors resembled other ancient features of the landscape, such as prehistoric burial mounds and dolmens which began to attract a growing archaeological interest. These were areas not merely of professional and scientific curiosity but visible symbols of ancient time-spans in an age increasingly conscious of differing rates and modes of historical change. Stonehenge, for instance, had long held a fascination for observers of England. For Emerson it appeared, as 'the seat and centre of the British race', to confirm the ancient pastoral lineage of the rural shepherds of Wiltshire: Wiltshire:

> *On the top of a mountain, the old temple would not be more impressive. Far and wide a few shepherds with their flocks sprinkled the plain, and a bagman drove along the road. It looked as if the wide margin given in this crowded isle to this primeval temple was accorded by the veneration of the British race to the old egg out of which all their ecclesiastical structures and history had proceeded.*[15]

The ancient stone blocks seemed a tangible link with a pre-Christian and pagan past and it was fitting that Thomas Hardy should set the arrest of his heroine Tess, in *Tess of the d'Urbervilles* (1892), descendant of a decadent line of aristocrats, in the ruins as she lay asleep on a large stone, as if ready for sacrifice.[16] The ancient megalith was evidence of an even longer span of human history in England compared to both the span of identifiably "English" history stretching back to medieval knights and lords, and the more immediate span of rapid economic change in the Victorian countryside which threatened to disconnect the age from its past.

The late nineteenth-century travel and nature writers were thus already subconsciously aware of a tendency that J H Plumb came to call the 'death of the past'. The effort to forge out of the visible symbols of the past a national culture which bore some direct relationship to the past was a conscious effort at pre-empting this possibility of loss. Hudson felt the ruins of the ancient Roman town of Silchester, in *Afoot in England*, epitomised both the tranquillity of the English countryside and its ancient history as well as providing an historical link for its present-day neighbours:

> *The perfect sense of satisfaction, of restfulness, of peace, experienced here is very perfect; but in the wilderness, where man has never been, or has at all events left no trace of his former presence, there is even a mysterious sense of loneliness, of desolation, underlying our pleasures of nature. Here it seems good to know, or to imagine, that the men I occasionally meet in my solitary rambles, and that I see in the scattered rustic villages hard by, are of the same race, and possibly the descendants of the people who occupied the spot in the remote past - Iberians and Celt, and Roman and Saxon and Dane.*[17]

The English landscape appeared as a quintessentially tended and tranquil "middle landscape", which Leo Marx has designated as the ideal compromise between the lonely and remote 'wilderness' and the urbanised landscape of the city.[18] It provided for Hudson a means of psychological identification after his earlier isolated residence on the Argentinian pampas, and at the same time it denoted the continuation of at least part of the older rustic order in the new machine age.

The ideological significance of this suburban middle landscape ideal lay in the fact that it tended to relegate the more radical attacks on English gentility to the peripheries of political debate. A number of writers in the tradition of William Morris' Arts and Crafts movement sought a more direct return to nature and communal living outside the mainstream of society. Edward Carpenter established a rural commune at Millthorpe outside Sheffield and in a number of books attacked middle-class pretensions to gentility. Championing the ideas of Thoreau and Kropotkin, Carpenter actively sought a return to a simpler rural life where there was to be found the true sources of 'social brotherhood' and 'honesty'. He berated the seaside homes of the south coast *rentier* bourgeoisie and the 'polite villa residences' which 'like unwholesome toadstools dot and disfigure the whole of this great land', for these ' "noble" mansions of organised idleness were built upon the bent back of poverty and lifelong hopeless unremitting toil."[19]

In his struggle against the claims of bourgeois gentility in the make-up of what he termed the 'national conscience', Carpenter confronted a basic dilemma; namely that, by the 1880s, the English peasantry no longer existed as a cohesive social and cultural entity. Unlike that of Ireland, English peasant culture by the late nineteenth century remained a mere memory, and Carpenter was drawn more towards a comparison with simpler societies overseas. In *Civilisation: Its Causes and Cure* (1889) he invoked the idea of the romantic savage as he contrasted the seemingly corrupt English urban society with the apparent cohesion of 'savage society'.

> *The social life of the wilder races...within its limits is more harmonious and compact than that of the more civilised nations. The members of the tribe are not organically at warfare with each other; society is not divided into classes which prey upon each other; nor is it consumed by parasites. There is more true social unity, less of disease.*[20]

However, such romantic ideas were out of keeping with the mood engendered by late nineteenth-century imperial expansion, which tended to exacerbate more racist notions of black and brown inferiority in combination with Darwinian conceptions of evolutionary struggle and "survival of the fittest". With the growing interest in colonial adventure fiction such as that of G A Henty and Rider Haggard, "savage" societies were not ones to be emulated as ideal social models but rather to be "civilised" and, as far as possible, "uplifted". By the late 1890s a number of liberal critics of imperialism such as J A Hobson and L T Hobhouse became worried by the manner in which imperialism and jingoism had found a base in the "villa toryism" of the suburban middle and lower middle classes.

The incorporation of some aspects of the rural and pastoral ideal in the suburbanisation of late-Victorian England seemed to forge a new aggressive national consciousness which masked internal social and economic differences. For a writer like H G Wells, who was familiar with the developments in scientific thought, this emerging intellectual trend behind the popular "social imperialism" filled him with concern. His time traveller in the scientific romance *The Time Machine* (1894) enters a future England in which class differentiation has followed evolutionary lines leading to two separate "races" which, in terminology reminiscent of T H Huxley, Wells called the Eloi and Morlocks. The supposedly peaceful and tranquil agrarian order of the Eloi above ground has high price for the small hairy Morlocks living beneath the ground have been thoroughly brutalised in the same manner as sections of the English working class. The Morlocks physically feed off the Eloi, whose culture is decadent, as literacy and books have been abandoned.

Wells' writing at this time reflected an underlying anxiety about the nature of imperial conquest, which he saw in more universal terms than the conventional idea of white Anglo-Saxon domination of black races. His novel *The War of the Worlds* (1898) awakened the Victorian reading public to the experience of colonial conquest as the Martian invaders of a placid rural England took on many of the trappings of British colonial intruders in Africa.

The domination of the heroic and chivalric in English historical consciousness by the end of the century was such that the warnings of writers like Wells tended to be understood by only a few. If there were a lesson to be learnt from the construction of the English national past it was generally one that emphasised the making of an imperial nation by both military conquest and the blending of racial stocks. The Darwinian writer Grant Allen, who Wells later held to have been an important influence on his own thought, in a popular survey of English country history, *Country and Town in England* (1901), depicted a pattern of racial settlement derived from the work of the physical anthropologists and archaeologists. Dorset was still an area of semi-Celtic survivors of the old Dorsetae tribe from the time of the Roman conquest, while Sussex was 'one of the most purely Teutonic counties in England'. As with most imperial history, this was a pattern dictated by boundaries and frontiers, and Berkshire marked:

*...the final great northern extension of the West Saxon power, when
the English colonists began to cross the ridge of the North Downs and
descend into the valleys of the Kennet and the Thames. The White
Horse formed the standard of the invading Teutons, as it still does
both of Hanover, when they came, and of Kent, where, perhaps, they
first landed in Britain.*[21]

Such interest in English racial survivors continued to preoccupy the
"experts" in archaeology and anthropology until at least the end of the
First World War, and would be introduced to a newer generation by such
authorities as H J Fleure and Harold Peake.[22] But already, by the end of
the Anglo-Boer War, the mood was one of growing disenchantment with
imperialism. The resurgence of liberalism in Edwardian England led to
a search for more indigenous English values to the exclusion of the wider
colonial empire. Indeed, W H Kent in the liberal *Westminster Review*
argued, in February 1902, that 'patriotism' and 'imperialism' were 'two
incompatible and mutually destructive ideas' and argued for an
'enlightened and practical patriotism' which concentrated on the tasks of
domestic social reform.[23]

In the years after the Liberal election victory in 1906, G K Chesterton
and a number of anti-imperial writers began to popularise many of the
concepts of England and Englishness which had been developed over the
previous two or three decades, though not always with the same
enthusiasm for English racial ancestry, which Chesterton tended to
decry as bogus pseudoscience[24]. The movement united the appeals of
English history and rural values in an attempt to undermine the
pretensions to imperial grandiosity. It was, however, largely
unsuccessful in demolishing the dominant school of Whig history at
Oxford and Cambridge which was so important for turning out new
recruits to the colonial service and India office. Chesterton's *History of
England* was written without a single date, and his weekly column in
The Illustrated London News was accepted by him on condition that he
steered clear of political topics. As both journalist and critic, Chesterton
was never treated with too much seriousness by his fellows intellectuals,
and his eminence was tarnished with charges of anti-Semitism, despite
his denials. Nevertheless, Chesterton's voluminous output marked a
certain intellectual celebration of Englishness, smallness and
parochialism, and he became most popularly known as a writer
championing certain recognisable codes of common sense.[25]

For a number of writers over the following generations the experience
of the First World War marked an indelible hiatus in the English
national experience, destroying forever the seemingly placid and
tranquil pre-1914 world. The memory of long hot summer days in green
English villages, in which tea was served during a cricket match and fish
could be caught in cool, unpolluted streams running through quiet
meadows, became the stuff and substance of novels, short stories and

poetry. 'The past is a foreign country,' L P Hartley wrote in his celebrated novel *The Go-Between* in 1953, 'they do things differently there.' This sense of loss and regret belies the degree of continuity in English thought concerning the apparently rural and pastoral qualities of national identity. Loss had always been a central theme in the English rustic ideal. In *The Heart of England* (1907) Edward Thomas lamented the decayed image of suburban streets as he left the town for the countryside, for 'an artist who wished to depict the Fall, and some sympathy with it in the face of a ruined Eden, might have had little to do but copy an acre of the surviving fields.'[26]

The nostalgic and sad English pastoral ideal proved all too successful in surviving the modernity of the twentieth century and two World Wars. By the 1920s the Conservative Prime Minister, Stanley Baldwin, cultivated the image of a country gentleman (to be adopted by Harold Macmillan in the early 1960s) and a new motorcar age began to discover the delights of the English terrain on the summer tour. H V Morton's popular *In Search of England* (1927) ensured the continuation of the myth for a new generation of more mobile tourists by carefully skirting the industrial towns and urban heartland for an older England, since 'the village and the English countryside are the germs of all we are and all we have become: our manufacturing cities belong to the last century and a half; our villages stand with their roots in the heptarchy.'[27]

The cultural roots of English resistance to industrialisation may thus be found at a considerably later date than the mid-Victorian period, for it was only in the last quarter of the Victorian age and in the Edwardian one following it that a strong movement to cultivate the nostalgic, pastoral ideal emerged in the context of growing political crisis accompanying imperial expansion. Though the empire continued as a Commonwealth into the 1960s and 1970s, a more nationalist age in recent years has seen a partial restoration of many of the earlier themes discussed in this chapter. Movements for the restoration of real ale, bread and cheese have proved very popular. There is a growing resistance to factory farming, while such pagan symbols as Stonehenge have become an arena for an annual summer struggle with authority. This movement back to the English landscape has become a powerful theme in English national identity. Its entrenchment in popular consciousness and the English cultural tradition suggests that it is stronger than a mere compensation for the loss of great power status, as has been the case with the Royal Family. The English pastoral ideal has proved to be an especially enduring quality within modern English culture.

The Impact of Immigration

The settlement of Jewish, Irish and black minorities has established different historical and cultural traditions within British society which have to a considerable degree undermined the older notion in Whig history that Britain was a homogeneous society shaped by the evolutionary structures of parliamentary government.[28]

The emergence of a new school of black British historiography, has revealed that black ethnic minorities have played an important role in British history from at least the Elizabethan age. Together with a number of other minority communities such as the Irish, the Jews, the Chinese and Germans, British society has been a complex mosaic of different communities and cultures that has belied the notion of the single national culture of the Whig historians, who have only looked at the operation of politics among the elite.[29]

The response from the dominant political establishment during the course of the twentieth century has been mixed. Commitment to the imperialist ideal by the late nineteenth century afforded space for a number of responses to people of different colour and culture. As A P Thornton has pointed out, the ideas of imperialism tend to be 'less ideas than instincts, the sum of a series of factors which cannot be precisely calculated'.[30] In general they were defined through the three dominant doctrines of power, profit and civilisation, though each had varying degrees of influence at any particular point in time, with the doctrine of power declining along with that of the imperial edifice itself.[31] It became possible for a number of varying climates of opinion to emerge, some of which proved remarkably willing to try to understand the position and disadvantage of African, Asian and other minority groups. Here was laid the basis of a liberal concern, which at its worst was a new form of paternalism and at its best a conscious and deliberate effort to change attitudes on race and supposed race differences. This tradition gained a fillip with the revival of liberalism after the Anglo-Boer War and the Liberal election victory of 1906. In the wake of attacks on the war by the Liberal anti-imperialists, there was increasing discussion on the position of black races, though this was often based on the geographical view that Europe was a continent in which black people would not be able to survive for any length of time. The revival of this liberalism also led to the search for a definition of "Englishness" which forms the theme of chapter one of this volume.

One of the most important events in this reassessment of the Victorian imperial ideal forms the subject of the third chapter of this book: the 1911 Universal Races Congress. This was an important international gathering in London of liberal and ethical opinion and needs to be contrasted with the activities of the mainstream missionary societies of the time. The Congress acted as a vital focus for a number of organisations, some of them black, and the determination of the organisers to attack systematic doctrines of racism makes the Congress an important forerunner of later international forums, such as UNESCO, in the period after the Second World War.[32] The Congress was not repeated, however, and racist doctrines did continue to get a "scientific" and "expert" airing in the period before the Second World War. Chapter two discusses the impact of eugenic ideas after the First World War and the significance of the ideas of the anthropologist Sir Arthur Keith, the curator of the Hunterian Museum of the Royal College of Surgeons. As Nancy Stepan has recently pointed out, Keith was an important figure in the dissemination of Darwinian ideas on war and evolutionary progress. However, as the chapter in this volume shows (it was written before Stepan's article appeared) Keith was also an important figure in the development of sociobiological and ethological notions of human fitness.[33]

Social anthropology in Britain was slow to mobilise intellectual resistance in Britain to racist doctrines. Its generally negative and undecided attitude on race in the 1930s prevented it from putting up any strong opposition to the emergence of Hitler and Nazi race doctrines in Central Europe. [34] The British anthropological school was not in the same position as Central European intellectual opinion on race, partly because the British intelligentsia has traditionally been treated with a considerable degree of scepticism by an empirically-minded establishment. The net effect was that racial ideas tended to be developed more from the practice of colonial administration than from social theorists, though many of the latter's ideas were shaped by the colonial experience either directly or indirectly.

Chapter four looks at a neglected dimension of this colonial administration in the form of the doctrine of segregation which found especial favour in the colonies of white settlement in Africa such as Southern Rhodesia and South Africa. Segregationism was a powerful and resilient ideology, and John Cell has cogently argued that it can be seen as one of the most successful ideologies of the first half of the twentieth century.[35] In Britain, it gained some following among a number of race theorists who could see in its symmetry a means of maintaining white power at a time when it appeared likely to be challenged by a nascent black nationalism. Segregationism was never officially imported into Britain itself, though compromises were made with segregation in the U S Army during the Second World War.[36] The involvement of Britain in a struggle against Nazi racism during the war made segregationism an increasingly unacceptable doctrine by the 1940s and this was to be further stimulated by the growing attacks on the newer form of segregationism in South Africa after the victory of D F Malan and the Nationalist Party in 1948 with its policy of apartheid.

This shift of opinion in the course of the 1930s and 1940s was by no means due to pressure from white liberal and philanthropic opinion alone. As chapter six points out, black students too had an important and pivotal role at this time and, in the case of the West African Students Union (WASU), often got into confrontation with the older style paternalism of the Anti-Slavery Society and the Rev. John Harris. The emergence of a group of black intellectuals in Britain in the 1930s and

1940s was partly linked to the growing pressures for colonial nationalism in West Africa. At the same time it was important for developing discussion on race issues within the metropolis itself. By the 1950s, this issue was becoming national in scope with the arrival of New Commonwealth immigrants. By this time many of the earlier black student generation had departed for their home countries and more traditional forces began to reassert themselves in response to the immigrants' arrival. The wave of wartime altruism began to decline and the Festival of Britain in 1951 marked the emergence of a new generation of "carnivores" who were far less open to humanitarian ideas than the previous era which had been dominated by the Labour and Liberal "herbivores".[37] As chapter six points out, the liberal efforts to gain a sympathetic response to the black immigrants' arrival were short-lived and calls for immigration control soon mounted.

The race card has traditionally been a powerful one in British politics, and is guaranteed to force a quick establishment response compared to other issues which can be either delayed or shelved altogether. By early 1955, it was clear that pressures for immigration control were mounting at local level and there were calls for the government to divert the immigration issue by focusing on the economic development in the colonial territories themselves.[38] The processes underlying the pattern of immigration were not well understood at this time and it was possible for Harold Chapman to write in *The Daily Telegraph* that 'it only needs a few well known families to cancel their passages to Britain for the whole movement to lose its enthusiasm.'[39] The government, as is now known from the Cabinet papers in the Public Record Office, had considered immigration control legislation as early as 1950-51, but had shelved it because the numbers were not considered extensive enough to warrant legislation that would antagonise a number of Commonwealth countries.[40] This was a theme on which the opponents of immigration control played during the 1950s. In September 1955 Norman Mackenzie wrote in *The New Statesman* that immigration restrictions could create a 'political shock' that would be 'bad enough among the coloured peoples of the Commonwealth' but 'would create an explosion in Jamaica, causing bitter frustration and resentment among the articulate and ambitious young workers'.[41]

Liberal concern with the issue was increasingly isolated by the late 1950s, despite the fact that, as chapter five shows, there was mounting interest in overseas race issues, especially South African apartheid. The development of the apartheid programme in the 1950s under Dr Vorwoed led to a growing debate in British liberal circles, though at this stage there were no serious proposals for a coherent programme of sanctions. These were suggested only in the wake of the Sharpeville shooting in 1960 and the banning of the ANC and PAC. For the most part, the activists involved in the campaign against white minority rule in Southern Africa were white liberal and radical activists, and little support was drawn from the black immigrant communities in Britain who were still engaged in more basic struggles to establish their presence within British society. As chapter seven points out, there was still a need for British black communities to achieve an historical identity of their own and it was difficult to be drawn into international issues.

Some analysts have tried, in a very simplistic fashion, to draw comparisons between the position of blacks in South Africa and the position of those in Britain. The compartmentalisation of black urban groupings into the cheaper housing areas of the inner cities has led to obvious analogies with the system of urban apartheid in South Africa. However, the "segregation" that can be perceived in the patterns of ethnic residence in Britain really bears little resemblance to the institutionalised pattern of group areas segregation in South Africa. Chapter eight examines the debate on urban segregation in Britain and looks in particular at Birmingham, for it is in this city that ethnic compartmentalisation is exceptionally high. In many instances, ethnic minorities choose to live in their own communities and it has been difficult to enforce policies of "dispersal" in the interests of achieving an ethnically mixed balance.

There are a considerable number of issues relating to ethics and notions of social justice in the politics of race and ethnicity in Britain. Chapter nine seeks to initiate such a discussion by examining the liberal tradition of pluralism in British political philosophy as this is an area that has been generally neglected by political theorists, though in the United States the area has become one of growing interest to scholars of race. An ethnically plural society leads to minorities claiming group rights as well as convential individual ones. Members of the British liberal establishment, exemplified by Lord Scarman, have been reluctant to spell out the nature of such a society. Scarman has not been encouraged by examples of plural societies in the international context, seeing them as politically unstable. But the educational debate on multiculturalism is a critical pointer to the need for greater awareness of as well as individual rights in the legal process.

The redefining of British national identity:

The essays in this book seek to show that race has played an important role in the debate on British national and cultural identity since the latter part of the nineteenth century. It is likely to continue to do so well into the next century, though the terms in which this will occur may be substantially different as British culture and politics become increasingly integrated into a nascent European polity centred on the European Union (EU).

The meaning of "race" has also shifted over this time as the imperial definition of an Anglo Saxon race ruling a "Greater Britain" gave way to a more insular definition of Englishness by the inter-war years. It was during this period that a close linkage became established between national identity and certain essential racial attributes, indicating that what some analysts have seen as a "new racism" emerging during the 1980s was not really so new when looked at over a longer time span.[42] A national culture became consolidated during this period that embedded notions of inherent English racial and cultural superiority before the advent of New Commonwealth immigration in the 1950s and 1960s. It was secured too by the pattern of post-war politics that successfully insulated the British electorate from the realities of imperial decline well until at least the late 1960s and Enoch Powell's "rivers of blood" speech.

The strength of this racial component of British – and more particularly English – nationalism has made the project of incorporation of black minorities into mainstream society far more difficult than for previous immigrant groups such as the Jews and Irish. The segregation and ghettoization that black communities have come to experience in Britain's inner cities threaten also to be replicated at the academic level with the progressive transformation of the traditional area of liberal concern – "race relations" – into "black studies" on a pattern reminiscent of the United States some two decades ago. If such a process develops it would tend to isolate debate over the political and social status of Britain's black communities from the rest of social science research and debate. At an historical level it would perpetuate too, the peripheralisation of black British history from the rest of British and imperial historiography.

The central intellectual challenge confronting analysts of Britain's racial minorities is to integrate their historical experiences of moving from the imperial periphery to the metropolitan core into a wider pattern of British involvement and retreat from empire.[43] When looked at in this context, black communities in Britain form an essential and intrinsic part of the forging of the contemporary British national identity. Such a perspective also gives historical depth to the project of multi-culturalism, which risks otherwise being a shallow political doctrine trying vaguely to link together a polyglot series of social groups bound together by little more than the fact that they live side by side with each other in the same physical space.

The theme of this book, therefore, is that historical understanding is crucial towards overcoming the alienation induced by racist stereotyping and cultural "otherness". It should not be assumed of course that historical knowledge per se can always act as a panacea for racial and ethnic hostilities. The upsurge of ethnic warfare in Georgia and the former Yugoslavia indicates that it is only too easy for some societies to be dominated by memories of the past and various historical myths. If taught sensitively, however, history can provide the basis for groups within a society to reassess their relationships with each other. In the British instance, this issue relates not only to black ethnic minorities but

the re-writing of post-imperial British history that reassesses the role of
the Scots, Welsh and Irish. This is a time in fact when the whole issue of
the way that the British national identity has been forged is being
subjected to an increasingly critical historical scrutiny.[44]

The teaching of history in schools, however, has undergone a serious
process of decline as it has been replaced in many instances by social and
cultural studies. This has reinforced for many children and young adults
a sense of their disconnection from the past and an alienation that all too
often serves as the breeding ground for the inculcation of racist
mythologies. The charge that history is no longer relevant in a society
struggling to reach a level of post-industrial modernity is also reinforced
by the assertion that teaching British history is anachronistic at a time
when Britain is becoming ever more closely integrated into a wider
European Union.

This argument undoubtedly has some weight, though it needs to be
seen in the context of a wider debate about the changing nature of
European history as a whole. Even the emergence of a fully united
Western European polity is unlikely to see the disappearance of the
teaching of local, regional and national histories. Indeed, these will be
vital as the ugly spectre emerges of a new pan-European racism
emerging, resurrecting much of the ideology of inter-war fascism that
many analysts in the post 1945 period hoped had been banished for good
from European politics. British history will need to be increasingly
integrated into a wider curriculum of European-centred history and with
it the role played by ethnic minorities. In the longer term it should be
hoped that a more comparative historical pespective will emerge, looking
at the different patterns of migration into Europe of individuals and
communities from Asia, Africa, the Caribbean, the Middle East and
Eastern Europe.

The history of migration in Europe is a vast and expanding one and is
increasingly likely to influence the nature of the debate on race in British
politics and society. It will be of particular importance for widening the
debate on racism and showing that racist ideologies do not simply have
colonial roots as has often been argued by sociologists of race relations in
the British instance[45]. The protracted civil war in the former Yugoslavia
suggest that modern forms of racism have expanded beyond defence of
pigmentation and race into defence of "culture", however variously this
can be described. The virulence with which this can be used to mobilise
group support suggests that it can be as emotive an issue as older
patterns of racial identification. It raises major theoretical issues for the
late twentieth century that analysts of race will sooner or later be
compelled to confront.

NOTES

1. See for example Gareth Stedman Jones, "Working Class Culture and Working Class Politics in London, 1870-1900", *Journal of Social History*, 7 (1973), pp. 460-508; John M Mackenzie, *Propaganda and Empire*, Manchester University Press, Manchester, 1984.
2. Anthony Clayton, *The British Empire as a Superpower, 1913-39*, The Macmillan Press, London and Basingstoke, 1986.
3. CUP, Cambridge, 1986.
4. Charles Wentworth Dilke, *Greater Britain*, Macmillan Press, London, 1890; see also *Race and Empire in British Politics*, pp. 12-26.
5. Edward A Freeman, "Imperial Federation", *Macmillan's Magazine*, LI (1885), p. 441. See also C J W Parker, "The Failure of Liberal Racialism: The Racial Ideas of E A Freeman", *The Historical Journal*, 24, 4 (1981), pp. 825-46.
6. Martin J Weiner, *English Culture and the Decline of the Industrial Spirit*, CUP, Cambridge, 1980. See also Herbert L Sussman, *Victorians and the Machine: The Literary Response to Technology*, Harvard University Press, Cambridge (Mass), 1968.
7. Frank Cass, London, 1986.
8. Mark Girouard, *The Return to Camelot: Chivalry and the English Gentleman*, Yale University Press, New Haven and London, 1981.
9. Jonathan Mendilow, "Merrie England and the Brave New World: Two Myths of the Idea of Empire", *History of European Ideas*, 6, 1 (1985), pp. 41-58; Hugh Cunningham, "The Language of Patriotism, 1750-1914", *History Workshop*, 12 (August 1981), pp. 8-33.
10. Richard Jefferies, *The Story of My Heart*, Longman Green and Co, London, 1904, pp. 137-8.
11. Parker, *op. cit.*; Asa Briggs, *Saxons, Normans and Victorians*, Bexhill, 1966; Reginald Horsman, "Origins of Racial Anglo-Saxonism in Great Britain before 1850", *Journal of the History of Ideas*, 37, 3 (July-September 1976), pp. 387-410; *Race and Manifest Destiny*, Harvard University, Cambridge (Mass); Hugh MacDougall, *Racial Myth in English History*, Harvester Press and University of New England Press, Montreal and Hanover, 1982.
12. T H Huxley, "On Some Fixed Points in British Ethnology", *Collected Essays*, Vol. 11, Macmillan, London, 1910, pp. 253-70.
13. RW Emerson, *English Traits and Other Essays*, JM Dent, London, 1908, p. 26.
14. W H Hudson, *Hampshire Days*, J M Dent, London, 1923, p. 228. Late in his life Hudson became a supporter of the sociobiology of Arthur Keith whom he considered 'our leading anthropologist', Hudson to RB Cunningham-Graham, 5 August 1920 in Richard Curle (ed), *W H Hudson's Letters to R B Cunningham-Graham*, The Golden Cockerel Press, London, 1941, p. 155.
15. Emerson, *op. cit.*, p. 137. W H Hudson, on the other hand, felt no especially strong link at Stonehenge for 'there is no shaking hands with the ancients of Britain - or Albion, seeing that we are on chalk. To our sons they are as strange as the builders of Tinhuernaro, or Mitla or Ilzana, and the cyclopean ruins of Zimbabwe...', *Afoot in England*, J M Dent, London, 1924, pp. 266-7.
16. Bruce Johnson, " 'The Perfection of Species' and Hardy's Tess", in U C Knoepflmacher and G B Tennyson (eds), *Nature and the Victorian Imagination*, University of California Press, Berkeley and London 1977, pp. 259-77.
17. *Afoot in England*, p. 91.
18. Leo Marx, *The Machine in the Garden; Technology and the Pastoral Ideal in America*, OUP, London, 1964. See also Weiner, *op. cit.*, pp. 9-10.
19. Edward Carpenter, *England's Ideal and Other Papers On Social Subjects*, Swan Sonnenschein, London, 1887, p. 5.
20. Edward Carpenter, *Civilisation: Its Causes and Cure*, Swan Sonnenschein, London, 1889, p. 9; see also Stanley Pierson, "Edward Carpenter, Prophet of a Socialist Millenium", *Victorian Studies*, 13 (March 1970), pp. 301-18; Chushichi Tsuzuki, *Edward Carpenter, 1844-1929; Prophet of Human Fellowship*, CUP, Cambridge, 1980.

21. Grant Allen, *Country and Town in England*, Grant Richards, London, 1901, p. 25.
22. See in particular Harold Peake, *The English Village*, Benn Bros, London, 1921. For Fleure and Peake see *Race and Empire in British Politics*, pp. 110-11.
23. W H Kent, "Patriotism or Imperialism?", *Westminster Review*, 157 (February 1902), p. 127, p. 135.
24. G K Chesterton, for example, attacked 'the modern madness for biological or bodily metaphors'. 'It is convenient,' he went on, 'to speak of the British Lion. But Britain is no more an organism than Britain is a lion. The moment we begin to give a nation a unity and simplicity of an animal, we begin to think wildly. Because every man is a biped, fifty men are not a centipede.' *What's Wrong with the World?*, Cassell, London, 1910, pp. 3-4.
25. For Chesterton's intellectual impact on British thought, see Margaret Canovan, *G K Chesterton: Radical Populist*, Harcourt Brace, New York and London, 1977; John Coates, *Chesterton and the Edwardian Cultural Crisis*, Hull University Press, 1984.
26. Edward Thomas, *The Heart of England*, J M Dent, London, 1906, repr. in David Wright (ed), *Edward Thomas, Selected Poems and Prose*, Penguin Books, Harmondsworth, 1981, p. 52.
27. H V Morton, *In Search of England*, Methuen, London, 1927, p. 2.
28. Reba Soffer, "Nation, Duty, Character and Confidence: History at Oxford, 1850-1914", *The Historical Journal*, 30, 1 (1987), pp. 77-104; John W Burrow, *A Liberal Descent*, CUP, Cambridge, 1981.
29. See the discussion in Tim Cloke, " 'Old England' and Other Perspectives (historical traditions and teaching)", *New Community*, XII, 2 (Summer 1985), p. 249-58.
30. A P Thornton, *Doctrines of Imperialism*, John Wiley, New York, 1965, p. 47.
31. *Ibid.*
32. Paul B Rich, "The Politics of 'race relations' in Britain and the West", in Peter Jackson (ed), *Race and Racism*, Allen and Unwin, London, 1987, pp. 103-4.
33. Nancy Leys Stepan," 'Nature's Pruning Hook': War, Race and Evolution, 1914-18" in H M W Bean (ed), *The Political Culture of Modern Britain*, Hamish Hamilton, London, pp. 129-48.
34. *Race and Empire in British Politics*, pp. 116-17.
35. John Cell, *The Highest Stage of White Supremacy: The Origins of Segregation in South Africa and the American South*, CUP, Cambridge, 1984.
36. *Race and Empire in British Politics*, p. 154.
37. Michael Frayn, "Festival" in Michael Sissons and Philip French (eds), *The Age of Austerity*, Hodder and Stoughton, London, 1963, pp. 317-38.
38. *The Daily Express*, 11, 19 and 29 January 1955.
39. *The Daily Telegraph*, 13 December 1955.
40. Paul B Rich, "The Politics of 'Surplus Colonial Labour': Black Immigration to Britain and Governmental Responses" in Colin Broch (ed), *The Caribbean in Europe*, Frank Cass, London, 1986, pp. 36-61.
41. Norman Mackenzie, "The West Indian in Britain", *The New Statesman*, 17 September 1955.
42. Martin Barker, *The New Racism*, London, Junction Books, 1981; Paul Gilroy, *There Ain't No Black in the Union Jack*, London, Hutchinson, 1987.
43. James Walvin, "From the Fringes: The Emergence of Black Historical Studies" in Jagadish S. Eundava and Ian Duffield (eds) *Essays on the History of Blacks in Britain*, Aldershot, Avebury, 1992, p. 231.
44. A factor now recognised by historians on the right as well as the left. See Max Beloff, *An Historian in the Twentieth Century*, New Haven and London, Yale University Press, 1992, esp. pp. 25-42.
45. See in particular, John Rex, *Race Relations in Sociological Theory*, London, Weidenfeld and Nicolson, 1970.

Chapter One

British Imperial Decline and the Forging of English Patriotic Memory, 1918-1980

The search for an historical anchorage for more recent manifestations of populist patriotism in British politics hinges on the social interpretation of the First and Second World Wars in contemporary British history. In both these conflicts, considerable shifts in British international status and power occurred and, as a consequence, major dents were made in the self-confidence and *esprit de corps* of the British governing class. The earlier imperialist climate inherited from the late-Victorian and Edwardian periods became considerably undermined, though the recent work of John Mackenzie has shown that imperial propaganda continued to exert a wide-ranging and protracted influence on British social life and thought via films, school textbooks and pro-imperial bodies well into the 1950s.[1] However, the demise of the earlier imperial self-confidence meant that, from the end of the First World War, a concerted shift occurred within governing circles towards a more favourable orchestration of notions of British, or more specifically English, national homogeneity and popular patriotism. The objective of this chapter, is to examine the evolution of this national ideology in the 1920s and 1930s. It seeks to assess the ideology's significance in more recent phases of British politics in the period since the 1950s, characterised by full-scale retreat from empire and the emergence of "Powellism" and a populist English patriotism on the right.

The Sources of the English National Ideology

The symbols and rhetoric of English national homogeneity were already embedded within the political culture well before the ending of hostilities in November 1918. At one level, the conception of a coherent "English ideology" went back to the emergence of a body of Whig historiography centred around Oxford and Cambridge in the middle nineteeth century.[2] The development of this school ensured that earlier radical notions of patriotism, inherited from the eighteenth -century attack on aristocratic corruption, became blunted and fused with a wider body of public doctrine linking the evolutionary emergence of parliamentary good government and liberal ideals of political liberty. This Whig vision was often underpinned in the writings of such figures as Froude, Dilke and Freeman by a racial conception of the supremacy of Anglo-Saxon and Teutonic races who were perceived as especially fitted to continue a parliamentary tradition of government rooted in tribal folk moots of the forests of North Germany.[3] In some cases, this racial conception even took precedence over the idea of the nation as it interlocked with wider imperial notions of Anglo-Saxon race fitness to govern and dominate weaker races. For Walter Bagehot, for example, writing in 1864, no 'great race' ever acted upon the principles of nationalism for 'every great country is peopled by different races. Each race has conquered weaker races right and left, and great nations have grown up from the results of these conquests.'[4] The idea fed, too, into the mid-Victorian conception of a "Greater Britain" which formed a key part of the imperialist visions of Charles Dilke and J R Seeley.

The disasters of the Anglo-Boer War encouraged a reassessment within governing political circles concerned not only with British imperial fortunes but also those in European politics, given the growing fear of German military rivalry.[5] At the same time, some of the thinking on the right began to echo the rhetoric of the mid-Victorian critics of industrialism through a growing interest in the sources of English village life, the disappearance of the peasantry and the search for the folk roots of English literature and culture.[6] Some of this interest occurred in aristocratic and military circles and related to a eugenic fear that the urban working class was breeding such an inferior line of stock that it needed to be replenished from a healthy rural yeomanry who would prove fitter and more able soldiers. Although the reasons for the rejection of many applicants to the army during the Boer War were environmental, the idea persisted that there was a long-term threat to the "national character" from the processes of urbanisation.[7] W M Flinders Petrie considered, in his widely-read *Modern Janus* in 1907, that the causes related in part to the emigration from Britain of superior biological stock and the immigration into it of eugenically inferior immigrants from Eastern Europe. This anti-Semitism was a defence of a traditional aristocratic gentility that Petrie saw as under attack from the rise of a new business and middle class that did not have the strong cultural roots of the old landed gentry.[8]

Petrie's suspicions of external colonisation were echoed more loudly by Edwardian liberal anti-imperial opinion. The dramatic triumph of the Liberal Party in the election of 1906 led many to believe that a revision of Britain's imperial role, which had come so disastrously unstuck on the South African veld, was needed. For many in this group, such as G K Chesterton and Hilaire Belloc, imperialism and patriotism were incompatible and, as one of the ardent anti-imperialists, Arthur John Butler, wrote in *The Speaker* in 1905, 'the "imperialist" who really knows what he is about, who has an aim beyond a mere election cry or an increased sale for his newspapers, is as likely as not a person of alien blood, to whom the tradition and surroundings...can have no meaning', citing as an example 'the German Lord Milner'.[9]

The policy of the Liberal governments before the First World War proved a great disappointment to the Liberal anti-imperialists, who remained a peripheral group after failing to exert much impact on government policy. The Westminster–Whitehall centre of power was closely wedded to the imperial ethos up to the First World War, though during the course of the hostilities a considerable undermining of the imperial ideal took place. By the 1923 Imperial Conference, it became clear that, despite the creation in 1917 by the Lloyd George government of an Imperial War Cabinet in which dominion statesmen like General Smuts from South Africa played a prominent role, the lurch towards dominion autonomy would prevent the establishment of any close imperial federal body.[10] With the demise of the ideal of a federal empire one of the central imperatives of Victorian imperialism had been essentially blown apart by the war, and the rhetoric of the pre-war school of imperial literati, such as Rudyard Kipling, seemed out of tune with the post-war mood.

In the first half of the 1920s, a relatively fluid period ensued in which a number of traditions of political rhetoric competed to define the make-up of the official doctrine of the government elite. On the left, the tradition of liberal internationalism was strongly articulated within Labour and Liberal circles and this contributed to attacks on imperialism as one of the major reasons for the war. There was often a strong sense of moral obligation involved in this tradition. It was well articulated by *The Daily Herald* in 1919 when it urged support for the nationalist movements in India, Egypt, Persia and South Africa for 'if our nation welcomes and aids these movements, if our British Labour movement will stand by all these rightly struggling to be free, our children and their children will be saved the shame which today is ours in regard to Ireland, and instead we shall see coming into actual being the Commonwealth of nations which is the Federation of the World.'[11] This translated the Tennysonian vision in *Locksley Hall* into one of high moral purpose. It was not, however, a view shared by all sections of the left at this time for, as Bertrand Russell argued in the ILP organ *The New Leader* in 1921, 'if "patriotism" means desiring the welfare of our country, I agree; but as symbolised by the Union Jack, it becomes a more sinister memory. The Union Jack is the symbol of imperial pomp, and helps us to generate the emotions which lead us to cause misery to countless millions in Asia and Africa. Nationalism and imperialism are the most crude and destructive features of modern civilisation.'[12]

In Conservative circles, on the other hand, there occurred a protracted and grudging recognition that the older Victorian imperial ideal was becoming anachronistic. 'The old narrow nationalism and the old brazen imperialism must pass,' declared one writer in *The Nineteenth Century* in 1921. 'They have played their part. None but men of minds mechanised, circumscribed, visionless, will gird at their passing...Our nationalism and imperialism will not die; but they will change, grow more human, more a "bulwark for the cause of men".'[13] In the course of the 1920s a reassessment began to take place on the right of the role of imperialism and its dissemination to wider public opinion. Crucial to this reformulation was the figure of the Conservative Prime Minister for a considerable part of the interwar period, Stanley Baldwin.

Baldwin and the Pursuit of the English Ideal

The figure of Stanley Baldwin is a vital one for understanding the evolution of English patriotic ideology in the 1920s and 1930s. Not only did this Bewdley iron master, with strong roots in the late nineteenth-century paternal culture of the West Midlands, imprint his name on a whole era of recent English history, but he also managed, as Bill Schwartz has pointed out, to link an abstract English constitutionalism with a popular view of the English "national character".[14] The dominating feature of the rise of Baldwin in Conservative politics was a reaction against the Lloyd George coalition government which appeared to embody both corruption in high places and a threat to the long-term hopes of the Conservative Party. As Baldwin reminded his Conservative audience in the famous 1922 Carlton Club speech, the Lloyd George government was a 'dynamic force' which was a 'very terrible thing'. His provincial style and adoption of the pose of a country gentleman acted as a consoling and steadying force, which could, at least for a period, act as a stabilising factor in British politics. Nevertheless, the phenomenon of Baldwinism was never strong enough to act as a hegemonic vision in British, or more specifically English, civilisation that could successfully incorporate the labour and trade union movement.[15]

The reasons for the Baldwinite politics of the interwar years need to be understood at the level of the provincial basis of much English intellectual and cultural life during this period. The imperially-minded intelligentsia had acted as a fairly cohesive force at the centre of English politics in the years before the First World War, anchored around interlocking groups of Milnerites, imperially-minded Fabians and Oxford-educated Round Tablers. [16] The influence of these groups started to decline in the 1920s in the face of a general post-war loss of faith in imperial ideals and the rise of a mass electoral franchise and industrial trade unionism. In their place emerged a disparate group of advocates for an indigenous tradition of English patriotism which lacked the intellectual cohesion of many continental nationalist doctrines.

English intellectual life had not depended upon a coherent social theory to support the transformation of parliamentary government in the nineteenth century. Sociology of the Durkheimian variety, stressing the nature of social and organic cohesion, did not have the same impact on insular English society as it had on France in the revolutionary climate of so much of the nineteenth century. The English governing class felt able to continue plodding along with the same bland mixture of positivism and empiricism that has continued to puzzle a number of analysts of English social thought. [17] The major social theory of the first half of the nineteenth century was utilitarianism. By the middle years of the century, however, this had become progressively overladen by a Whig liberalism, and the earlier philosophical radicalism was eclipsed by an emerging faith in parliamentary "good government". [18] In the latter half of the century the Hegelian idealism of T H Green and Bernard Bosanquet gave a strong stimulus to this liberalism and helped hasten an intellectual accommodation within governing circles to the idea of an organic and collectivist state.[19]

The rise of the late-nineteenth-century "new liberalism" built upon the earlier growth of government in so far as the state was not seen as a revolutionary phenomenon, despite the protracted resistance by the "diehards" to reform of the House of Lords. By the early twentieth century, political ideologues on the right tended to be confined to the fringes of British political life. This meant that, by the interwar years, fascist groups remained peripheralised despite the social connections of the one British fascist leader of note, Oswald Mosley.[20]

The orchestration of ideas conducive to English "national character" and a distinctive patriotic style developed from a more diffuse and regionalised intellectual class than in many other European countries. Eschewing coherent social theory, this motley collection of local intelligentsias generally turned to literature as a means of expressing its ideas and feelings on the nature of the "English genius" (as the critic Hugh Kingsmill termed it) and its particular relationship to landscape, regional "types" and local character. A full historiography of this interlocking set of local traditions will depend upon a series of microstudies to portray a coherent picture of English regional thought that, in varying degress, remained unmoved by the sophisticated literary styles of Bloomsbury and the Auden generation of public-school radicals.

The tenor of these local intellectuals was mainly low church, with a strong element of cultural nostalgia for the previous century and a deferential view of the English class system and social status.[21] Many wrote in a near-mystical style of the English national and patriotic make-up, having important consequences for the later formulation of English patriotic ideals during the Second World War. The poet John Drinkwater, for example, writing in 1924 on patriotism in literature, argued that patriotism was 'something more than the utilitarian compact between the citizen of a state for the purposes of a defence against foreign encroachment' for it was a 'spiritual force, a mood, an energy that aims at no material advantage, a delight as natural and uncalculating as the pleasure we take in sunlight or sound limbs.' For Drinkwater, patriotic emotion formed an organising force around which to construct a literary vision of reality.[22]

This local tradition of English patriotism imbibed many of the values of the Victorian age concerning the hideousness of cities and urban life. Reflecting a more widespread commitment to gentility in English cultural life, this anti-urbanism had important political implications in the post-war period and the mounting industrial/class conflict. 'It is queer to see the revolutionary look in people's eyes everywhere in the cities,' wrote the Shropshire-born poet John Masefield to his American patron Florence Lamont in 1920. In Birmingham and Shrewsbury, he detected a 'kind of anger screwed up to spitting point. So little would set both sides spitting, or biting the thumb.' Masefield preferred to look back to a tradition of 'quality' inherited from the past when

> *you could tell the officers from the men by the face alone. You could tell the lady from the not-quite at a glance. There was here a race of people committed to a way of life and manners by both birth and tradition, in which a distinguished quality alone mattered. They were not very wise, perhaps, nor very broad-minded, nor very generous, but they had a high standard of courtesy and breeding and good manners, a fine tact of exclusion as Pater calls it .....*[23]

Such status-consciousness reflected George Orwell's observation that 'English regional snobberies' were 'nationalism in miniature'.[24]

If this was a defence of traditional snobbery, it nevertheless acted as an important guide to the survival of a provincial sense of social hierarchy and place despite the massive economic and social changes induced by advancing urbanisation. There was a strong element of nostalgia for a way of life that seemed to be passing, though there were still some inherently innovative features which indicated that this was a cultural and intellectual tradition that was by no means completely played out. The pursuit of what Tom Nairn has termed a 'myth community' in English social thought served as a vital buttress to an ideology of rusticity that contained a vision of an English patriotism.[25] It served as a means for neutralising a conception of class warfare and emphasising the homogeneous nature of English society rooted in small town and village life and spreading up through the shires and counties to that of central government and the organs of national power. To some writers within this tradition, the overwhelming nature of this provincial rusticity could, on occasions, prove burdensome. Writing from Rushdene in Northamptonshire to Edward Garnett, H E Bates, for example, complained in 1926 of 'dying of solitary loneliness... God knows how people keep alive here. It must be easier for bananas to grow in their gardens than for them to live or what happens to them. Everything's so silly and dull – one has to flirt with every conceivable girl and gibe at the pious and interest myself in the local Labour Party and trespass myself in other people's woods in order to get anything out of the business. I can't write, I can't read or think.'[26]

Unmasking the myth of peaceful "merrie England" could be disconcerting, since it threatened to reveal a culture of boredom and indolence. It was difficult for those committed to this indigenous myth to equal the more grandiose visions of overseas adventure offered by the imperialist tradition of popular fiction of Henty, Haggard and Kipling. However, the leitmotif of English pastoral fiction and poetry of the interwar period is a degree of charm and simple style which had appeal for a generation exhausted and sickened by the ravages of war. One such example was Mary Webb, whose novel, *Precious Bane* (1924), carried a strong eulogistic preface from Stanley Baldwin in the 1928 edition, following her death the previous year. Like Masefield, Mary Webb came from Shropshire and she wrote of a rural society in touch with the passing of the seasons and the life cycle of animals and people. In some respects, the image of England discerned in Mary Webb's writing was a Burkean one of continuity through generations. As she wrote in her foreword to the novel:

> *We are tomorrow's past. Even now we slip away like those pictures painted on the moving dials of antique clocks – a ship, a cottage, sun and moon, a nosegay. The dial turns, the ship rides up and sinks again, the yellow painted sun has set and we, that were the new thing, gather magic as we go. The whirr of the spinning wheels has ceased in our parlours, and we hear no more the treadles of the loom, the swift, silken noise of the flung shuttle, the intermittent thud of the batten. But the imagination hears them, and theirs is the melody of romance.*[27]

There was thus a romantic element to the image of the English rustic and picturesque which could partly make up for the loss of the imperial adventurer tradition. At the same time, the search for the rural served as a consoling theme to those seeking to confront the horrors of the First

World War. Dean Inge in his book *England*, for example, believed that the importance of the poetry of the war lay in its emphasis on rural life and its 'revelation of the national character'.[28]

The impact of the literature of the war on popular memory was, however, ambiguous and double-edged. As Paul Fussell has pointed out in his important study *The Great War and Modern Memory*, one crucial feature of the war lay in its heightening of an adversarial tone in English literature which was to have lasting ramifications through the Second World War and beyond.[29]

This adversarial quality of English literature was a reflection of a more general disintegration of the moral order which had underpinned so much literary writing from the Victorian era. The catastrope of the war, as John McCormick has remarked, 'brought into modern society a sense of urgency and a new tempo; it made for a new consciousness of self and of the place of self in society; it created an atmosphere in which the loss of old certainties, the presence of new anxieties, and the thrusting forward of public issues combined to isolate man from man and group from group.'[30]

In this new situation of apparent cultural disintegration, so well expressed by the modernist poetry of Eliot and Pound and the lambasting tone of Wyndham Lewis, the efforts of the provincial literati to effect a cultural return to normalcy seemed doomed to failure. Even some of the Conservative ideologues themselves were driven to admit a general crisis of political ideas. As Lord Eustace Percy confessed in his book *Democracy on Trial* in 1931, there was no 'national idea in which we any longer believe. We have lost the easy self-confidence which distinguished our Victorian grandfathers and still distinguishes our American contemporaries.'[31]

This reflected a disillusionment, in considerable sections of the political and cultural elite, with the pre-1914 posture of romantic patriotism and a world role for Britain as the hub of an empire. However, the personnel who occupied many of the dominant positions in public life in the interwar years were still the products of the same public school tradition which had infused the naive romanticism and gentlemanly idealism which had died on the Somme.[32] In most cases, this elite remained committed to imperial ideals, though they expressed them in more cautious terms and in a language that accorded with post-war norms of "trusteeship". If the romance had been removed from the posturing on an external imperial plane, it was to some extent being rediscovered within the English cultural and political landscape. The legacy of Matthew Arnold's Christian idealism, which had shaped much of the mood of late nineteenth-century imperialism, fed back into the English heartland. Aided by the poet's visions of the pre-war Georgians, it found solace and comfort in the quest for a new set of local identities.

The close links between this indigenous quest for "merrie England" and the older imperial ideal were not immediately apparent. Some of the features of the merrie England ideal were derived from late nineteenth-century critics of empire such as William Morris and Edward Carpenter. For example, the radical and pacifist leader of the Labour Party in the early 1930s, George Lansbury, articulated an ideal of a socialist and pastoral England similar to that of his nineteenth-century forebears. 'I do not want Dowlais or Merthyr, Poplar or Canning Town, the Black Country or the coal fields of Lanarkshire, or anywhere else like them replanned,' he wrote in *My England* (1937). Industrial communities, he argued, should rather be transformed to accord with the ideal of 'reclaiming, re-creating England' where he could 'see the village greens with the maypoles once again erected and the boys and girls, young men and maidens, all joining in the mirth and folly of May Day'.[33] Similarly, Walter Greenwood's important industrial novel *Love on the Dole* (1933) manifested at certain points a pronounced anti-urban tone, for all its adeptness at penetrating the culture of working-class community life in Salford. Describing Dawney's Hill, for instance, Greenwood invokes the rural past before the two cities were built and contrasts the present industrial hideousness with the former pastoral cleanness;

> *From its brow, if you sit with your back to the setting sun, the huge stricken area of the Two Cities sprawls away east, north and south. Like a beleaguered city from which plundered incendiaries have recently withdrawn a vast curtain of smoke rises as from smouldering ruins. And the tall chimneys standing in clusters like giant ninepins, sprouting forth black billowing streamers, write their capricious signatures on the smudgy skies. The same today as in the not-long-ago when old people told tales of cows being called home from where below were once lush meadows: days when the soaring larks beat wings against spotted skies, and, of a night, gawmless calves, the daft loons, stood gaping at the moon, and, aloft, the stealthy midnight owl sharply eyed the moonlit green below.*[34]

The passage is a good example of what Fussell has called the dichotomising of the modern literary imagination as a result of the Great War. The urban and the industrial landscape of the Two Cities is counterposed to the pastoral heritage before they were built. The Two Cities are depicted in imagery born of the conflict in the trenches where 'plundered incendiaries' have recently withdrawn the 'vast curtain of smoke' from the 'smouldering ruins'. In contrast, the surrounding pastoral countryside is described as timeless, gentle and tranquil where only 'soaring larks' beat their wings against the 'spotted skies'.

The persistence of the pastoral and rustic within the imagination of radical writers in England to some extent blunted the impact of the literary modernists in the interwar years. It also reinforced the efforts of the conservative provincial literati to define the nature and scope of the

English patriotic ideal. This became especially evident by the time of the
Second World War when the pastoral theme became a dominant
leitmotif of a popular patriotism mobilised in pursuit of war.

England as a Parish: The Second World War and Popular Patriotism

The achievements of the Baldwin era in establishing an ideology of
English national homogeneity in the popular imagination have been
eclipsed by subsequent attacks on the policy of appeasement. The figure
of Baldwin passed into history widely discredited and blamed for the
failure of Britain to rearm adequately in the 1930s. However, Baldwin's
conception of England was important for linking it to rustic and country
roots and a constitutional view of political compromise and consensus. It
was also significant for avoiding a pseudoscientific vision of the nation
derived from neo-Darwinist theories of struggle and survival of the
fittest. As a consequence, the writings of the curator of the Hunterian
Museum at the Royal College of Surgeons, Sir Arthur Keith, did not gain
an extensive following in the interwar period, since they linked the
process of national unification with warfare and armed conflict.[35] By
contrast, the political vision of Baldwin was anchored in a nostalgic ideal
of English independence which he saw as having essentially spiritual
qualities. Speaking, for instance, to the Federation of British Industries
in 1937 he confessed to dreading 'the loss of that independent
individualist character which has made this nation what it is. I dread the
growth of that materialist view of life which, to my mind, is a danger both
to body and to soul. We must see to it that in some way we can preserve
the character of our people to meet the changed conditions of the age, and
see that our character triumphs over our environment.'[36] This is a very
different Conservative ideal from the more recent radical Thatcherite
vision which has been principally concerned with transforming the
national character in a more materialist direction and creating an
'enterprise culture'. The main continuity in Conservative thought thus
lies in the stress on English individualism, though this has revealed
more of a Smilesian "self-help" ideal in the Thatcherite project compared
to the Baldwinite harkening back to a more traditional yeomanry notion
of individual self-reliance.

By the end of the 1930s, nevertheless, there were growing tensions in
the Baldwinite consensus as elements in the national intelligentsia
began looking for a more active vision of the patriotic ideal. The writer J
B Priestley was notable for including in some of his urban novels, such as
The Good Companions (1929), a strong presence of the Pennine
landscape. But he, too, by the end of the 1930s, was eager for a dynamic
element to enter into the definition of the English patriotic make-up, as
he lamented the loss of the rich culture of urban working-class
communities with the expansion of an apparently sterile and conformist
suburbia. In his autobiography *Rain Upon Godshill* in 1939, written

after extensive foreign travels, he called for a creative society that would act as 'a bridge that will take us from yesterday to tomorrow, from the end of one system of communal life to the beginning of another and better one, safely across the iron and sterile gulfs of an enforced economy that has neither true politics nor community'.[37] This feeling of cultural exhaustion at the end of the 1930s was echoed by the travel writer H V Morton, who had written in the 1920s the popular guide *In Search of England* that had carefully skirted round the industrial and urban centres in pursuit of an older England located in the villages and countryside. However, in *I Saw Two Englands*, published in 1942 and based on travels immediately after the outbreak of war, Morton confessed to a despair at the apparent indolence of a society in need of being woken up:

> *So upon a winter's day I returned from my journey through war-time England, vaguely disturbed by the apathy of a nation that lacked a leader, a nation that was not even half at war, a nation sound as a bell, loyal and determined, warlike but not military, a nation waiting, almost pathetically, for something – anything – to happen.*[38]

In 12 months, however, Morton detected a different mood as the formerly localised and isolated villages that had made up his traditional vision of England became transformed through the impact of a popular patriotism. 'One of the most remarkable things about this war is the quiet gay England has ceased to be a country or even a county for many of us, and has become a parish. All over our land, villages once proclaimed dead and done for have awakened to arms. People scarcely on speaking terms have come together to organise defence.'[39] The image of the English village landscape, cultivated since the decline of the imperial myth at the end of the First World War, had been successfully fostered and revitalised behind the Churchillian war effort.

Despite the apparent political disconnection with the coming to power of the Churchill government in May 1940, there was an important continuity in patriotic imagery which the propaganda of the war ably fostered. The developments in popular tourism in the interwar period had led to a growing interest in the preservation of a distinct ideal of the English landscape. The cult of preservationism, as Patrick Wright has pointed out, has vital ideological functions in that it plays a role in the nationalisation of history and enables the state, in times of crisis, to project an idealised image of the nation.[40] This certainly occurred in the course of the 1920s and 1930s when an extensive literature developed on the nature and development of "the legacy of England". In a collection of essays published under such a title in 1935, the poet Edmund Blunden, famous for his pastoral poetry from the First World War, wrote of the importance of 'landscape consciousness' in which the preservation of ancient monuments had a key place.[41] Charles Bradley Ford went on to write of the importance of the English village which had an inner harmony 'based on the Englishman's love of his soil and the house he has built upon it'. Further, this image was linked to a wider constitutional development for 'such freedom and content as have flourished in this country do still, notwithstanding many reverses, find their best material expression in the quiet beauty of many English villages.'[42] R H Mottram also described the country town with its specifically English roots for there was 'nothing in the country town of Celtic Twilight or Celtic fairyland, nor of that savage nobility that redeems and makes uncomfortable the small towns of Ireland and the Highlands.'[43] The colonial imagery lay just beneath the surface of this landscape literature and indicated its close connection with an indigenous patriotic quest for cultural roots.

The advent of the Second World War, was crucial in defining a movement of neo-romanticism in English art and literature which had close affinities with a popular patriotism.[44] The Tory historian Arthur Bryant was able to give this mood an historical definition with his *English Saga, 1840–1940* published in 1940. Here the "green land far away" of England is described as having a culture

> *that was not founded on courts and cities but on the green fields and growing earth, like a tree it spreads upwards. Walking among the water meadows at Bemerton one could see its roots: the Spire of Salisbury cathedral tapered skywards out of the cup of the downs and the cottage folk spoke of a pious man named George Herbert whose grave was forgotten but whose books they still read. In men's hearts there dwelt a novel called the Past; its chapters were their own earliest memories, hallowed by repetition and loving association, and the tales their fathers and the old wives of the village had told them.*[45]

The symbol of the cathedral spire had considerable importance in the reworking of the English myth in the early 1940s. It accorded with the revival of religious poetry in the idiom of Edith Sitwell's *Still Falls the Rain* and T S Eliot's *Four Quartets*. In a similar manner the fighter pilot Richard Hillary recalled in his autobiography *The Last Enemy* that driving up to his aerodrome 'the road running up to the Mess took us close by Salisbury, and the towering steeple of its cathedral was a good landmark from the aerodrome. The countryside lay quiet in the warm glow of the summer evening. A few minutes' flying to the south was the sea, and across from it France, equally peaceful in the quiet of the evening: within a few weeks Britain's army was to be struggling desperately to get back across that narrow stretch of water, and the France that we knew was to be no more.'[46] The use of pastoral contrast in order to understand the full horror of the war had been fully explored, as

Fussell has pointed out, in the First World War. Hillary's depiction of a placid pastoral landscape in southern England was much in this tradition, though it also emphasised the ultimate underpinning of this view by a Christian faith symbolised by the spire of Salisbury Cathedral.[47]

This religious vision grew into the near-mystical with Michael Powell and Emeric Pressburger's film *A Canterbury Tale* (1944) in which the action is dominated by the spire of Canterbury Cathedral standing out from the bombed ruins of the surrounding city. Though attacked by a number of film critics at the time of its release for its abstruseness, the film is an important reflection of neo-romanticism in British cinema in the war years. It especially manages to portray the idea, as H V Morton put it, of England as a parish. The film is a pastoral poem to the countryside of Kent and clearly identifies the obvious signs of Englishness within the landscape: the map of Chaucer's England, the village of Chillingbourne, the Colpeper Institute, the old village craftsmen. The film celebrates the essential continuity of English history, from the opening scene of the falconer transformed into a modern firewatcher and his falcon into a spitfire. Within what is essentially a feudal vision of the English landscape, the figure of Colpeper is crucial as the "natural" interpreter of the law. As Nannette Aldred has suggested, there are Kiplingesque overtones to Powell's film, indicating that the notion of the "law" conceived in the context of India and the frontiers of an empire have been brought back to the imperial metropolis at a time of crisis to portray an organic and homogeneous ideal of England.[48]

The conservative religious symbolism of English patriotism was by no means unchallenged in the course of the Second World War. New influences from Hollywood and the intrusion of the American GIs from 1942 onwards had long-term effects on the make-up of English society. From 1942-43 there were some 12,000 black GIs in Britain and for the first time a nationwide pattern of race relations began to grow up in British towns and cities. Before the war this had mostly been confined to the seaport towns.[49] As one Commonwealth Relations Office memorandum pointed out in 1943 it was important 'not to speak of "the empire" to denote the overseas parts of the empire alone. Such a usage implies that the United Kingdom...is not part of the Empire and might be thought to suggest an attitude of "ownership" on the part of the United Kingdom which is neither in accordance with the facts nor good propaganda'.[50] The softer conception of "Commonwealth" began to overtake official parlance during the course of the early 1940s, underpinned by the doctrine that the objective of colonial policy was now the promotion of a "partnership" of the colonised peoples with the governing power, rather than the older ideal of imperial "trusteeship".[51]

There were efforts by the Churchill government to try, as far as possible, to restrain and control the degree of liberalisation in political debate during the war. This was exemplified by the decision of the Ministry of Information to ban the BBC broadcasts of J B Priestley in 1941 and Churchill's attempt to suppress the Powell and Pressburger film *The Life and Death of Colonel Blimp*.[52] But the force of public mood was against such efforts and, in the long run, it is possible to see the period as a critical one for the emergence into political and cultural life of a more humanitarian and benign group of opinion leaders who were to exert their sway until at least the early 1950s. This new "middle opinion" had come of age in the period following the First World War and had been impressed, in varying degrees, with a less grandiose vision of British political aims and ambitions. It came to dominate the leadership of the Labour Party and imbibed ideals of mild socialist public ownership and an attack on the material values of Victorian capitalism. For such groups of "herbivores", to employ the phrase of Michael Frayn, the role of Britain in the post-war era lay in promoting the ideals of both the United Nations and the British Commonwealth. It sought, through such liberal organs as the *News Chronicle*, *The Guardian* and *The Observer*, a more benevolent ideal of public administration in which the values of the welfare state were to have a high prominence. For a period at least, it appeared that the values of British patriotism that had been emphasised during the war years were to be replaced by the ideal of welfare as a means of promoting both internal social harmony and managing the pattern of class conflict.[53]

The Welfare State and the Decline of Patriotism

The post-war period to 1956 and the Suez crisis was a disorientated one in which the more conventional ideals of patriotism no longer seemed to have the same political resonance. Jimmy Porter in John Osborne's play *Look Back in Anger* (1956) probably spoke for a good many of the post-war National Service generation who envied the older generation's chance to fight for causes like the International Brigade and the war against Hitler, as well as lamenting the fact that there seemed to be no good causes left. The older imperial idealism was now confined to a fringe on the right and a few Labour enthusiasts like Ernest Bevin who continued to hope as late as 1946 that India would be kept in the empire.[54] For the elderly Attlee cabinet, the purpose of overseas colonial policy became one of economic development of British colonial territories. There was, as one of its information pamphlets endeavoured to explain, no 'sinister imperialism' involved in this enterprise for 'all of us who have a common loyalty to the throne are honestly trying to create a better world not only for ourselves but for mankind generally.'[55] Right-wing critics of the Labour policy often dwelt less on the new definition of aims but rather on the degree of central government planning involved stemming from the 1940 and 1945 Colonial Development and Welfare Acts. As the *Round Table* argued, there was no necessary virtue in 'uniformity' in policy and there should be a more pragmatic accommodation to different local circumstances.[56]

The commitment to trying to build up the Commonwealth as a third force in post-war international relations became progressively undermined by a growing lack of political credibility. By the end of the 1940s the emergence of the United States as a superpower seemed to many critics of the government confirmation that British policy was being increasingly forced to bend to dicates from Washington. The devaluation of the pound in 1949 also reflected the growing imbalance in the Atlantic Alliance and many younger intellectuals entered the following year with a good deal of cynicism. 'Not only is the intellectual importance of England growing daily less than that of the United States,' complained Peter Laslett in the *The Cambridge Journal*, 'but the Anglo Saxon attitude itself gets more and more backward rather than forward looking.' There was an increasing obsession with the Royal Family in England that rivalled that of Anglophile Americans, he argued, perhaps because of the drabness of post-war London, but also because of a feeling that Britain counted for less in the world. There was thus a need to recognise that 'the peace of the world depends...on the Englishman being able to reconcile himself to a continuous diminution in the consequence of his country.'[57]

Plans for the 1951 Festival of Britain were geared to take people's minds off the austerity of post-war Britain, as well as to promote the name of England in the cultural and artistic sphere. In the event, the popularity of the Festival marked the end of an era rather than the start of a new injection of post-war idealism into British politics and culture. Later the same year Labour was defeated by the Conservatives and the return of the Churchill government signalled the departure of the "herbivores" from such public prominence and the emergence of a new and harder generation of "carnivores".[58] Though committed to the continuation of many aspects of the welfare state, the apparent moderation of the resulting Conservative policy of "Butskellism" covered a more pronounced difference of approach to British politics than its predecessor. It led to the initiation of a debate on the condition of England that was to have repercussions within Conservative circles as late as the 1970s.

After the Labour victory in 1945, thinking in the Conservative Party had been confused. While a small minority tried to resist accommodation to the general collectivist tide in post-war Britian, the political rethinking in the party led to an Industrial Charter in 1947 that was broadly favourable to government intervention in a mixed economy and Keynesian demand management.[59] By 1947/48, a high water mark was reached in the government's nationalisation policy and strong resistance was mounted in Conservative circles to the nationalisation of the steel industry.[60] From this period it is possible to date the slow emergence within the party of a libertarian right wing that placed increasing faith

in the liberation of the market forces through the diminution of state
control and intervention in capitalist market processes. These ideas were
frequently expressed at a provincial rather than national level, as in the
case of the Birmingham Unionist Association where the pre-war old
guard began to lose out by the late 1940s to a more radical lower-middle-
class element with free market ideas.[61] At the political centre these
trends tended to be masked by a more paternalist leadership whose
authority had been partly restored by the party reforms in the late 1940s
by R A B Butler and Lord Woolton.

At a deeper level, though, there was a crisis of Conservative political
faith in the 1950s as Britain's international political status continued to
decline. The domination of the party's thinking throughout the 1950s by
what Andrew Gamble has called the 'right progressives' concealed a
deep-seated malaise in sections of the right at the loss of British imperial
prestige which, it was felt, rationalised and legitimised the authority of
the party in domestic politics.[62] As late as 1953 the imperial enthusiast
Julian Amery could still justify the Commonwealth on the grounds that
it provided a "mystique" in English political life and an outlet for the
energies of British landowning and middle-class families who might
otherwise have been drawn to fascism under the post-war Labour
government.[63] The Suez crisis of 1956 seemed to dash such ideals.
Though the party was able to recover under the leadership of Harold
Macmillan with an appeal to affluence and consumer values ("You've
never had it so good"), for sections of the Conservative right the era was
one of growing national complacency. Peregrine Worsthorne pointed out
in a penetrating article in *Foreign Affairs* that it was 'difficult to recall a
period in modern British history when a nation felt so passive about its
role in the world'. This Worsthorne ascribed to the half-baked nature of
the post-war social revolution which 'merely confused the existing

> ....*much more thought and experience in the field of race relations
> and forms of government in the Colonial Empire. Especially is this
> needed in multi-racial societies, like those of East and Southern
> Africa where the simple question, 'National self-government or not',
> at once breaks into the sharp splinters of who is to govern, and how
> are the rights of the different communities to be balanced.*[22]

The retention of at least the forms of older class domination,
such as the public schools and Oxbridge, meant that no new
national equilibrium had been established by pragmatic
social engineering since the mid 1940s. As a consequence,
there had been a cramping of the old national posture without
the release of new energies in Britain's "stalemate state". All
this had been at least momentarily revealed at the time of Suez and the
consequence had been the articulation of a growing mood of
dissatisfaction by the younger generation of "Angry Young Men",

epitomised by John Osborne's *Look Back in Anger*, though this discontent had not found an automatic place in the Labour Party.[64]

There was much in Worsthorne's perceptive analysis which rang true, for the Macmillan years did come to manifest a failing in Conservative political ideals and were associated with corruption and dishonesty in governing circles through the Profumo Affair of 1963. For many on the right, there appeared to be a loss of political direction and almost a politics of make-believe. The novelist John Wain wrote in *Encounter* that there were 'too few people in responsible positions...who have disentangled dream from reality. Our insularity prevents us from seeing ourselves as others see us. And our national mixture of idealism, vague grand memories, vanity, the old habit of world supremacy, and sheer mental laziness prevents us from being candid with ourselves.'[65] This general disparagement of the "state of England" question was very typical of intellectuals of the period and perhaps reflected their own marginalisation from serious influence within the British political process. The exploration of the state of the nation in governing circles did indeed go on, but it tended to take place behind closed doors. Indeed, it was only with the general frustration at the restricted and exclusive nature of this debate that a wider popularisation began to ensue in the 1960s. This was partly the result of a growth of television audiences and the withering nature of such satire as *That Was The Week That Was* and partly the consequence of a more aggressive and impatient style of a new generation of right-wing radicals in Conservative circles, whose lower-middle-class origins put them out of tune with the older landed and aristocratic establishment or "magic circle", as they were acerbically called by Iain Macleod.

Even before the advent of this popularisation of the state of England issue in the 1960s many of its chief features were explored within Conservative clubland. One of the most significant features of right-wing political concern was the linkage of New Commonwealth immigration to Britain in the 1950s with the decline of great power status. There was not, though, any unanimous agreement on the need for immigration control legislation, for some departments such as the Commonwealth Relations Office had a vested interest in trying to make its overseas colonial development programme viable, and so opposed measures that might erode the goodwill of nationalist leaders in the territories concerned. Nevertheless, the more traditionalist Lord Salisbury, as undersecretary of state at the CRO, saw immigration as a 'fundamental problem for us all' which threatened in time to reach American proportions. Salisbury saw the welfare state as the reason for the immigration and it was necessary to 'recognise that this coloured problem is potentially of a fundamental nature for the future of our country' even though it was 'only just beginning to push its ugly head above the surface of politics.'[66]

Salisbury's interest in the issue was a reflection of his involvement in decolonisation and the thinking of what kind of society "England" was to be in years ahead. In one respect, as a senior peer of the realm, he was in a good position to see black immigration in terms of the traditional aristocratic conception of English national identity. As Worsthorne later argued, those who rejected that yardstick of identity were left with no alternative national ideal to follow.[67] Thus the settlement of significant communities of black immigrants who did not appear to share the same cultural values as the surrounding society represented a long-term threat to this aristocratic definition of Englishness. 'We are faced with a problem,' Salisbury thus warned, 'which, though at present it may be only a cloud the size of man's hand, may easily come to fill the whole political horizon.'

The weakness in the debate on the Conservative right up to the middle 1960s was that it possessed no national ideal of England other than the older imperial one. In the decade from Suez in 1956 to the second election victory of the Labour Party under Harold Wilson in 1966 there was a strong element of gracious and gentlemanly withdrawal of the Conservative old guard, punctuated by periodic upsurges of conflict such as Harold Macmillan's cabinet purge in 1962 and the refusal of Enoch Powell and Iain Macleod to serve under Sir Alec Douglas-Home when he was appointed Macmillan's successor as Prime Minister in the autumn of 1963. But with the electoral defeat of 1964, albeit by the narrow margin of five, the traditionalist right went into full-scale retreat and the way was opened for the right progressives under Edward Heath, the first Conservative leader to be elected by the parliamentary party. It was thus in the context of the rise to eminence of the new technocratic element in the Conservative Party in the middle 1960s that the challenge of Powell to the dominant post-war political consensus was made. This was to be in terms of a new conceptualisation of the English patriotic ideal.

Enoch Powell and the Vision of the English Nation State

The crisis among the Conservative traditionalists following Suez occurred at the same time as the older pre-war Baldwinite ideal of the English landscape started to be radically undermined by the post-war welfare state. The dominant 1930s myth of England had built on the pastoral visions of the late-Victorian back-to-nature enthusiasts and widened them to accord with a new motorcar age. But the myth had left the basic ideal of picturesque village communities and rolling landscapes essentially intact. Some of the contributors to the magazine *Country Life* even hoped that this ideal could continue in the post-war era, including a return to the culture of the country house.[68] However, it soon became clear that the developments in farming and post-war town planning were going to make this ideal even more far-fetched than it had been in the interwar years. Agricultural mechanisation, the speeding up of popular mobility and the creation of new towns in the late 1940s and 1950s indicated that the English rural landscape was changing fast.

For some traditionalists this was a matter of deep regret, but one that had to be understood. H E Bates lamented the pace of agricultural mechanisation which seemed like a disease which progressively enveloped everything. There were compensations, however, for the new planned scenery of the post-war welfare state was eliminating much of the "decay" of the 1930s, leaving in its place a 'pattern of rural, urban and semi-urban – that neat, fresh, tightly woven almost garden like weave of grass and woodland and hill and stream and village and valley and moor and orchard and hedgerow, so undramatic and unspectacular and yet so profoundly satisfying, that we have to think of it as our God-given rather than our man-given inheritance – [which] seems more fully planted than ever.'[69] For Bates there was a new permanency to the English landscape that was born out of the nationalisation of the aristocratic and genteel ideal during the war years. In his post-war novels that dealt with the retreat from empire, such as *The Scarlet Sword* (1950) set on the north-west frontier of India, Bates used this new national conception of the English landscape as a stabilising factor in a situation of political turmoil and social upheaval. The very landscape of the Kashmir in which the Catholic mission is located appears to reflect the surrounding instability of the partition of the Indian subcontinent. As Father Anstey digs in the mission garden he could never fail to look at the mountains in the distance

> *without remembering that once, more than a thousand years before, the whole of the mountain before it had fallen, obliterating the valley below. He did not know why that, even so far away as almost to be legendary and happening in any case to a mountainside that had otherwise nothing more spectacular to it than the hills of his native Yorkshire, should always disturb him so much.*[70]

This was an ideal that was not concerned with drawing out internal regional divisions within the English landscape or trying to locate the source of English identity with the southern or "Anglo-Saxon" as opposed to "Celtic" people. It was more interested in drawing out an English national ideal from the specifics of an island landscape that now appeared to be threatened with eclipse with the rise of Russia and the United States to superpower status. George Orwell, for instance, saw Britain in his novel *1984* as Airstrip One of the great continental landmass Oceania (the United States).

The decline in interest in regional peculiarities reflected the increased domination of London in English literary and cultural life and the decline of the older provincial intelligentsias. Many of the newer provincial literary figures were notable for their swift removal from their Midlands or northern roots and their orientation towards the capital.

Thus novelists such as Kingsley Amis, John Braine, John Wain, Alan Sillitoe and Stan Barstow were notable for writing novels about provincial life with a strong emphasis on the hero, usually working or lower middle class, moving out and upwards, often in a London direction. This phenomenon was exacerbated by the films that were made of these novels. They reinforced a middle-class and London view of provincial working-class life and culture that verged on the patronising. One prominent exception could perhaps be made to this general trend in the poet Philip Larkin, who obstinately resided in Hull where he worked as a university librarian. But Larkin was born in Coventry and chose to reside on Humberside where his writings could reflect a provincial idea of England, but one strongly orientated in a London direction. The poet of *Whitsun Weddings* is on a train speeding to London and, though he feels himself very distanced from the provincial rituals of the multiple wedding ceremony, closely identifies with the nationalised and increasingly urbanised English landscape:

> *We hurried towards London, shuffling gouts of steam*
> *Now fields were building plots, and poplars cast*
> *Long shadows over major roads...*

Nevertheless, the poet can make one last gesture towards seeing London in pastoral terms:

> *I thought of London spread out in the sun,*
> *Its postal districts packed like squares of wheat...*

It is clear that this was an increasingly homogeneous ideal of England which Larkin, as one of the most prominent figures in post-war English poetry, attempted to see in terms freed from the older gentility stretching back to the Georgians.

The connection between the literary imagination and political thought is always a tenuous one and it is arguable that very little of this post-war literary writing had much to do with political ideology. For Enoch Powell, anyway, as Tom Nairn has pointed out, the main concerns of his own poetry lie with the Georgians and in opposition to the interests of more recent movements in English poetry.[71] However, the connection can be seen to lie at a more oblique level in that the ideas Powell came to espouse by the 1960s grew out of a political and cultural situation in which a more nationally-orientated intelligentsia had emerged in England since the Second World War, aided by the growth of radio and television and popular mobility. It was these factors which contributed to the message he was able to give in the late 1960s to an audience already attuned in some degree to a populist language that believed the survival of the English nation to be in jeopardy through the advent of black immigration.

For Powell, black immigration was only one feature of a far wider and more grandiose project for transforming the British political landscape and what he termed 'The Empire of England'.[72] As one of the key spokesmen of the new right in the Conservative Party in the 1960s, Powell sought to undermine the dominant ideology of the right progressives and reorientate the party around an ideology that emphasised a strong British patriotism, a free market economy with a minimum of state intervention and an independent foreign policy that was not tied to the dictates of either the Atlantic Alliance or Western Europe. In effect, Powell sought to offer a new national strategy to the Conservatives based upon both a politics of power to reorganise the state as well as a new politics of support to win the consent of the electorate.[73] The appeal to an English patriotism was undoubtedly a key feature in this effort to win electoral support after it had proved itself increasingly fickle in the 1964 and 1966 elections by voting in Labour governments. No longer could the middle ground of politics, especially among the new groups of salaried middle-class employees, be taken for granted and politics was increasingly a matter of ideological warfare rather than one anchored in traditional voting patterns. Powell was thus important for emphasising the mythology of the nation for 'the life of nations, no less than that of men, is lived largely in the imagination.' The nation was a 'mysterious composite being' which had its own hopes and fears. The definition and make-up of this entity was seen in strictly populist terms, for the 'corporate imagination' of the nation was often more important for many people's happiness than their own private imagination.[74] Here the experience of the last war was especially apposite for Powell, for the national patriotism of that period exemplified the point that people could identify their own fortunes with those of the nation. What nations think about themselves, furthermore, was determined by their conception of their past history, which was always myth:

> *The moment a fact enters into history it becomes mythical,*
> *because it has been taken and fitted into place in a*
> *set of ordered relationships which is the creation of the*
> *human mind and not otherwise present in human nature.*[75]

However, for Powell the point was that two false national myths had entered into the popular imagination: first, that Britain had been a great imperial power and had then in the course of the twentieth century lost this position; and secondly, that she had been a great industrial power and had been superceded by other nations. Both myths amounted to a vision of national decline; but both, for Powell, were wrong, for the empire had been a relatively late and transitory phenomenon occurring only in the late 1890s after Victoria's Diamond Jubilee, while even in Britain's industrial heyday in the 1860s she had been importing manufactured goods. Both the empire and the Industrial Revolution needed to be seen in terms of a longer time span; the essential continuity of English history throughout had remained unbroken:

> *Thus our generation is like one which comes home again from years of distant wandering. We discover affinities with earlier generations of English, generations before the "expansion of England", who felt no country but this to be their own. We look upon the traces which they left with a new curiosity, the curiosity of finding ourselves once more akin with the old English.*

The dominant consideration stemming from this conception of English history thus lay, for Powell, in the country's unity accruing from the 'unlimited supremacy' of the Crown in Parliament and 'the homogeneity of England, so profound and embracing the counties and regions making it a hobby to discover their differences and assert their peculiarities.' There grew from this the ethological observation that the 'deepest instinct' of the 'Englishman' lay in continuity.[76]

Powell's vision of an ascent of English national feeling came eventually to founder, as far as he was concerned, with the apparent betrayal of English sovereignty after the Heath government's decision to join the Common Market in 1971. In turn, Powell removed himself from the centre of the political debate in the Conservative Party by voting Labour in 1974 and eventually coming to reside as an Ulster Unionist MP until his defeat in the 1987 general election. However, his political message was important for injecting a strong dose of English patriotic fervour into post-war British political debate and laying the foundations for a populist appeal by the Conservatives in the late 1970s by Heath's successor, Mrs Thatcher.[77] The Powellite message acted in some respects as a prototype for the later Thatcherite package as it reflected the injection of a new right political movement into the Conservative Party. The effect was that, by the early 1980s, the Conservatives had been able to win back the mantle of the national party after it appeared to have been momentarily lost in the early 1970s with the electorate's disillusionment with the Heath government.

By the late 1980s, however, patriotism had become linked with a British version of Gaullism and a strong state-initiated drive for radical social engineering involving massive privatisation and the erosion of the post-war consensus.[78] At the root of this national ideal there lay, though, not the vision of "One Nation" but of a society divided between north and south. The success of the populist strategy accorded with electoral geography as the capture of seats in the south and the Midlands by the Conservatives in both the 1983 and 1987 elections proved sufficient to ensure a comfortable parliamentary majority despite the loss of support in the north and Scotland. In the pursuit of this reordering of British society the Thatcher government has not needed, as some analysts on the left have imagined, to live on the nostalgia of the imperial past which was ostensibly invoked at the time of the Falklands War. The significance of the Thatcher government lies rather in that, building on the national vision of English continuity formulated by Powell but stretching back to earlier versions under Baldwin in the 1920s and 1930s, the imperial mystique has been to a considerable degree removed from the central mind of the British body politic. A new, more hard-headed realism entered into British foreign policy as the old obligations East of Suez were removed and, in many ways, the older sentiments for empire have been not so much revived as relegated to grand media epics such as *The Raj Quartet* and *Far Pavilions*.[79] In contrast to the marginalisation of the imperial mystique, though, a more basic set of colonial attitudes and values survived in the treatment of ethnic minorities in the inner cities. But this colonialism was a more amorphous set of societal ideologies rather than a state-fostered pseudoreligion like the old imperial faith. For this reason it remains more difficult for it to be tackled through state legislation, though undoubtedly the emergence of a political debate about the nature and direction of the English national ideology would make it possible for governments to give a strong political lead on an apparently intractable political issue.

NOTES

1. John M MacKenzie, *Propaganda and Empire*, Manchester University Press, Manchester, 1984.
2. Reba Soffer, "Nation, Duty, Character and Confidence: History at Oxford, 1850-1914", *The Historical Journal*, 30, 1 (1987), pp. 77-104;
John W Burrow, *A Liberal Descent*, CUP, Cambridge, 1981; Abraham D Kriegel, "Liberty and Whiggery in Early Nineteenth Century England", *Journal of Modern History*, 52 (June 1980), pp. 253-78.
3. Burrow, *op. cit.*
4. Walter Bagehot, "The Meaning and Value of the Limits on the Principle of Nationalism", *The Economist*, 18 June, 1864 repr. in Norman St John Stevas (ed), *The Collected Works of Walter Bagehot*, volume 8, London; *The Economist*, 1974, p.149; G R Searle, *The Quest for National Efficiency in Britain*, The Clarendon Press, Oxford, 1971.
5. Searle, *op. cit.*; Paul Kennedy, *The Rise of Anglo German Antagonism, 1860-1914*, Allen and Unwin, London, 1980.
6. Alun Howkins, "The Discovery of Rural England" in Robert Colls and Philip Dodd (eds), *Englishness: Politics and Culture, 1880-1920*, Frank Cass, London, 1986, pp. 62-88; Jan Marsh, *Back to the Land: The Pastoral Impulse in Victorian England from 1880 to 1914*, Quartet Books, London, 1982.
7. Gareth Stedman Jones, *Outcast London*, Penguin Books, Harmondsworth, 1984, pp. 331-6.
8. W M Flinders Petrie, *Janus in Modern Life*, Archibald Constable, London, 1907, p. 14. The yeomanry ideal continued into the interwar years, see Christopher Hussey, "The Decay of English Country Life", *The Quarterly Review*, 24, 479 (April 1924), pp. 340-1.
9. Arthur John Butler, review of L Oldenshaw, *England: A Nation*, in *The Speaker*, 1 April 1905.
10. Paul B Rich, *Race and Empire in British Politics*, CUP, Cambridge, 1986, p. 64. It was the Canadian Prime Minister, MacKenzie King, who especially opposed the idea of a single imperial foreign policy and a common imperial cabinet in council. See John M Carland, "Shadow and Substance: MacKenzie King's perceptions of British intentions at the 1923 Imperial Conference", in Gordon Martel (ed), *Studies in British Imperial History*, The Macmillan Press, London and Basingstoke, 1986, pp. 187-200.
11. *The Daily Herald*, 27 October 1919.
12. *The New Leader*, 21 November 1921.
13. Cyril Falls, "The Future of our Race", *The Nineteenth Century*, April 1922, pp. 567-8.
14. Bill Schwartz, "The Language of Constitutionalism: Baldwinite Conservatism" in Bill Schwartz *et. al.*, *Formations of Nation and People*, Routledge and Kegan Paul, London, 1984, p. 3.
15. *Ibid.*, p. 2.
16. Rich, *op. cit.*, pp. 54-64.
17. Thomas Philip Schofield, "Conservative Political Thought in Britain in Response to the French Revolution", *The Historical Journal*, 1, 29, 3 (1986), pp. 601-22. For the impact of the French Revolution on French sociology see Robert A Nisbet, "The French Revolution and the Rise of Sociology in France", *American Journal of Sociology*, 59, 2 (1943), pp. 156-64. See also Noel Annan, *The Curious Strength of Positivism in English Political Thought*, OUP, London, 1959 and Robert Eccleshall, "The Identity of English Liberalism", *Politics and Society*, 9, 1 (1979), pp. 1-32.
18. Burrow, *op. cit.*
19. See, for example, S Collini, "Hobhouse, Bosanquet and the State: Philosophical Idealism and Political Argument in England, 1880-1918", *Past and Present*, 72 (1976), pp. 86-111.
20. 'The fact that Britain had neither a co-ordinated integral nationalist populist movement, nor was influenced significantly by romantic nationalism before 1914, helps

explain the uphill task which British fascists faced in their later attempts to revolutionize society', Richard Thurlow, *British Fascism: A History, 1918-1985*, Basil Blackwell, Oxford, 1987, pp. 20-1.

21. Tom Nairn, "The English Literary Intelligentsia" in Emma Tennant (ed), *Bananas*, Quartet Books, London, 1977, pp. 57-83.

22. John Drinkwater, *Patriotism in Literature*, Williams and Norgate, London, 1924, p. 233.

23. John Masefield to Florence Lamont, 1 February and 23 October 1920 in Corliss and Lansing Lamont (eds), *Letters of John Masefield to Florence Lamont*, The Macmillan Press, London and Basingstoke, 1979, pp. 91, 109.

24. George Orwell, *The Road to Wigan Pier*, Penguin Books, Harmondsworth, 1966, p. 102.

25. Nairn, *op. cit.*, p. 66.

26. *H E Bates Papers*, Humanities Research Centre, University of Texas at Austin, H E Bates to Edward Garnett, 19 March 1926.

27. Mary Webb, *Precious Bane*, Jonathan Cape, London, 1933, p. 11.

28. Williams Ralph Inge, *England*, Ernest Benn, London, 1926, p. xi.

29. Paul Fussell, *The Great War and Modern Memory*, OUP, New York and London, 1975, esp. chapter three.

30. John McCormick, *Catastrophe and Imagination*, Croom Helm, London, 1957, p. 41.

31. Lord Eustace Percy, *Democracy on Trial*, John Land, London, 1931, p. 38.

32. Corelli Barnett, *The Collapse of British Power*, Eyre Methuen, London, 1972, p. 36.

33. George Lansbury, *My England*, The Mayflower Press, Plymouth, 1937, p. 58. Significantly, it was precisely this pastoral vision which *The Seaman*, the jingoist organ of the National Union of Seamen, castigated at the time of the General Strike. 'When the British Empire goes,' it declared, 'this country will be of small importance. Of course that does not matter to [A J] Cook, he hopes to see grass growing round the pits, the railways, the factories, mines, our ships rotting in the docks and millions of our people starving.' *The Seaman*, 3 July, 1926.

34. Walter Greenwood, *Love on the Dole*, Penguin Books, Harmondsworth, 1969, p. 79.

35. Paul B Rich, *Race and Empire in British Politics*, pp. 116-17; for Keith's ideas see Nancy Leys Stepan, " 'Nature's Pruning Hook': War, Race and Evolution, 1914-18" in H M W Bean (ed), *The Political Culture of Modern Britain*, Hamish Hamilton, London, 1987, pp. 129-48; chapter two, "The Long Victorian Sunset: Anthropology, Eugenics and Race in Britain, c. 1900-1948."

36. Stanley Baldwin, *Service in our Lives*, Hutchinson, London, 1937, pp. 116-17.

37. J B Priestley, *Rain Upon Godshill*, Heinemann, London, p. 219.

38. H V Morton, *I Saw Two Englands*, Methuen, London, 1943, p. 282.

39. *Ibid.*, p. 288.

40. Patrick Wright, *On Living in an Old Country*, Verso, London, 1975, p. 49.

41. Edmund Blunden, "The Landscape" in Adrian Bell *et. al.*, *The Legacy of England*, Batsford, London, 1935, p. 26.

42. Charles Bradley Ford, "The Village" in *ibid.*, p. 100.

43. R H Mottram, "The Country Town" in *ibid.*, p. 131.

44. See the guide to the Barbican art exhibition by David Mellor (ed), *A Paradise Lost: The Neo Romantic Imagination in Britain, 1935-55*, Lund Humphries in association with the Barbican Art Gallery, London, 1987. See also Simon Featherstone, "The Nation as Pastoral in British Literature of the Second World War", *Journal of European Studies*, xvi (1986), pp. 155-68.

45. Arthur Bryant, *English Saga, 1840-1940*, Eyre and Spottiswoode, London, 1940, p. 37.

46. Richard Hillary, "Spitfires" in Ronald Blythe, *Components of the Scene*, Penguin Books, Harmondsworth, 1966, p. 89.

47. Fussell, *op. cit.*, p. 231 and *passim*.

48. Nannette Aldred, "A Canterbury Tale" in Mellor, *op. cit.*, pp. 118-20. See also Noel Annan, *op. cit.*

49. Rich, *op. cit.*, pp. 149-50.
50. DO 35/1205, Memo on "nomenclature: 'British Empire' and 'British Commonwealth' ", 1943.
51. Rich, *op. cit.*
52. Angus Calder, *The People's War: Britain 1939-1945*, Granada Pub, London, 1969.
53. Michael Frayn, "Festival" in Michael Sissons and Philip French (eds), *Age of Austerity*, Hodder and Stoughton, London, 1963, pp. 317-38.
54. Ernest Bevin, "My Dream of Empire", *News Chronicle*, 21 January, 1948; see also Kenneth O Morgan.
55. *Britain and the Colonies; A Catalogue of Matters About the Colonies Available to Scholars and the Public*, HMSO, London, 1946, p. 3.
56. *The Round Table*, June 1945.
57. Peter Laslett, "On Being An Englishman in 1950", *The Cambridge Journal*, III, October 1949-September 1950, pp. 491-4.
58. Frayn, *op. cit.*
59. Andre Gamble, *The Conservative Nation*, Routledge and Kegan Paul, London and Boston, 1974, pp. 43-7.
60. Godfrey Hodgson, "The Steel Debates" in Sissons and French, *op. cit.*, pp. 295-316.
61. At the national level in the late 1940s the British Housewives League became a forum for strong resistance to state controls and generally supportive of Conservative policies. See Paul Addison, *Now The War Is Over*, BBC and Jonathan Cape, London, 1985, pp. 40-4. For more details on the Birmingham Unionist Association see chapter eight.
62. Gamble, *op. cit.*, p. 102 and *passim*.
63. Julian Amery, "A Conservative View of the Commonwealth", *The Political Quarterly*, xxxv, 2 (April-June 1959), p. 168.
64. Peregrine Worsthorne, "Class and Conflict in British Foreign Policy", *Foreign Affairs*, 37, 3 (April 1959), pp. 419-31. See also Robert Skidelsky, "Lessons of Suez" in Vernon Bogdanov and Robert Skidelsky, *The Age of Affluence, 1951-1964*, Macmillan and Co, London and Basingstoke, 1970, pp. 168-91.
65. John Wain, "Our Situation", *Encounter*, XX, 5 (May 1963), p. 14.
66. DO 35/5216 Lord Salisbury to Lord Swinton, 20 March, 1954.
67. Worsthorne, *op. cit.*, p. 426.
68. *Country Life*, 8, 23 and 30 November and 14 December, 1945.
69. H E Bates, *The Face of England*, Batsford, London, 1952, p. 44.
70. H E Bates, *The Scarlet Sword*, Penguin Books, Harmondsworth, 1974, pp. 5-6.
71. Tom Nairn, "English Nationalism: The Case of Enoch Powell" in *The Breakup of Britain*, Verso, London, 1981, pp. 256-90.
72. Enoch Powell, "The Empire of England" in *Tradition and Change*, CPC, London, 1954, pp. 41-53.
73. Gamble, *op. cit.*, p. 115.
74. John Wood (ed), *A Nation Not Afraid: The Thinking of Enoch Powell*, Hodder and Stoughton, London, 1965, p. 136.
75. *Ibid.*, p. 137.
76. *Ibid.*, pp. 144-5.
77. Though Powell had doubts on Mrs Thatcher, see J Enoch Powell, "Who Speaks for England Now?", *The Spectator*, 11 October 1980.
78. Peter Riddell, *The Thatcher Government*, Martin Robertson, London, 1983, p. 11.
79. Salman Rushdie, "The Raj Revival", *The Observer*, April 1984.

Chapter Two

The Long Victorian Sunset: Anthropology, Eugenics and Race in Britain c.1900-48

The political manipulation of ideas about racial differences forms a vital and complex part of European history which has been principally defined by the experience of the Third Reich and the years of the Final Solution, 1942-45. There is a danger, as a number of analysts have warned, of seeing all European thinking on race through the lenses of this catastrophic period and imposing present-day values on historical periods when race was not necessarily consciously discussed as part of a political ideology linked to National Socialism.[1] This problem of "presentism" should not lead to neglect of the way that ideas discussed by well-intentioned and benign scholars and analysts could become part of a wider climate of opinion in which more coherent and consistent political ideologies of race flourish. The first three decades of the twentieth century are an especially important example of this. During this time many scholars with roots in the Victorian period became challenged by the mobilisation of racial populism and the prostitution of their ideas in previously unimagined directions.

This chapter looks at the development of anthropology in Britain from the early years of the century up to the late 1930s when the rise of National Socialism forced a number of anthropologists to consider the political consequences of their use of race. This period is frequently associated with both the methodological developments in field work by Bronislaw Malinowski at the London School of Economics and a shift from the measuring of skulls and body anatomy to that of the study of the structure and function of human societies. However, alongside this rise in social anthropology there was a protracted resistance by the more traditional school of physical anthropology which was remarkably adept at adapting to the rise of both Darwinism and Mendelian genetics until the 1930s. Indeed, contrary to the view that the older anthropological theory of racial "types" left no room for the modes of explanation introduced by Darwin and Mendel,[2] the typological theorists continued to exert a strong influence in the discussion of "race" and the "race problem" in educated circles well into the twentieth century.

One of the significant features of this physical anthropological school was its ability to publicise and propagate its ideas. Frequent use was made of honorary lectures or rectorial addresses to university students, many of whom would become significant civil servants, businessmen or colonial administrators. These talks would often be published in cheap pamphlet form and would thus gain a wide circulation amongst the reading public. Similarly, the school was successful in penetrating new areas of disciplinary enquiry such as geography, where their ideological influence is only now beginning to be assessed by social historians of race. In addition, the older anthropological school was revitalised in the Edwardian years through the rise of eugenics and the pursuit of "race fitness". The term "eugenics" was originally coined by the great Victorian anthropometrist, explorer and cousin of Charles Darwin, Sir Frances Galton, as 'the study of agencies under social control that may improve or impair the racial qualities of future generations either physically or mentally'. Eugenic ideas had a special appeal to a particular section of the professional middle class in the years after the disasters of the Anglo-Boer War. There was a campaign for "national efficiency" to revitalise the resources of the nation and empire in order to meet growing international competition from Germany, France and the USA.[3] For a number of intellectuals on both right and left, eugenic ideas and methods seemed to represent a "scientific" means of national regeneration. In 1910 even Harold Laski wrote that eugenics represented 'an attempt adequately to estimate the extent of the social problem in its biological aspect, and an indication of the scientific means for its solution'.[4] He was, however, careful to point out that the study of human nature could not be separated from environmental considerations, for 'we have learnt now the correlation between the two, and we realize that, however excellent the social heritage may be, it does not outweigh the importance of the natural inheritance.'[5]

This appeal of eugenics continued after the First World War, despite the decline in eugenic ideas of "motherhood" and selective breeding in the wake of the carnage in the trenches and the loss of faith in the establishment of a white imperial race.[6] Eugenic ideals reinforced much of the work in physical anthropology in the light of the decline of belief in rational social reconstruction. The senselessness of the First World War led a number of theorists to explain it in terms of ethological analogies derived from animal behaviour. One of the most popular of these, though frequently misunderstood, was the work of Wilfred Trotter, *Instincts of the Herd in Peace and War*, first published in 1916. It went through ten impressions over the following decade. Trotter articulated an irrationalist thesis of human behaviour based on the analogy of the herd which looked back to the late Victorian reaction to Darwinism in such works as Benjamin Kidd's widely successful *Social Evolution* of 1894. Trotter's analogy with animal "gregariousness", however, was qualified by a carefully stated reluctance to use it to explain the human resort to war, unlike his successors, Robert Ardrey and Konrad Lonrenz. 'The doctrine of the biological necessity of war,' Trotter wrote, 'may...be regarded as open to strong suspicion on theoretical grounds of being contrary to the evolutionary tendency already plainly marked out for the human species.' Furthermore, it was to be distinguished from racial theory, for Trotter dismissed the 'pseudo-scientific dogmas of political biologists' and

> *the facile doctrines of degeneracy, the pragmatic lecturings on national characteristics, on Teutons and Celts, on Latins and Slavs, on pure races and mixed races, and all the other ethnological conceits with which the ignorant have gulled the innocent for so long.*[7]

Despite this strong stand against the racial use of his herd instinct thesis, its simplicity and neatness continued to appeal to writers and informed a number of popular thriller writers from John Buchan to Ian Fleming. The latter used it to portray the "wolf" character of Mr Big in the James Bond story *Live and Let Die* (1954).[8]

The notion of "instincts", whether of the herd or the tribe, was used extensively to explain human social behaviour in the following years. The anatomist and curator of the Hunterian Museum of the Royal College of Surgeons, Arthur Keith, was particularly successful in linking behaviour to a biological and racial theory of nationality. In 1919, as the president of the Royal Anthropological Institute, Keith developed this theory in the Robert Boyle Lecture at the Oxford University Junior Scientific Club. He sought to link race to an evolving theory of nationality which he saw as an inextricable part of the new world order being constructed on the basis of the Versailles Peace Settlement of the same year. His theory represented an important conservative retort to the liberal hopes for a world order based on a universal "modern conscience" between nation-states which had been forcibly expressed in the 1911 Universal Races Congress.[9] For Keith, the key issue was to fit race into the post-war discussions on nationality, for while 'the problems of Race and of Nationality...arc by no means new ...in their modern form they are new.' In particular,

the far-flung lines of the British Empire and the mobilization of the
popular spirit by means of the press and propaganda have compelled
our statesmen, historians, publicists, psychologists and
anthropologists to re-examine the nature of the forces which lie
behind racial movements and national agitations.[10]

Keith was particularly impressed by the instinct model of human
behaviour and went on to argue that 'in our modern racial strifes and
national agitations we see men's inherited tribal instincts at war with
his present-day conditions of life.'[11] In this maelstrom, there was an
interrelationship between race and nationality, for each had its own
separate 'frontiers':

a marriage across a racial frontier gives rise to an offspring so
different from both races that it gives rise to a progeny which may
pass as a member of either parent's nationality. Further...nationality
is the incipient stage in the process which leads on to racial
differentiation.[12]

In the course of time, therefore, if the French in Canada maintained
continued isolation and did not marry with other groups 'a racial
differentiation would be produced within their territory.'[13] In the case of
Britain, 'statesmanship has succeeded in raising up in the minds of all
the inhabitants of the British Isles – all save a greater part of Ireland – a
new and wider sense of nationality, a spirit of British nationality.'[14]
Keith explained the failure of Ireland to be incorporated in terms of a
Celtic 'tribal instinct' which stood outside the main forces of 'commerce,
communication and the building of massed populations' which moved the
rest of Britain beyond the stage of tribal bonds into one nation.[15]
   Keith fortified the language of late nineteenth- and early twentieth-
century anthropology with that of ethnology and 'tribal instincts' at a
time when conceptions of nationality had a growing appeal to the British
ruling class. Parts of this discourse rejected an exclusivist conception of
nationality, preferring to see the make-up of the British nation in
cultural rather than racial terms. Before the war, attacks on racial
prejudice had been made at the 1911 Universal Races Congress on the
basis of arguments developed by the Frenchman, Jean Finot, in his book
Race Prejudice. These were taken up by John Oaksmith in an important
study entitled *Race and Nationality* in 1919. He argued for a British
'national character' defined, not in racial terms, but as a 'community of
interest developed in the course of time into a characteristic traditional
culture which gradually creates for itself machinery, legislative,
administrative and other, for effecting its end in the world of human
action.'[16] As a consequence, there was in Britain 'no possibility of a
legitimate racial pride, except perhaps in the number of different peoples
from whom our blood is drawn.'[17]

However, a patriotic discourse did exist that was not averse to the employment of racial categories, using them in the context of an historical nationalism based upon an invented historical legitimacy of British institutions. The years following the Russian Revolution were a time of growing panic among a considerable section of the upper and middle class about an international "Bolshevik menace", culminating in the Zinoviev "Red Letter" scare during the 1924 general election. While this did not lead to the patriotic discourse of the ruling class being completely taken over by a racial and conspiratorial ideology, as the somewhat sceptical reception by mainstream opinion of the *Protocols of the Elders of Zion* indicated,[18] there was still a strong conspiratorial and anti-Semitic theme in the thinking of clubland at this time. This often emerged in the form of the popular novel, such as John Buchan's *The Three Hostages* which had a powerful ideological influence on the attitudes of the London establishment.[19]

Keith's theory of race and nationality was ultimately not successful in capturing mainstream establishment thinking. This was probably due to its secular nature and its resort to the irrationalist basis of tribal behaviour to explain the policies of modern nation-states.[20]

A more successful populariser of the eugenic tradition was the Dean of St Paul's, W R Inge, who became a well-known public figure in the interwar years through his radio broadcasts and frequent newspaper articles. Unlike Keith, Inge sought to develop a version of patriotism that was rooted in a rationalist outlook. He had little time for 'irrationalist prophets' like Benjamin Kidd and G K Chesterton and declared that 'the anti-scientific temper is our enemy today – a worse enemy than the Germans'.[21] Inge distrusted "scientific" ideologies of race such as those of Houston Stewart Chamberlain, whose beliefs, Inge argued, had helped lead to the First World War.[22] His patriotism was of a more traditional kind. It looked to the eventual destruction of large urban conglomerations created by industrialisation and a return to a more pristine rural condition. As a eugenicist, Inge linked this to a reduction in the national population:

> *The masses in this country will have to take their choice between giving up their ambition to secure for themselves a comfortable and civilized life, and a drastic limitation of their numbers ...I look forward without the slightest regret to the time when the site of East and West Ham will be reclaimed for the plough, for I would rather see 35,000,000 happy, healthy and contented Englishmen than 60,000,000 of embittered visionaries crying for the moon.*[23]

This retreat to a pre-industrial pastoralism was rooted in a nostalgia for the Middle Ages, which Inge saw as containing the model for a new international order free from militarism.[24] While this nostalgia was fairly common in the intellectual life of Britain in the 1920s – it is evident, for example, in R H Tawney's *Religion and the Rise of Capitalism* (1926) – Inge linked it to a more basic racial pessimism. Taking up some of the racial categories developed by physical anthropology, he saw the predominantly Nordic racial stock of Britain being undermined in the towns by a 'Mediterranean race', so that the English were 'becoming darker in each generation'.[25] Inge's racial categorisation was a version of the Anglo-Saxonist ideology of the nineteenth century which was being given a new lease of life in the United States by, among others, Madison Grant in *The Rising Tide of Colour* (1920).[26]

Inge's racial pessimism was really a coded form of expressing a more basic anxiety in the future of the English upper and middle class, which he saw as threatened by a militant, internationalist socialism.[27] This he saw as the main enemy; at this time black immigration into Britain was not seen as a significant political issue. 'We are not threatened by coloured immigration,' Inge wrote, 'and we have nothing to fear from the armies and fleets of Asia.'[28] Furthermore there was 'not much danger to Europe from the African blacks.'[29] The main threat came from the internal decay within the "English Race" itself, for 'as regards quality, the outlook at present is bad':

> *...the destruction of the upper and professional classes by taxation directed expressly against them has already begun, and this victimization is certain to become more and more acute, until these classes are practically extinguished. The old aristocracy showed a tendency to decay even when they were unduly favoured by legislation, and a little more pressure will drive them to voluntary sterility and extermination. Even more to be regretted is the doom of the professional aristocracy, a caste almost peculiar to our country. These families can often show longer, and usually much better pedigrees than the peerage; the persistence of market ability in them for several generations is the delight of the eugenist.*[30]

However, Inge did see a new force for stabilisation in the emergence of the labour aristocracy, and showed a considerable development of thought over most pre-war eugenicists. For them the emergence of a prosperous working class enjoying material benefits was a matter of regret since it appeared to be, as the headmaster of Eton had noted, 'inconsistent with the kind of domestic life which seems to be a necessity for people in that situation'.[31] For Inge this development was a matter for some regret, but it did give some hope for racial survival without complete eugenic deterioration:

The power will apparently be grasped by a new highly privileged class, the aristocracy of labour. This class, being intelligent, energetic and intensely selfish, may retain its domination for a considerable time. It is a matter of course that, having won its privilege of exploiting the community, it will use it. In other words, it will become an exclusive and strongly conservative class, on a broader basis than the territorial and commercial aristocracies which preceded it. It will probably be strong enough to discontinue the system of State doles which encourages the wastrel to multiply, as he does multiply, much faster than the valuable part of the population.[32]

This was a far more subtle and sophisticated employment of eugenic and racial concepts. It related to the strategy of class incorporation which underpinned the moves for a corporatist consensus in the 1920s as successive governments, especially following the 1926 General Strike, sought to build up a network of mutual political bargaining and institutionalised consensus between the state, business and organised labour.[33] In contrast, Arthur Keith's vision of tribal struggle at the root of national identity was not in keeping with the general mood of pacifism in the interwar years and the hope for a new era of world peace based upon the League of Nations. In his rectorial address, "The Place of Prejudice in Modern Civilisation", to the students of Aberdeen in 1931, he defended human prejudices as 'part of the scheme of human evolution – the scheme whereby Nature, through the eons of the past, has sought to bring into the world ever better and higher races of mankind'.[34] Keith opposed the idea of "universal brotherhood" epitomised by the League of Nations for, insofar as this meant a 'scheme of universal deracialization' it stood in opposition to his interpretation of Darwinian human evolution and the notion that race prejudice was essential to human progress:

Without competition Mankind can never progress; the price of progress is competition. Nay, race prejudice, and, what is the same thing, national antagonism, have to be purchased not with gold but with life. Nations throughout the past have demanded that a people who seek independence as well as peace can obtain these privileges only in one way – by being prepared to sacrifice their blood to serve them.[35]

This plea for war as an instrument of human progress found little favour in Britain, although with the rise of fascist political ideologies in the late 1920s and 1930s it found a wider resonance in Europe. Keith, however, remained an isolated and politically uncommitted figure – more a legacy of Victorian liberalism and anti-imperialism than anything else. With other British theorists of racial segregation such as J W Gregory, Professor of Geology at the University of Glasgow, he was, nevertheless, significant in keeping alive the notion of race as an important biological factor in world politics. 'What do we Londoners know of race feeling?' Keith asked in a preface to Gregory's lecture, "Race as a Political Factor", delivered at the Conway Hall, Red Lion Square in April 1931 and later published in pamphlet form. 'We are as ignorant as babies in this aspect of life. You have to live on a racial frontier before you realize the feelings and passions which race contact may engender.'[36] Though he called London at this time 'a menagerie of races',[37] Keith was significant for seeking to instil strong notions of race before the emergence of an indigenous race relations situation in Britain with the advent of New Commonwealth immigration in the 1950s and 1960s.

Keith was also helped in developing a folk wisdom on racial differences by the neutral and blunted position of much mainstream academic anthropology at this time. In Cambridge in 1924, for example, Alfred Court Haddon wrote in *The Races of Mankind and Their Distribution* that natural selection combined with 'isolation areas' produced 'stocks with certain associated characters and it is to such stocks that the term races can be applied.' While not altogether happy with the notion of "racial type", Haddon nevertheless considered that 'continued geographical isolation in areas of characterization does tend to produce a general uniformity of physical appearance.'[38]

Further support for this idea came from the geographer and anthropologist Herbert John Fleure, Professor of Geography and Anthropology at the University of Aberystwyth from 1917-30. Fleure became an influential figure in anthropology in the 1920s and he was notable for keeping alive the original classification of European racial types, made by the American William Z Ripley in 1900, into Mediterranean, Nordic and Alpine. He saw the British population as an overlap of the Mediterranean and Nordic races, though some were derived from neither, being 'a survival of old long-headed types remaining incompletely differentiated into one or the other but later influenced by later immigrants of both these stocks.'[39] Fleure was especially disposed to interpret British history through racial factors, seeing the Nordic racial type, which was 'tall, strong-boned, with his fair hair and blue eyes', as an important contributor to the landed aristocracy and poorly adapted to living in towns. The Nordic race's influence was strong in the country house and hunting tradition of rural England and thus contributed towards "civilisation".[40] Commercial imperialism in the nineteenth century drew off many of these Nordic elements and, he argued, there had 'been a call for a great increase of the fundamental elements of the population, which seem specially able to withstand the difficulties of industrial towns'.[41] The notion that the Nordic race's roots were in the countryside and on the landed estates was taken a stage further by Fleure's colleague Harold Peake. In his book entitled *The English Village* in 1922, Peake saw the origins of the Nordic race as being on the steppes of Central Asia where patriarchal government had been developed which 'had deeply impressed upon the race the importance of the family and in all their doings in subsequent times the lord played for the advantage of the family rather than for that of the individual'.[42]

This racial anthropology influenced generations of students in geography and anthropology and helped perpetuate the myth, already well-developed by the end of the nineteenth century, that the essential core of English culture lay not in the urban civilisation of the industrial towns but in the countryside dominated by the values of the landed gentry and the estate.[43] This belief was not well disposed towards a *völkisch* interpretation of English history for it accepted the permanence and reality of urban industrial culture and did not seek any return to rural folk roots beyond studying rural populations, such as those in Wales and the Scottish Highlands, as a means of locating the racial origins of the British population. On the other hand, this kind of anthropological work was suitable for use in a more propagandistic form by popularisers like Arthur Keith, who saw the anthropological support for British racial types as proof of his theory of history as being the struggle of races through natural selection.[44] 'My fellow tipsters have hardly done justice to the entrants for the Grand National of the World,' he wrote in the *Evening Standard* in 1927. 'They speak as if there was only one kind of horse concerned, whereas there is an enormous field of the most varied kind. The Caucasian stable alone has saddled a wealth of candidates and mounted them in national colours. I am putting my money on horses from the Caucasian stable – particularly the British breed.'[45]

By 1930, Fleure became increasingly anxious at the way the "Nordic type" had been used to foster a political ideology which he saw as the 'Nordic myth',[46] and over the following years British anthropologists became aware of the danger of anthropological ideas of race being used for ideological purposes. While eugenics had lost its hold on the imagination of the British intelligentsia, it was still being enthusiastically propagated in the media and in public discussion.[47] In a radio broadcast in a series "What I Would Do With the World" in 1931, Sir Basil Blackett, the president of the eugenist British Social Hygiene Council, urged that:

> *In biology...we have a potential instrument for improving the human race and we are not using it. The study of anthropology and eugenics ought to be a compulsory item of training of every man and woman who is destined to take up administrative service in any part of the world'.*[48]

In the same year Arthur Keith too felt that the times boded well for eugenics to be taken up as a serious issue in public discussion, although its possibilities depended 'on the extent to which human nature can be rationalized'.[49]

The rise of National Socialism in Germany in the 1930s and its use of eugenics in a vicious programme for German "race fitness" forced anthropologists to rethink the nature of race and the possibilities of applying eugenic methods to improve biological heredity. In 1935 a joint committee of the Royal Anthropological Institute published a report, *Race and Culture*, which reflected the general uncertainty over race definition. While a number of people in the discussions continued to use the conventional anthropological categories to distinguish racial types, there were warnings of the difficulty of a truly scientific application of the concept. The biologist J B S Haldane pointed out that the physical characters of existing populations tended to be derived from the crossing of certain "pure" racial types such as the Nordic, Mediterranean and Alpine in Europe, though this could not account for all possible features:

> *The presence of a certain proportion of red-haired individuals is a feature of some populations, but I doubt if any anthropologist has yet postulated a red-haired ancestral race...Hence any attempt to describe a population as say 60 per cent Alpine, 10 per cent Nordic, 10 per cent Mediterranean and 20 per cent Dinaric will inevitably omit certain facts.*[50]

One prominent anthropologist, G M Morant, also admitted that 'our present knowledge of human biology appears to be insufficient to furnish a definition which will satisfy theoretical needs and, at the same time, be capable of actual application.'[51]

Race and Culture was notable for paying some attention to genetics in the scientific classification of gene pools. However, it was not until the publication of the joint work of Julian Huxley and A C Haddon, *We Europeans,* later in 1935, which urged that if race had any scientific meaning it was only in terms of a genetic analysis, that the anthropological notion of typology was rendered meaningless. Analysis shifted to the study of statistical aggregates:

> *...our knowledge of genetics assures us that once mixture has taken place it is impossible, without applying the stockbreeder's method of rigorous selective breeding for a large number of generations, to reconvert the population into anything approaching either of the ancestral types. The very word 'race' applies to a hypothetical past, or to a problematical future, not to the actual present...the only way to measure the genetic relationship of ethnic groups would be by ascertaining the quantitative values of their coefficients of common ancestry, which would be based entirely upon the statistical methods of probability theory.*[52]

Huxley and Haddon, in seeking to debunk the Nazi use of race, undermined it as a worthwhile anthropological or biological category, preferring to use instead the term ethnic group. This presaged a significant shift in social science nomenclature in the years after 1945.[53] However, this project did not meet with unanimous approval from British anthropologists who continued, as far as possible, to use the term race, despite the manner in which it had been manipulated for political purposes. Even after the outbreak of the war, G M Morant declared that the lack of agreement among anthropologists over the 'methods of racial analysis' need not have prevented them from making a protest at the way "race" was being misused.[54]

The experience of the Second World War was, however, a profoundly sobering one for British anthropologists and eugenicists who, for the most part, tried to sanitise their discourse and remove the racial terminology which had been so prevalent in the 1930s. The new mood was epitomised by H J Fleure on his retirement from the University of Manchester in 1946 when he warned of 'arguments about the diversity of "race" that have sometimes crept into political discussions'. He continued

...let us beware of giving support to propaganda about so-called superior and inferior races, and let us try to see that this dangerous nonsense is effectively condemned by UNO and UNESCO in the most public manner possible.[55]

Even Arthur Keith, living in somewhat obscure retirement in Charles Darwin's village of Downe in Kent, wrote now of a 'group spirit' as the key element in human evolution and his earlier praise of 'prejudice' as a factor in nationalism gave way to the notion of 'patriotism'. This he interpreted in a manner that would be taken up more systematically by a later generation of socio-biologists, for 'group patriotism' could be regarded 'as an expansion of family patriality'.[56] Similarly, Keith sought to reconcile his position with the earlier liberal and pluralist view of nationality enunciated by John Oaksmith in 1919. Recognising, after Fleure, that 'race' was an 'incendiary term', Keith formulated a more sophisticated conception. This saw race at two different levels: that of a local or race-making group and at a more general level as a product of evolution and the differentiation of people. While Oaksmith was seen as using race in the physical sense as a finished product, Keith argued that he had used it 'to designate a group or a people involved in the process of differentiation'. His conception of race was as 'a thing which is consciously and vitally alive', while Oaksmith (along with the mainstream of anthropology) saw it as 'inert, unconscious and passive'.[57]

Keith's redefinition of race brought him into line with Huxley and Haddon, who saw race as an entity that had a past and might be realised in the future but could not be seen as a distinct phenomenon in the

64

present. Keith had isolated one aspect of his thinking from a more politically contentious set of notions regarding nationality, promoting war as a means for achieving human evolution through natural selection. By 1948 this had been redefined in terms of the notion that 'man's patriotism lies at the root of war',[58] so laying the basis for the later ethology of Desmond Morris, Robert Ardrey and the popularisers of human group competition in the 1960s and 1970s. In Keith's case, however, the firm racial connection between his earlier thinking and the later body of theory remained. He acted as a crucial link between Victorian racial anthropology and more recent ethology and socio-biology, despite the fact that some later practitioners of the methodology, such as Pierre van den Berghe, disclaimed his influence because the latter subjects do not involve a specifically racial view of human group behaviour.[59]

The intellectual history of this debate, as this chapter has sought to show, demonstrates a firm tradition of racial analysis, despite the hopes of some earlier ethologists such as Wilfred Trotter. Moreover, the historical understanding of the debate illuminates the protean quality of race as both an analytical tool and a political ideology which still surfaces in anthropological analysis in the light of genetical research. In 1978, for instance, a former president of the Royal Anthropological Institute, J S Weiner, saw the issue of racial variation and sociology as a critical part of anthropology in its current state 'beyond' physical anthropology. With the decline of the older typology 'the debate on aggression and territoriality...represents in the field of palaeo-anthropology yet another and very large extension of traditional physical anthropology.'[60]

In this manner, the interwar debates between biology and anthropology have left a long-lasting legacy in an area burdened by new sets of political and ideological pressures and conflicts. They also served as an important British parallel to a phenomenon detected by the American scholar, E B Reuter, in 1945, when he came to assess the scholarly impact on "racial theory" in Europe and America over the preceding decades. 'Serious study and competent analysis,' he noted, 'have gone on in the midst of an elaborate, emotionally deep-seated, and continuing body of popular philosophy.' Furthermore, this study had in no manner undermined these beliefs for 'more often they have revitalized the old doctrines and brought them to new periods of activity.'[61] His warning regarding this capacity for the revitalisation of racial ideas is one that still deserves attention from scholars in the sciences and humanities.

NOTES

1. George M Stocking, "The Limits of 'Presentism' and 'Historicism' in the Historiography of the Behavioural Sciences" in *Race, Culture and Evolution: Essays in the History of Anthropology*, Free Press, New York, 1968, pp. 1-12; Michael D Biddiss, "Myths of the Blood", *Patterns of Prejudice*, vol. 5, no. 5, September-October 1975, pp. 11-19; Michael Banton, "The Idiom of Race: A Critique of Presentism", *Research in Race and Ethnic Relations*, no. 2, 1980, pp. 21-42.
2. Banton, "The Idiom of Race", p. 23.
3. G R Searle, *The Quest for National Efficiency*, Clarendon Press, Oxford, 1971.
4. Harold Laski, "The Scope of Eugenics", *Westminster Review*, no. 174, 1910, p. 27.
5. *Ibid.*, p. 30.
6. Anna Davin, "Imperialism and Motherhood", *History Workshop*, no. 5, 1978, pp. 9-65.
7. W Trotter, *Instincts of the Herd in Peace and War*, London, 1942, p. 132. See also Greta Jones, *Social Darwinism and English Thought*, Harvester Press, Sussex, 1980, pp. 120-39, for the role of Trotter in the emerging irrationalism and "instinct" theory of Kidd, Graham Wallas and William McDougall.
8. For the significance of Fleming's Bond novels in developing a Cold War ideology of racial differentiation see Margaret Marshment, "Racist Ideology and Popular Fiction", *Race and Class*, no. 19, 1978, pp. 331-44.
9. For an analysis of the Congress see Michael D Biddiss, "The Universal Races Congress of 1911", *Race*, vol. 13, no. 1, July 1971, pp. 37-46; and chapter three.
10. Arthur Keith, *Nationality and Race from an Anthropologist's Point of View*, Twenty-first Robert Boyle Lecture delivered before Oxford University Junior Scientific Club, 17 November 1919, OUP, Oxford, 1919, p. 5.
11. *Ibid.*, p. 8; Arthur Keith, *An Autobiography*, Watts and Co, London, 1950, p. 40.
12. Keith, *Nationality and Race*, p. 9.
13. *Ibid.*, p. 10.
14. *Ibid.*, p. 22.
15. *Ibid.*, p. 35.
16. John Oaksmith, *Race and Nationality*, Heinemann, London, 1919, p. 4. For the influence of Finot see chapter three.
17. *Ibid.*, p. 30.
18. Colin Holmes, *Anti-Semitism in British Society, 1876-1939*, London, 1979, p. 151. Once *The Times* exposed *The Protocols* as a forgery, their influence after 1921 was mostly on the political fringe.
19. Norman Etherington, "Imperialism in Literature: the Case of John Buchan", ICS seminar paper, London, 1979; see also Paul B Rich, "Milnerism and a Ripping Yarn: Transvaal Land Settlement and John Buchan's novel *Prester John*, 1901-1910" in Belinda Bozzoli, *Town and Countryside in the Transvaal*, Ravan Press, Johannesburg, 1983, pp. 412-33.
20. Keith recalled that his 1919 lecture *Nationality and Race* 'brought me no scalps. It was a jumble of arguments. It cost me a quarter of a century to bring its jumbled parts into a coherent whole,' *Autobiography*, p. 399.
21. William Ralph Inge, "Eugenics" in *Outspoken Essays* (2nd series), London, 1922, p. 255.
22. William Ralph Inge, "Patriotism" in *Outspoken Essays* (1st series), pp. 48-9.
23. Review article in *Eugenics Review*, vol. 10, April 1918. Searle has seen Inge's employment of eugenics to support an anti industrial case as refutation of the Marxist argument that eugenics was simply an ideology of bourgeois social engineering, G R Searle, *Eugenics and Politics in Britain, 1900-1914*, Leyden, 1976, p. 112.
24. W R Inge, "Patriotism", pp. 55-6.
25. W R Inge, "The Future of the English Race", *Edinburgh Review*, no. 468, April 1919, p. 84.
26. W R Inge, "The White Man and His Rivals", in *Outspoken Essays* (2nd series), pp. 210-16.

27. W R Inge, "Patriotism", p. 54.
28. W R Inge, "The White Man and his Rivals", p. 226.
29. *Ibid.*, pp. 318-19.
30. W R Inge, "The Future of the English Race", pp. 98-9.
31. The Rev. Hon. Edward Lyttelton, "Racial Responsibility as a Factor in Formation of Character", *Eugenics Review*, 5 April 1913, p. 35.
32. "The Future of the English Race", p. 99.
33. Keith Middlemas, *Politics in Industrial Society*, André Deutsch, London, 1979, especially pp. 174-213.
34. Arthur Keith, *The Place of Prejudice in Modern Civilization*, Benn Bros, London, 1931, p. 26.
35. *Ibid.*, p. 48.
36. Sir Arthur Keith, "Foreword" to J W Gregory, *Race as a Political Factor*, Seele and Co., London, 1931, p. 10.
37. *Ibid.*, p. 5.
38. A C Haddon, *The Races of Man and Their Distribution*, CUP, Cambridge, 1924, p. 139.
39. H J Fleure, "The Racial History of the British People", *Geographical Review*, no. 5, January-June 1918, p. 217.
40. *Ibid.*, pp. 216, 230.
41. H J Fleure, *The Races of Mankind*, Benn Bros, London, 1927, p. 77.
42. Harold Peake, *The English Village*, Benn Bros, London, 1921, p. 190.
43. Martin Weiner, *English Culture and the Decline of the Industrial Spirit*, CUP, Cambridge, 1980.
44. See, for example, Sir Arthur Keith, "How did Britain's Racial Divisions Arise?", *Discovery*, January 1929.
45. *Evening Standard*, 14 October 1927.
46. H J Fleure, "The Nordic Myth", *Eugenics Review*, no. 22, 1930, pp. 117-21.
47. G R Searle, "Eugenics and Politics in Britain in the 1930s", *Annals of Science*, no. 36, 1979, p. 163.
48. Sir Basil Blackett, "What I Would Do With The World", *The Listener*, 28 November 1931.
49. "Urgency of Eugenic Reform", address given to the International Federation of Eugenic Organizations, 11 September 1930, MS, Arthur Keith Papers, Royal College of Surgeons.
50. Royal Anthropological Institute and the Institute of Sociology, *Race and Culture*, Le Play House Press and RAI, London and Malvern, 1935, p. 10.
51. *Ibid.*, p. 19.
52. Julian S Huxley and A C Haddon, *We Europeans*, Cape, London, 1935, p. 134.
53. *Ibid.*, p. 108.
54. G M Morant, "Racial Theories and International Relations", *Journal of the Royal Anthropological Institute*, vol. 69, 1939-40, p. 161.
55. H J Fleure, "The Institute and Its Development", *Journal of the Royal Anthropological Institute*, vol. 76, 1946, p. 2.
56. Sir Arthur Keith, *A New Theory of Human Evolution*, London, 1948, p. 51. For a more recent statement of this view see Richard Lynn, "The Sociobiology of Nationalism", *New Society*, 1 July 1976, pp. 11-14, and the critiques by Eric Hobsbawm, "Lynn and Nationalism", *New Society*, 8 July 1976, p. 84 and Henry Tajfel, "Against 'biologism' ", *New Society*, 29 July 1976, pp. 240-2.
57. *Ibid.*, p. 320.
58. *Ibid.*, p. 47.
59. Pierre L van den Berghe, "Ethnicity and the Sociobiology Debate", paper presented to the Conference on Theories of Racial and Ethnic Relations, St Catherine's College, Oxford, 19-23 March 1984, p. 9.
60. J S Weiner, "Beyond Physical Anthropology", *RAIN*, 31 June 1979, p. 7.
61. E B Reuter, "Racial Theory", *American Journal of Sociology*, 50, 1945, p. 452.

Chapter Three

'The Baptism of a New Era': The 1911 Universal Races Congress and the Liberal Ideology of Race

Despite the scale of its deliberations, the 1911 Universal Races Congress has attracted relatively little interest from historians of race. The Congress held its main discussions at the Imperial Institute in London between the 26 and the 29 July during a hot English summer. There were an estimated 1,200 "active" members of the Congress and a further 1000 "passive" members. The eight main sessions were on too general a scale to produce any significant scholarly discussion, but a considerable number of people went away with a heightened degree of enlightenment on the current state of thought on race in a number of disciplines, especially those of economics, anthropology and politics. The long-term effects of the Congress on more general attitudes towards race and "race relations" may thus be considered to be of some significance. The Congress can be considered as one of a number of important agents in the development of liberal thought in Europe and North America away from the Victorian consensus that there was a hierarchy or chain of different racial stocks, with the Anglo-Saxon or "Teutonic" races foremost, towards a more pluralistic view of racial differences governed by notions of cultural "advancement" and "backwardness".

The historiography of the Congress has tended rather towards downplaying its long-term political and ideological significance. George Shepperson, for example, has been most impressed by the attendance at the Congress of W E B Du Bois and has placed the

Congress within the Pan-Africanist political tradition. However, although Du Bois was a secretary of the Congress and the gathering provided an important meeting ground for a number of black nationalist leaders, including Duse Mohammed Ali from Egypt, John Tengo Jabavu from South Africa, G K Gokhale of the Indian Congress Party and ex-President Legitime of Haiti, the main thrust of the Congress was not in any specifically Pan-Africanist, Pan-Slavist or pan-any-other direction at all. Indeed, the main ethos of the Congress was one of liberal internationalism rooted in a concern to transcend national divisions in the promotion of a world order that could ensure the perpetuation of peace.

The original idea for the Congress developed following an international peace conference at the Hague in 1899 and was first mooted in 1906 by Felix Adler, Professor of Political and Social Ethics at Columbia University, during an international conference of ethical societies at Eisenach, Switzerland. These roots in the ethical movement became allied with the internationalism of the Inter-Parliamentary Union which was founded at the Paris World Fair in 1889 and which held a series of conferences in succeeding years. The President of the Congress, Lord Weardale, an ex-Liberal MP, had been President of the Inter-Parliamentary Union since 1906. He represented a more secular liberal interest in the interracial issues in contrast to the traditional anti-slavery and missionary bodies. The Anti-Slavery and Aborigines Protection Society (APS) declined involvement in the Congress since it saw the whole scheme as too ambitious in nature, and E D Morel's Congo Reform Association also avoided attending.[2]

This general divorce from the main welfare bodies in Britain at the time perhaps explains why the Congress has not received more attention from liberal historians. Michael Biddiss, in an important article assessing the Congress and its debates, sees the Congress as ultimately eclipsed by international events. Although it provided a forum for 'characters of courage striving through whatever muddle to be more humane than the generality of men or even the generality of intellectuals in an age addicted consciously or otherwise to racist idioms and modes of explanation',[3] it was unable to repeat itself before the First World War struck. Plans for a second Congress on the ostensibly multiracial terrain of Honolulu in Hawaii did not reach fruition due to lack of funds, and further plans for a meeting in Paris in 1915 ended with the outbreak of war. With this, Biddiss has concluded, perished the 'brave hopes' and 'generous aspirations'[4] of those who sought to use the Congress to help build a new world order or, as Lord Weardale declared in his opening address, 'the baptism of a new era, a new humanity'.[5]

The idealistic aspirations of those organising the Congress were not shared, however, by many prominent liberals and it may be too partial an assessment of the Congress to judge it solely in terms of its own professed objectives. L T Hobhouse, the first Martin White Professor of

Sociology at the London School of Economics, was on the initial committee to arrange the Congress, but gave no further assistance beyond being a member of the Executive Council and a donor towards its funds.[6] Other prominent liberals such as James Bryce, who had written and lectured extensively on "interracial" matters, and J L Hammond were also not present at the Congress. Several members of the Liberal Rainbow Circle (which met for monthly meetings at the Rainbow Tavern in Fleet Street), such as the sociologist J M Robertson, G P Gooch, J A Hobson and Sydney Olivier, the Fabian governor of Jamaica between 1907 and 1913, did take a significant part in the discussion, though Olivier did not consider the Congress a great political success.[7] The Congress tended to reflect a radical and anti-war liberalism which had developed in the wake of the Anglo-Boer War. It was anxious to free itself from the more benevolent liberal imperialism of the latter part of the nineteenth century which was still anchored to the notion of a specifically racial or "Teutonic" capacity for holding and maintaining empires. Bryce, for example, likened the British empire in India to that of ancient Rome.[8] Although there were still scattered references to Teutonism in the Congress (Charles Bruce, the former governor of Mauritius, linked the 'Teutonic race' to 'the principle of liberty'), the debates were noteworthy more for their disconnection of race from any particular system of imperial control and their perception of races in their totality within a single world order. To this extent, the main ethos of the Congress upset several assumptions about race within particular disciplinary spheres. The discussions were noteworthy in three specific areas: in anthropology and the debate between monogenists and polygenists; in economics and the discussion on the removal of barriers to international capital investment; and in politics and the capacity of non-western races for parliamentary government. All three areas were of current liberal interest in Britain and the Congress's contribution to them will be discussed in turn.

The Anthropological Debate

The discussion on anthropology began in the first session on the Wednesday morning of 26 July and to some extent set the tone for the rest of the Congress. It was marked by considerable acrimony between rival parties and attracted the attention of some sections of the press. Although anthropology was a very specialised profession which was only just beginning to gain academic recognition, it had a long pedigree going back to Victorian times and provided a "scientific" anchoring point for theorists of the varying capacities of fitness amongst different racial "types". In the nineteenth century this debate had been defined around rival schools of monogenists, who argued for the emergence of different human races from a single original stock, and polygenists, who argued for racial differences arising from a different set of racial stocks which had evolved separately from one another. The dispute had reached its peak in the 1860s when the polygenist and virulent racist Robert Knox led the Anthropological Society in opposition to the monogenist Ethnology Society. The division was resolved only after Knox's death, when the two societies merged to form the Anthropological Institute in London in 1871.[9]

The impact of Darwinian thought also suspended this debate to some extent as the focus of interest shifted to the mechanism of evolutionary change. It did not, however, lessen the interest in different racial types among physical anthropologists in the latter part of the century.[10] Craniometry and anthropometry became major obsessions among anthropologists in Europe and North America as the measurement of the human skull and anatomy were used to buttress nationalist ideologies in the wake of the American Civil War, Italian and German unification and in the advent of European imperial expansion.[11]

The development of physical anthropology from the 1880s onwards, in both Britain and North America, can be seen as contributing to a continuation of the polygenist tradition of anthropological argument in that it bore a certain set of assumptions regarding the origins of different racial stocks. Cultural anthropology, on the other hand, which developed under the intellectual influence of E B Tylor in Britain, represented more of a monogenist notion of racial difference and this had a considerable intellectual impact on early pioneers of social anthropology such as Alfred Court Haddon. By the turn of the century, therefore, the old monogenesis/polygenesis debate was by no means dead and, in so far as it represented what George Stocking has termed 'specific expressions of enduring alternative attitudes towards the variety of mankind',[12] was merely in a period of temporary eclipse.

The 1911 Congress was significant for the manner in which it popularised this old debate within anthropology. The Assistant Treasurer of the Congress was John Gray of the Anthropological Institute, an avowed anthropometrist, while Haddon was the director of an exhibition of slides at the Congress showing different races. The ensuing debate provided an opportunity for an attempted anthropological counterattack against the beliefs of the Congress organisers in the equality of races and the brotherhood of man. Harry Johnston, in an article in *The Contemporary Review,* had welcomed the Congress as an opportunity to defeat the traditional English reluctance to engage in discussion on 'racial questions' and to assert emphatically that there was only one human species living on the globe which was fertile and capable of interbreeding.[13] John Gray, on the other hand, saw the question of racial differences as being determined by both environment and the 'racial constitution of the stock' which nullified the idea of complete racial equality and limited the amount of 'improvement' which could take place through education. This did not imply, though, that each "race" should not be allowed to have 'the best obtainable opportunity for development'.[14]

Gray's somewhat benign anthropometric racism was eclipsed by a more virulently Darwinist attack on racial equality by Dr Felix von Luschan, Professor of Anthropology at the University of Berlin. He argued for a monogenist origin of human races, but explained their differences in terms of adaptability to different environments according to the law of the survival of the fittest. In contrast to the hereditarian and polygenist racism of Gray, which still allowed for the education of 'inferior' races, Luschan's theory implied a territorial basis for policies on races, as removing certain races from their 'natural' environment and transplanting them elsewhere might upset biological laws of natural fitness. The argument bore a close resemblance to those of the classic late nineteenth-century theorists of race differences such as Charles Pearson and Benjamin Kidd, although Luschan contributed a more specifically anthropological basis to the argument that 'racial barriers' should remain for 'The brotherhood of man is a good thing, but the struggle for life is a far better one.'[15] It meant also a resistance to the classic "race relations" situation of the emigration of rural peoples into an urban setting, for:

> *It certainly cannot be a matter of indifference to a nation, if great numbers of strangers come into their towns, take lower wages, live on a very low standard of life, and send home the greater part of their income.*[16]

For some liberals these anthropological arguments represented fundamental attacks on the objectives of the Congress, especially in so far as they implied a scientific basis for rejecting miscegenation as biologically harmful and reinforcing the notion that 'racial barriers' would 'never cease to exist'.[17] 'Races may once have been pure,' argued Alfred Haddon, 'but they are now so mixed that we had better speak of nations.'[18] Professor G Sergi of Italy went even further and argued against speaking of any differences of race and urged the Congress to pass a resolution in favour of all races being given the same rights on such matters as religion, custom and language.[19] The dispute was notable for the unease it produced in press comment on the Congress. *The Times* reported the debate with an element of mirth, seeing the Congress participants as quarrelling over 'trifling matters' such as 'whether the parents of the delegates hung by the tail from one tree or many trees,'[20] and undoubtedly helped to foster the view that the Congress's deliberations were of an esoteric nature. G K Chesterton, the Little Englander columnist of the *Illustrated London News*, doubted the value of any of the discussions on race which Harry Johnston had hoped would be fostered by the Congress. 'Anything that is soothing they call liberal,' Chesterton sneered, 'and anything that is liberal they call scientific...all this talk of oneness and Upwardness and Onwardness is really very bad for the sense of human brotherhood.' It was a fallacy of 'philanthropic anthropology,' he wrote, that races could 'come together'.[21]

Despite these reservations from some elements of the right-wing press, the anthropological debate did, to some extent, clear the air for the liberal protagonists of race, especially in so far as it confirmed their hostility to the conventional wisdom on miscegenation and to the belief that racial mixing would lead to a eugenic deterioration of the population. The liberal position on this had been forcibly stated in political terms by Sydney Olivier in the first edition of his book *White Capital and Coloured Labour* in 1906. A model of interracial relations had been outlined based on Olivier's experiences of colonial administration in the Westindies, where the brown middle class was seen as a stabilising element in a colour-class society that was free from the polarisation which Olivier perceived in the United States' and South African models of sharply defined black/white colour divisions.[22] This was born out of a long historical accommodation by the Westindian Creole elite of the colonial administration and the defeat of attempts at nationalism in the mid-nineteenth century. It was not until the 1930s that there was a renewed upsurge in Creole nationalist consciousness. This view, however, shaped some of the contributions on the issue of miscegenation in the second session.

Earl Finch, a black Professor at Wilberforce University in the United States, took up Olivier's arguments to defend interracial liaisons and shifted the general direction of analysis towards the economic and social deprivation behind the "inferior" status of mulattoes. For Finch, the examples of Booker T Washington, Frederick Douglass and W E B Du Bois served as proof of the 'remarkable intellectual power' attained by some people of mixed race.[23]

The thrust of the discussion at this point was away from anthropology, which Sydney Olivier attacked for its failure to throw much light on the issue,[24] towards an economic analysis of races and their positions within the social order. The ensuing debate commenced in the fourth session of the afternoon of Wednesday 27 July and here a new set of considerations was introduced.

The Economic Question

In constrast to the rather oblique and uncertain manner in which anthropological concepts had been introduced into the Congress proceedings, the debate on "Inter-Racial Economics" was of a more high-powered nature. This was partly because some of the principal figures in the intellectual revaluation of liberal economics, especially J A Hobson, were prominent in this debate and able to contribute a perspective derived from the "New Liberalism" of Edwardian England. It was also a result of the debate on the economic and political position of the American blacks which was reflected in the contribution of W E B Du Bois, representing the National Association for the Advancement of Coloured People (NAACP). He was distrustful of the more accommodationist standpoint of Booker T Washington and the reliance on simple economic, as opposed to political, pressures to transform the status of black Americans. The discussion was interesting for the way these two sets of political interests were brought into play, and their resulting ideological divergence.

The focal point of the session was the shift in English liberal thought on the nature of the relationship between overseas capital investment and imperial expansion. In his book *Imperialism* in 1902 and in successive articles after that, Hobson had propounded the underconsumptionist thesis that the high export of capital abroad had led to a reduction in domestic demand. This was the overriding cause behind the formation of imperialist expansion by gold and diamond mining interests which led to the Anglo-Boer War. Hobson's theory of imperialism had never been a completely economic one for, in *The Psychology of Jingoism* in 1901, he explained the mobilisation of popular enthusiasm for the war in terms of an early theory of mass psychology induced by the overcrowded life in towns and industrial cities.[25] Hobson's hostility to imperialism was born of a profound moral distaste for jingoism and its extreme nationalistic features rather than a simple economic analysis. In the tradition of Cobdenite radicalism, Hobson believed in progress and peace and it was as a result of the changing nature of his moral outlook that his views on overseas capital export began to change by 1909.[26] In the years before the First World War, finance capitalists acquired a vested interest in peace. In an article in the *Financial Review of Reviews* entitled "Do Foreign Investments Benefit the Working Classes?", Hobson began arguing that the export of capital had become a key means of securing a peaceful world order. There was a limit to the amount of capital which could be invested in international trade, and it was thus necessary that the excess go abroad otherwise there would be an 'epoch of rotten flotations with over capitalisation hurrying towards a financial crisis'.[27] The resulting development of international capitalism would not necessarily be antagonistic to the interests of the working class, as the resulting import of goods and raw materials into the home market would help domestic manufacturing, transport and distribution trades. To insulate the home market from these external trading markets would mean, as a result of a 'narrower, more exclusive nationalism',[28] that the British economy would be dependent upon extractive industries and therefore precariously dependent upon 'climatic and other natural fluctuations against which no provision could be made'.[29] Thus, while it was true that contemporary imperialism meant a set of warlike tendencies, due to its manipulation by the owners of foreign investments, this was 'an abnormal abuse of a normally pacific tendency' and, in general, external capital investment promoted both peace abroad and economic prosperity at home.[30]

The argument had some impact on the thinking at the Congress when it came to the question of the kind of economic policies necessary to promote harmony among races. A paper by the Professor of Political Economy at the University of Kolozsvar, Hungary, Dr Akos von Navratil, recommended Hobson's paper in support of the argument that foreign capital investments were 'one of the most powerful means of peaceful economic co-operation between races of different economic levels'.[31] Hobson too, in a paper on "Opening of Markets and Countries", applied the arguments from his 1909 paper to interracial relations. In the case of 'savage or semi-savage peoples', a long retention of imperial control by western states might be necessary in order to develop their economies and prevent their exploitation. The colonial administration needed, therefore, to be conducted by 'honest, independent and intelligent officials'. Reacting to the campaign against the rule of King Leopold in the Congo by E D Morel's Congo Reform Association (founded in 1904) and the resulting revelations of exploitation of the African peasantry by rubber syndicates, Hobson urged that 'a public sighted policy may prevail over the private short-sighted policy of traders'.[32] In the case of 'backward but civilised Asiatic states', however, Hobson argued for a policy of peaceful trading penetration, especially in countries like China, and opposed formal imperialism. Commercial expertise should be left to the 'free determination of Asiatic peoples' and Hobson condemned any ideas of acquiring 'white man's markets' in the Asian context.[33]

In some degree, Hobson helped to perpetuate certain stereotypes of black peoples in his distinction between 'savage' and 'Asiatic' peoples, especially when he doubted the capacity of 'negro and Indian races' for factory life – a view commonly held by liberals at this time.[34] This was the same creed as the segregationist ideology in the American South which, in the Jim Crow era, relegated American blacks to a secondary status on the basis of a folk-orientated economy structured around sharecropping. Hobson had been appalled, after visiting the United States in 1903, at the threat posed by Southern segregationism to American democracy, especially if it successfully allied itself to the new imperialist interest which had developed in the north in the wake of the war against Spain in 1898 and the acquisition of colonies such as the Philippines.[35] His pessimism regarding segregationism echoed the state of American liberal thinking at the time and even black American leaders such as Booker T Washington had emphasised, in the years after his famous Atlanta Exposition Address in 1895, economic as opposed to political advancement in order to promote black business enterprise by a 'talented tenth'.

This compromise with segregationism was not shared, however, by all black leaders in the United States and the formation in 1909 of the NAACP had led to an attack on Washington's political standpoint by a

more radical section of the black American political leadership led by W
E B Du Bois.[36] Washington toured Europe in 1910 and his views were
already familiar to British liberal opinion by the time of the 1911
Congress.[37] The NAACP put out a statement in 1910, "To the People of
Great Britain and Europe", attacking Washington's policy of
accommodationism. The Association believed that it was induced by his
dependence upon rich charitable bodies for funds for the Tuskegee
Institute in Alabama of which he was principal. The statement pointed
out that American blacks were actively discriminated against in
education, in housing, and in jobs, where half the American unions
refused to admit black members. This discrimination was undermining
American democratic principles and the statement sought the 'moral
support' of England and Europe 'in this recognition of manhood [sic]
despite adventitious differences of race'.[38] It was in this context that W E
B Du Bois decided to attend the 1911 Congress, despite commitments to
getting the NAACP started . The Congress was a means to combat some
of the political messages that had been disseminated in Europe by
Washington.[39]

Du Bois emphasised the discrimination suffered by blacks in the
United States, especially in employment, and introduced the element of
political struggle to the more deterministic cultural view propounded by
Hobson. Du Bois believed that the classical liberal model of international
free trade as a means of promoting harmonious race relations would only
apply in the USA if segregationist restrictions on learning skills and
higher wages were overcome:

> A southern negro, for example, could only get work in the shoe trade
> as a porter; he could not learn the trade. Only by co-operative
> financing, through a series of inevitable failures due to ignorance,
> could negroes manage to make a shoe store of their own succeed.
> Usually such a store supplied negro customers only. Economic
> intercourse between two countries or groups was of benefit to both
> only if the income arising from it was equally distributed between
> both.[40]

The notion of equal distribution between either racial groups or
countries was not successfully defined by the liberals at the Congress. It
had no model of universal economic distribution of goods and resources
to complement its notion of universal harmony between nations and
races.

In contrast to Du Bois, Sydney Olivier defended the workings of
peasant production in areas like West Africa as a means of avoiding a
'great black proletariat absolutely dependent on capital',[41] and was
unwilling to confront an emergent black working class in industrial
societies. It was only in the late 1920s, in works such as *The Anatomy of*

African Misery (1927) and the second edition of *White Capital and Coloured Labour* (1929), that he began a systematic analysis of capitalistic industrialisation in South Africa structured on a segregationist ideology and even then his critique was still mounted in terms of reviving and rejuvenating African peasant agriculture. It was maintained by some participants at the Congress, however, that international regulation could be ensured on the workings of international trade. The United States' delegate to the International Institute of Agriculture in Rome described its functions, in a paper in the fourth session, pointing out that since its foundation in 1905 its Treaty had been ratified by 47 governments and claiming that it covered 98 per cent of the world's population and 95 per cent of the world's land area. The chief objective of the Institute was to remove barriers from the operation of a free market of agricultural commodities and was in keeping with the general spirit of the Congress and its search for international amity between nations.[42] The basis of the Rome Institute, however, lay in treaties between nations and so did not tackle the political barriers rooted in the power interests of nation-states. It was to this latter area that the attention of the congress turned. The idea emerged of promoting a new international order based on what was termed 'the modern conscience'. The last main area of Congress debate asked how far political dimensions in race relations could be linked with humanitarian and ethical considerations.

Politics and the "Modern Conscience"

The Congress's origins in the international ethical movement ensured that any resolution of interracial relations would be seen within the framework of modern international ethical concern. This they termed the 'modern conscience' and the fifth session began with this theme on the morning of 28 July with an important paper by Professor Felix Adler, one of the original instigators of the Congress, entitled "The Fundamental Principle of Inter-Racial Ethics and Some Practical Application of It". Adler revealed how far the Congress had moved from the Victorians' more classically political notion of world order by his rejection of Tennyson's vision in *Locksley Hall* of a 'parliament of man and the federation of the world'. Parliament could not be a *terminus ad quem* for the Congress, argued Adler, for it could not be relied upon in itself to secure justice , for 'no parliament has as yet been free from the taint of class legislation and favouritism.'[43] Adler perceived the aims of the Congress as lying outside the terrain of traditional politics.[44] Instead he preferred the more idealistic notion of seeing humanity as a *corpus organicum spirituale* (an organic spiritual body) which could be best promoted through the idea of 'reciprocity of cultural influence' and the recognition of the greatest possible number of different cultural types.[45] This pointed beyond the tradition of static racial typologies bequeathed by nineteenth-century physical anthropology and towards social and cultural anthropology based upon detailed field work and local case studies. Through such a 'race pedagogy' it would be possible to understand different cultures, laws, customs, manners and religion in a way that would be of great use both to colonial administrators and to those concerned with promoting agricultural and industrial training.

For many this emphasis on improved cultural understanding represented the main purpose of the Congress. Introducing the fifth session, the Gaekwar of Baroda spoke of 'the evolution of a new moral vision' that should be applied in the sphere of race relations.[46] The demand for the peoples of the world to study 'sympathetically' the customs and civilisations of other peoples became one of the central resolutions of the Congress at its final plenary session on 29th July.[47] This objective, however, conflicted with the more overtly political objectives of many of the representatives from colonial territories, states such as Hungary, China and Japan and the Inter-Parliamentary Union interest. In the third session, for instance, Dr Christopher Lange, the Norwegian Member of the Second Hague Conference and General Secretary of the Inter-Parliamentary Union, had pointed out the growth in national consciousness in many parts of the world. This was represented by the Japanese defeat of Russia in the war of 1905, the political upsurge in Persia in 1906, which had led to the Shah granting a constitution, and the various nationalist forces in China, India and Egypt. Envisaging a series of international conferences, he hoped that the Congress would serve as an opportunity for promoting the idea of an International Parliament to encourage the parallel development of national legislation. The universal ideal of the Congress needed to take into account the reality of national states. 'I do not see any ideal in inter-national uniformity,' he concluded. 'On the contrary, national and racial diversity is in my opinion a condition of progress and life.'[48]

This split between the universal ethical element and the more politically orientated internationalist faction was compounded by a third element of individual nationalist spokesmen. W E B Du Bois foresaw the pattern of interracial contact in the United States as presaging the world pattern[49] and this impressed some of the other black representatives present, such as the two black South Africans, John Tengo Jabavu and Walter Rubusana. For them, the Congress was a useful opportunity to attack the myth of a "black peril" in South Africa. White colonial propaganda had succeeded in popularising this in Britain in the previous seven or eight years, especially via press accounts and popular adventure fiction such as John Buchan's novel *Prester John* (1910).[50] Rubusana attacked the notion that South Africa was a white man's country and argued, in language strongly reminiscent of black American political discourse, that 'there were only isolated cases of misbehaviour among the submerged tenth'.[51] Alongside this black South African interest, there were also white liberal interests with South African connections, such as Harold Polak of the South African British India Committee. This organisation was concerned with taking up the charges made at the Congress, by the Fabian Annie Besant, of abuse and exploitation of Indians in South Africa.[52] Polak urged all the races in South Africa to 'unite and assist the others in developing the country for their mutual benefit and advantage';[53] a plea that became common in later South African liberal rhetoric.

The South African debate, especially over the treatment of Indians, encapsulated a much wider attack on the liberal notion of harmonising separate communal interests through improved cultural understanding. The Indian nationalist position at the Congress was represented by the moderate figures of G K Gokhale, a former President of the Indian National Congress. His paper "East and West in India" was published simultaneously in India in the *Hindustan Review*. The Morley Minto Reforms of 1909 were, argued Gokhale, ultimately a constitutional cul-de-sac and the only way forward lay in further reforms, for while the mutual study by people from Britain and India of their respective cultures might help to improve their relationship, it was 'on the attitude of Englishmen towards the political advancement of India that these relations will mainly turn'.[54] Gokhale's paper reflected the fact that since 1907 at the latest more extreme nationalist elements had been making headway in the Indian Congress, especially after the imprisonment of the radical nationalist Bal Gangadhar Tilak in 1908. If there had ever been a moment for the emergence of a strong liberal movement in Indian politics, it was between 1905, when the Liberal, John Morley, first went to the India Office, and 1907, after which it effectively vanished for good.[55] Paradoxically, the Congress provided, despite its professed aims, a forum for the articulation of nationalist positions, especially Indian, which would ultimately help to destroy the universalist idealism of the Congress's instigators in the years after 1914.

The Legacy

The Universal Races Congress was without doubt an important event in raising the issue of comparative race relations to an international level and drawing the attention of a large number of governments, individual statesmen and public figures worldwide. Its hopes for creating a new world order were rooted in the idealism of the Hague Peace Conferences and international organisations like the Inter-Parliamentary Union. Alongside this Edwardian optimism, however, there was an underlying fear and foreboding for the future. This was typical of the time, which has often been seen as representing the break-up of the nineteenth-century liberal order. Lord Weardale warned prophetically of the 'centripetal and centrifugal forces' in the international order which 'have brought us face to face with a situation of grave difficulty, which, unless our disciplined humanity grapples with it successfully, threatens to end in the rebarbarisation of the world under huge military despotisms.'[56]

The Congress hoped its resolutions at least would have some effect, especially in so far as they stressed the roles of anthropological study and education. Much of this passed into the conventional wisdom of the 1920s as colonial powers like Britain and France became increasingly aware of the need for a more systematic industrial education in their colonies, especially Africa. The Phelps-Stokes Commission Report of 1922 brought home the importance of the American model derived from Booker T Washington's Tuskegee Institute. During the interwar years a number of measures were taken to promote the expansion of both missionary agricultural training and Jeanes Schools in East and Central Africa, as well as in South Africa in accordance with its policy of territorial segregation.[57] At one level, therefore, the Congress acted as a catalyst for new ideas which later passed into common currency and should not be judged solely on the more naive idealism of its original visionaries.

At another level, however, the Congress marked a rejuvenation of a nineteenth-century supranationalist liberal idealism at precisely the moment when such ideals were being overtaken by a resurgence of nationalist pressures in both Europe and what would now be termed the Third World. Despite the more pragmatic hopes of the Inter-Parliamentary Union, who desired an extension of Whig parliamentary ideals to the international plane (foreshadowing the devolution of power to nationalist movements in many British colonies in post-war years, leading to eventual independence under nominal parliamentary institutions), the Congress ultimately represented the more universalist ideals of its organisers. They had hoped that it would lead to local organisations spreading its message worldwide, the establishment of a *Journal of Comparative Civilisation* and an International Institute which could encourage 'in popular and other forms...sound and scientific investigations in appreciation of various civilisations of the world and to spread the same information through the medium of the press'.[58] Ironically, these objectives were taken up in the most concrete form by the Pan-Africanist *African Times and Orient Review*, edited by the Egyptian Duse Mohammed Ali, which was founded in 1912 in London to act as the Congress's mouthpiece.[59] While this journal initially presented many of the Congress's ideals in its articles, it acted eventually as a forum for the Pan-Africanist cause which had been expressed at the first Pan-African conference in London in 1900.[60]

The universalist liberalism of the Congress probably meant very little to most of the black representatives attending it; it was more significant for being an international conference willing to take up and debate issues concerning race and nationalism in the capital of the world's most important and powerful empire. The black representatives came originally as individual spokesmen for their countries and used the Congress to draw attention to their particular grievances. One example was the moving complaint of the Secretary of State for Liberia, F E R

Johnson, that in the past 30 to 40 years his country had been reduced by annexation from 80,000 square miles to 30,000.[61] The commanding intellect of W E B Du Bois helped focus the aspirations of many of these delegates to a more international level. There was, however, no overtly Pan-Africanist theme in any of the debates and Du Bois, at this stage in his career, was more concerned with the American pattern of race relations.

Events over the following decade gathered a momentum of their own and destroyed the illusions of those who attended the Congress. The experience of the war stimulated a growing nationalism among the black political elites in America, Africa and the Caribbean. In February 1919 a second Pan-African Congress was held in Paris with 57 delegates, 12 of whom were Africans from nine African countries. The NAACP played a leading role in the organisation of the Congress. This was a personal triumph for Du Bois in view of the difficulties he had encountered in gathering together a large number of delegates in the wake of the war and despite the suspicions of many European governments.[62] The era of universalist political ideals was now clearly over as more nationalist and colour-conscious political ideologies began to dominate the perspectives of the black political elites.

In Britain this shift was ably articulated by the Trinidadian Felix Hercules, editor of *The African Telegraph* and a leading figure in the Society of Peoples of African Origin. He recalled, in the article "The African and Nationalism" in 1918, that during the pre-war period he had been 'grasping blindly for a "something" that would transcend mere nationality, searching after the elusive "something" in humanity that would help men to meet in common and to remain linked without being narrowed by petty considerations of political frontiers or geopolitical barriers'. The experience of England's class divisions had destroyed these hopes, for he was confronted by 'barriers' and 'prejudices' which amounted to a 'caste system as rigid as any practised by the Hindoos'. As a consequence he felt driven back 'to the refuge of my own people'.[63]

Despite these nationalist reactions, the 1911 Congress did have a long-term effect on liberal political thought on race over the succeeding decades. It marked an important counter to the tradition of Fabian parochialism and disinterest in external political issues in the period before the establishment of the Fabian Colonial Bureau in 1940. This narrowness of Fabian preoccupations often spilled over into outright racism, as in the case of the Webbs after their tour of the Far East in 1911-12,[64] and reinforced the general reluctance of the Labour Party to take up colonial and racial issues. The 1911 Congress helped to stimulate a concern with racial discrimination among liberal philanthropic groups. One individual attending the Congress, Harold Polak, became the Chairman of the Joint Council to Promote Understanding Between White and Coloured People in Great Britain in the early 1930s, a body which eventually became absorbed into the League of Coloured Peoples, established by Harold Arundel Moody. Another liberal whose interest was stimulated by the Congress's discussion of race was Frank Norman who, after a career at the International Labour Organisation and in the Colonial Office as Labour Adviser in the Westindies, was instrumental in stimulating a sociological interest in race relations in the late 1940s through the Racial Relations Group of the Institute of Sociology. In the early 1950s this group merged with the Racial Unity Movement which championed many of the 1911 Congress's ideals. It encouraged an educational drive to counteract racial prejudice and championed legal measures to outlaw racial discrimination in public places.[65]

The long-term legacy of the Congress was important. It can be seen as a milestone in the development of a liberal conscience seeking to humanise racial relations in Britain and to develop a wider public knowledge to dispel ignorance and prejudice on an increasingly sensitive political issue.

NOTES

1. George Shepperson, "Pan-Africanism and 'Pan-Africanism': Some Historical Notes", *Phylon*, XXII, 4, Winter 1962, p. 354.
2. MSS Brit Emp S22 G441, R Felkine to Travers Buxton, 7 December 1909; Z G Harrington to Buxton, 10 December 1909.
3. Michael D Biddiss, "The Universal Races Congress of 1911", *Race*, XIII, I (1971), p. 45.
4. *Ibid.*
5. *Record of the Proceedings of the First Universal Races Congress*, PS King, London, 1911, p. 23.
6. Anti-Slavery Papers, Rhodes House, Oxford, MSS Brit Emp S22 G441. Notes on gathering of Universal Races Congress dated 22 December 1909. The initial organising meeting was at the Westminster Palace Hotel on 13 December and was attended by eight people including Hobhouse, W T Stead, a representative of the South Africa British India Committee, a black man, Dr Garnett, and 'some Indian gentleman'.
7. J A Hobson, *Confessions of an Economic Heretic*, The Harvester Press, Sussex, 1976 (1st edn 1938), pp. 94-5. For Olivier's criticisms see *The Times*, 6 August 1911.
8. James Bryce, "The Roman Empire and the British Empire in India", *Studies in History and Jurisprudence*, Vol. I, Clarendon Press, Oxford, 1901. See also Raymond F Betts, "The Allusion to Rome in British Imperialist Thought of the Late Nineteenth and Early Twentieth Centuries", *Victorian Studies*, XV, 2 December 1971, pp. 149-59.
9. John W Burrow, "Evolution and Anthropology in the 1860s: The Anthropological Society of London, 1864-1871", *Victorian Studies*, 7, 1963, pp. 137-54; Ronald Rainger, "Race, Politics and Science: The Anthropological Society of London in the 1860s", *Victorian Studies*, 22, 1978, pp. 51-70.
10. J W Burrow, *Evolution and Society*, CUP, Cambridge, 1966, p. 263.
11. Andrew P Lyons, "The Question of Race in Anthropology From the Time of Johann Friedrich Blumenbach to that of Franz Boas With Particular Reference to the Period 1830-1890", D.Phil. Thesis, University of Oxford, pp. 108-9; Philip Graham Reynolds, "Race, Nationality and Empire: Aspects of Mid Victorian Thought", Ph.D. Thesis, Queens University, Ontario, 1972; Daphne Herzstein, "Anthropology and Racism in Nineteenth Century Europe", *The Duquesne Review*, 14, 2, Fall, 1969, p. 123.
12. George M Stocking, "The Persistence of Polygenist Thought in Post Darwinian Anthropology" in *Race, Culture and Evolution: Essays in the History of Anthropology*, Free Press, New York, 1968, p. 45.
13. H H Johnson, "Racial Problems and the Congress of Races", *The Contemporary Review*, April 1911, p. 160.
14. *Record*, p. 25.
15. Prof. Felix von Luschan, "Anthropological Review of Race" in *Papers on Inter-Racial Problems Communicated to the First Universal Races Congress held at the University of London, July 26-29, 1911, edited, for the Congress by G. Spiller, Hon. Organiser of the Congress*, P S King, London, and The World's Peach Foundation, Boston, 1911, pp. 13-24.
16. *Ibid.*, p. 22.
17. *Ibid.*, p. 23.
18. *Record*, pp. 25-6.
19. *Ibid.*, pp. 26-7.
20. *The Times*, 28 July 1911.
21. *The Illustrated London News*, 5 August 1911.
22. Sydney Olivier, *White Capital and Coloured Labour*, I L P, London, 1906, pp. 38-41.
23. Prof. Earl Finch, "The Effects of Racial Miscegenation", *Papers*, pp. 111-12.
24. *Record*, p. 32.
25. J A Hobson, *The Psychology of Jingoism*, Grant Richards, London, p. 8 and *passim*.
26. Norman Etherington, "The Capitalist Theory of Capitalist Imperialism", *History of Political Economy*, 15, I, 1983, pp. 59-60.

27. J A Hobson, "Do Foreign Investments Benefit the Working Classes?", *The Financial Review of Reviews*, VII, March 1909, p. 25; see also Avner Offer, "Empire and Social Reform: British Overseas Investment and Domestic Politics, 1908-14", *The Historical Journal*, 26, I (1983), pp. 121-2.

28. Hobson, *op. cit.*, p. 28.

29. *Ibid.*, p. 29.

30. *Ibid.*, p. 30.

31. Dr Akos von Navratil, "Investments and Loans", in *Papers*, p. 211.

32. J A Hobson, "Opening Markets and Countries", in *ibid.*, p. 231.

33. *Ibid.*, p. 232.

34. *Ibid.*, pp. 231-2.

35. J A Hobson, "The Negro Problem in the United States", *The Nineteenth Century*, 54, October 1903, pp. 581-94.

36. For an analysis of the debate see August Meier, *Negro Thought in America 1880-1915*, The University of Michigan Press, Ann Arbor, 1973, esp. pp. 171-89.

37. Herbert Aptheker (ed), *The Correspondence of W.E.B. Du Bois*, Vol. I, The University of Massachusetts Press, 1973, p. 173.

38. The National Negro Committee on Mr Washington, 1910 statement, "To The People of Great Britain and Europe", in Herbert Aptheker (ed), *A Documentary History of the Negro People in the United States*, The Citadel Press, New York, 1964, pp. 884-6.

39. W E B Du Bois to Dr Ettie Sayer, 28 February 1911, in Aptheker (ed), *Correspondence*, pp. 173-4.

40. *Record*, p. 44.

41. Lord Olivier, *The Anatomy of African Misery*, The Hogarth Press, London, 1927; *White Capital and Coloured Labour*, The Hogarth Press, London, 1929. For a discussion of Olivier's thought see Paul B Rich, *Race and Empire in British Politics, 1890-1962*, ms, RUER, University of Aston, 1984, pp. 76-80.

42. David Lubin, "The International Institute of Agriculture at Rome", in *Papers*, pp. 254-8.

43. Dr Felix Adler, "The Fundamental Principle of Inter-Racial Ethics and Some Practical Applications of it", in *ibid.*, p. 262.

44. Stefan Collini, Donald Winch and John Burrow, *That Noble Science of Politics*, CUP, Cambridge, 1983, pp. 3-21.

45. Adler, *op. cit.*, p. 266.

46. *Record*, p. 47.

47. *Ibid.*, p. 8.

48. Dr C L Lange, "Tendencies Towards Parliamentary Rule", in *Papers*, p. 123.

49. *Record*, p. 61.

50. Paul B Rich, "Milnerism and a Ripping Yarn: Transvaal Land Settlement and John Buchan's Novel *Prester John*, 1901-10", in Belinda Bozzoli (ed), *Town and Countryside in the Transvaal*, Ravan Press, Johannesburg, 1983, pp. 412-33.

51. *Record*, p. 61.

52. *Ibid.*, p. 54.

53. *Ibid.*, p. 79.

54. Hon G K Gokhale, "East and West in India", in *Papers*, p. 164.

55. I R J Moore, *Liberalism and Indian Politics, 1872-1922*, Edward Arnold, London, 1966, p. 97.

56. *Record*, p. 24.

57. Kenneth King, *Pan Africanism and Education*, Pall Mall Press, London, 1971; Paul B Rich, *White Power and the Liberal Conscience*, Manchester University Press, Manchester, 1984, pp. 18-22.

58. *Record*, pp. 8-9.

59. *A.C. Haddon Pap*, University of Cambridge, 5406, Duse Mohammed Ali to A C Haddon, 30 April 1912.

60. Owen Charles Mathurin, *Henry Sylvester Williams and the Origins of the Pan African Movement, 1869-1911*, Greenwood Press, Westport, 1966, pp. 60-82.

61. *Record*, p. 52.

62. Clarence G Contee, "Du Bois, the NAACP, and the Pan African Congress of 1919", *Journal of Negro History*, LVII, 1 January 1972, pp. 13-28.

63. F E M Hercules, "The African and Nationalism", *The African Telegraph*, December 1918; see also W F Elkins, "Hercules and the Society of Peoples of African Origin", *Caribbean Studies*, January 1972, pp. 47-9.

64. J M Winter, "The Webbs and the Non-White World: A Case of Socialist Racialism", *Journal of Contemporary History*, 9, 1974, pp. 181-92.

65. MSS Brit Emp D 10/5 f 5, Frank Norman to Commander Fox-Pitt, n.d. encl. life history.

Chapter Four

Doctrines of Racial Segregation in Britain: 1900-1944

The Rise of "White Anglo-Saxon" Racial Ideas

The study of the history of racial ideas in twentieth century Britain has, until quite recently, been seriously neglected by scholars. This has in part resulted from a division of labour between historians, who have generally focused upon the evolution of racial ideas and ideology in the eighteenth and nineteenth centuries, and sociologists of race relations, more interested in contemporary patterns of housing, employment, education, debates on multiculturalism and "institutional racism". This avoidance of the earlier decades of the twentieth century, however, represents a serious omission, for this was a period of dramatic political and economic change. The Victorian era of imperial confidence gave way to slow national decline; periods of sharp class conflict were followed by long years of Conservative government, and two World Wars led to substantial social change and the rise of a welfare state. It was during this era, too, that Victorian racial ideas were reinterpreted to fit a new social and political situation. If there is a "new racism" of the 1970s and 1980s that is rooted in the imperial past, [1] it is not necessarily to some amorphous "imperial legacy" that we need to turn, but to a more immediate and active contemporary history in which racial ideas and symbols are actively sifted and reinterpreted by conscious historical agents.

This does not imply that the history of racial ideology should be interpreted through the prism of contemporary historical "presentism", a mistake to which students of social science are all too prone.[2] The formulators of racial ideas in previous generations were motivated and shaped by a complex pattern of objectives and influences, and it was by no means clear to anthropologists and historians in the period before 1914 that many of their ideas would be taken up by fascist political movements on a systematic and horrendous scale.[3] The dangerous political implications of race did dawn on some analysts, such as the French anthropometrist Vacher de Lapouge who remarked in the 1880s: 'I am convinced that in the next century millions will cut each other's throats because of 1 or 2 degrees more or less of cephalic index.' It is, however, a distortion of European history to see the history of race solely from the vantage point of the Final Solution.[4] To a considerable extent, white Anglo-Saxon racism remained a separate strand of racial ideology from that of Central European racism and was only an indirect contributor to European fascism and National Socialism.

From the 1880s until the First World War British and American thought was dominated by a general consensus on the inherence of racial differences and the supposition that races could be graded along some form of "great chain of being", with the white Anglo-Saxon race in the topmost position, Mediterraneans and Southern Europeans in a lower position, followed by Indians, Chinese, Africans and non-white races in general.[5] The widespread similarity in racial attitudes among the white Anglo-Saxons was a phenomenon frequently commented upon by informed, if racist, commentators, especially the supposed aversion to intermarriage and a general drive towards racial "separation" and its institutional and legislative legitimation. As Alfred Holt Stone, a sociologist from the US south, noted in 1908:

> *The attitude of the so-called Anglo-Saxon people toward the Negro the world over is essentially the same. Eventually it will be sufficiently recognised to afford a basis for mutual toleration and respect among all white people, as regards their social and political relations with the Negro, and the other inferior or backward races with which they are brought in contact.[6]*

This growing consciousness of an overall white Anglo-Saxon racial identity in the early years of the century left a strong imprint on racial thought in Britain. It began, in some respects, to replace older notions of "Teutonic" race solidarity with Germany, as the latter power became a national rival for Britain in European and imperial power politics.[7] As this chapter seeks to show, this consciousness acted as an important mechanism for the instilling of segregationist ideas into sections of the British intelligentsia at a time when its members were themselves undergoing a crisis in intellectual and social identity. The more stable Victorian political consensus had begun to break up in the face of growing democratisation in Britain and sharp class conflict. For a number of eminent "experts" on racial matters, especially in the imperial context, segregationism represented a new and significant buttress to older ideas of racial differentiation. Indeed, for many it represented a liberal redefinition of the "race problem" in more intellectually acceptable terms. This avoided having to employ the cruder stereotypes of more populist racists, which offended the strong sense of social gentility that many members of the British "intellectual aristocracy" had at this time.[8]

The Significance of Segregationism

The *locus classicus* of segregationist ideology was the American South from the time of the Compromise of 1877 which ended the phase of Reconstruction after the Civil War. Over the following decades there occurred, as C Vann Woodward has observed, a process of restraint on the oppositional forces of Northern liberalism, Southern conservatism and Southern radicalism. This led to the progressive nullification of the Civil Rights Act of 1875, culminating in the crucial decision of the US Supreme Court in 1896 in the case of *Plessy v Ferguson* that legislation was 'powerless to eradicate racial instincts' and that separate facilities for blacks and whites in education could be equal.[9] Segregation was a product of the breakdown of a previous balance of power which, in the period immediately after the Civil War, had kept in check the forces favouring racial exclusion in Southern society. It was in turn greatly promoted by a new climate of opinion which was strongly racist, a consequence of growing "scientific" racism, rooted in anthropological and eugenic theories of racial difference and a new expansionist imperialism epitomised by the war against Spain in 1898. This encouraged notions of an Anglo-Saxon racial superiority over black, brown, yellow and even Southern European peoples, indeed anybody not of Nordic or Caucasian descent.[10] It is important to note that the actual formulation of the ideology of segregation came less from the extreme racial populists than from intellectuals and men of the professional class. They were keen for a strategy of social control which could defuse the more violent aspects of racial polarisation represented by the Ku Klux Klan and the increase in lynchings towards the turn of the century. As John Cell, an American analyst, has recently noted:

> ..*far from being the crude, irrational prejudice of ignorant 'rednecks',
> segregation must be recognised as one of the most successful political
> ideologies of the past century. It was, indeed, the highest stage of
> white supremacy.*[11]

In some respects segregationism can be interpreted as a "Leninist" ideology of white supremacist control by political ideologues keen to control the more diffuse, even anarchistic, racism of the grass-roots populists – the equivalent of what Lenin was later to term 'left wing Communism'.[12] As Cell has pointed out, while segregationism became closely intertwined with racism, it nevertheless contained a degree of flexibility which ensured that it would survive beyond the demise of the more overt aspects of racism in the 1930s and 1940s. This resilience needs to be taken into account by analysts of comparative race relations for, in so far as the ideology presupposed a model of separate racial behaviour and group destiny, it manifested a greater degree of subtlety and sophistication than the cruder racism of the populists, which simply maintained a notion of a gradient of racial superiority and inferiority. This is a concept that leads to either total racial exclusionism (such as the idea of some Southern racists of shipping all blacks back to Africa) or genocide, as in Nazi racism towards Jews and Gipsies. Segregationism fell into the mainstream political discourse of "middle opinion",[13] and it is important to recognise that for a significant period from the 1890s to the 1940s the concept seemed eminently reasonable even to people of moderate and liberal political persuasions.

One particularly important feature of segregationism was its international nature. The term was readily exportable and was taken up in a number of other societies with white colonial and "Anglo-Saxon" features, such as Australia and South Africa. In the case of the latter, the notion of territorial or "possessory" segregation between white and black races made South African segregationism unique. Although the notion of separate territorial residence in the US South had been periodically proposed by some racists, it was never seen as a particularly practical solution. However, one British commentator, the theatre critic William Archer, did propose a separate black state in the South.[14] In South Africa the pattern of "native locations", established in the course of white colonial expansion in the nineteenth century, provided a ready model for segregationists to promote a more fixed and rationalised pattern of territorial demarcation. One prominent segregationist in the Transvaal after the Anglo-Boer War, Howard Pim, employed the American pattern of segregation to indicate a general historical tendency for 'the two races' to 'steadily drift apart'. The reserves should be the abode of the black race, where a separate black agricultural economy could be fostered, for 'there can be nothing unhealthy or wrong in requiring the Native himself to cope with the increase in his own number or the increasing stress of outside competition'.[15] The reserves were limited, however, in order to facilitate the development of white capitalist agriculture using cheap black labour. It was on this basis that the Union government in South Africa passed the 1913 Natives Land Act, restricting the land area for blacks in the country to some nine per cent of the whole, effectively laying the foundations for the later policy of apartheid or "separate development" in the 1950s and 1960s.[16] The African, as the early nationalist Sol Plaatje noted in his classic book *Native Life in South Africa*, woke up to find himself 'a pariah in the land of his birth.'[17]

The segregationist model nevertheless had a fascination for analysts of race in other countries, not least in Britain. Even though British society in the early years of the twentieth century did not itself contain a sizeable number of black people beyond those in such seaport towns as Liverpool, Cardiff, South Shields and the East End of London, together with small groups of black students and itinerant pedlars, it was acutely colour-conscious. The Pan-Africanist writer and diplomat Edward Wilmott Blyden wrote in 1903 that, on a visit to Blackpool some years previously, he went to the Winter Gardens where there were some wild animals on exhibition. He continued:

I noticed that a nurse having two children could not keep her eyes from the spot where I stood, looking at first with a sort of suspicious if not terrified curiosity. After a while she heard me speak to one of the gentlemen who were with me. Apparently surprised and reassured by this evidence of a genuine humanity, she called to the children who were interested in examining a leopard, 'Look, look, there is a black man, he speaks English.'[18]

For other blacks, this English curiosity took more hostile or humiliating forms, and the Sierra Leonian, A B C Merriman-Labor, wrote in 1910 that in working-class areas 'the black man stands the chance of being laughed to scorn until he takes to his heels'.[19] The combination of English ignorance of race and a patriotic feeling of superiority over black and yellow races remained a prevalent feature in later years, as more recent accounts, such as that of the cricketer Learie Constantine, attest.[20] It was, however, accentuated in the early years of the century by a growing awareness within government and informed circles of a crisis of imperial confidence, especially after the disastrous campaign in the Boer War.

The significance of imperialism lies not only in its simple economic or material benefits but in the complex set of emotions invested in it. As A P Thornton has observed:

..Imperialism is less a fact than a thought. At its heart is the image of dominance, of power asserted; and power is neither used nor witnessed without emotion... Imperialism is therefore more often the name of the emotion that reacts to a series of events than a definition of the events themselves.[21]

It was a crisis in the emotional buttressing of the British imperial enterprise which created the ideological space necessary for the intrusion of ideas of racial segregation.

The Eclipse of the Victorian Liberal Tradition

In earlier years Victorian liberal opinion had been fairly hostile to ideas of strict racial differentiation. The controversy over the actions of Governor Eyre in Jamaica in 1865 had split Victorian opinion, with a number of prominent liberals such as Richard Cobden, T H Huxley and John Stuart Mill supporting the condemnation of Governor Eyre.[22] Similarly, some liberals championed the enfranchisement of the American blacks at the end of the Civil War on the grounds that it was 'against the principle of caste politics that a radical party in the United States has now taken its stand.'[23] Even after the Radical Reconstruction and the Compromise of 1877, some Victorian liberals still envisaged a continuous process of political advancement for American blacks. The liberal scholar, writer and diplomat James Bryce wrote in *The American Commonwealth* in 1889 that the American black was:

> *Growing into citizenhood and the time may not be distant when he will begin to exert that restless influence on the white oligarchy which unenfranchised masses always tend to exert upon leaders, however superior in intelligence and energy the leaders may be.*[24]

In the course of the 1890s, however, the advance of segregationism in the American South nullified some of these earlier British observations and hopes, and by the time of the Boer War a more favourable image of segregation began to emerge. It surfaced in British political discussion in the context of a more wide-ranging concern over the state of global race relations. As Bryce pointed out in 1900 in an important Romanes lecture at Oxford, the 'closer and more widespread contact' of 'advanced and civilised races with the more backward' could be 'deemed to mark a crisis in the history of the world.'[25] In the course of the 1890s a number of writers began expressing pessimism over the future of the white race in world politics. Under the impact of Darwinian thought, it began to appear that an international struggle for existence was taking place between different races, only the fittest of which would survive this global law of the jungle. The Australian writer Charles H Pearson, for example, articulated this view in 1893 in his *National Life and Character*, in which he envisaged that the 'black and yellow belt' of the tropical regions would expand at the expense of the white race, which could not survive in competition with the 'more vigorous life' of 'lower civilisation'.[26] A gradual loosening of white imperial control was likely as the black and yellow races of the tropics gained the monopoly of trade in their own regions and began 'circumscribing the industry of the European'.[27]

This view was not shared by all writers of the time for, as Benjamin Kidd argued in his book *The Control of the Tropics* (based on a series of articles in *The Times*) in 1898, it appeared more likely that an international struggle would take place between European imperial powers for control of trade with the tropical regions, which were still seen as geographical areas in which the white race could not flourish under the laws of natural selection.[28] By the turn of the century there was certainly a loss of the older imperial confidence; and even if, as writers like Bryce averred, the "higher" white race was destined for world rule for some years to come,[29] there was anxiety at the growth in black immigration into white-ruled areas such as Australasia, Southern Africa and North America, especially of people from Asia. A series of immigration statutes were implemented, based on a model in Natal to restrict Indian entry, and these were seen as the only means by which these population movements could be controlled, albeit on a basis of overt racial discrimination.[30]

The attraction of the American model of segregation lay in its "scientific" solution of many of the seemingly intractable racial problems pointed out in the 1890s. Bryce saw the elimination of yellow fever in Cuba by American medical practitioners as grounds for believing that advances in medicine could ensure that whites could live in tropical zones, and thereby offer a "scientific" control over the forces of natural selection.[31] These hopes were reinforced in the early years of the twentieth century by more concrete evidence from areas such as Queensland in Australia, where the development of the sugar industry provided increased employment for white labour. One theorist, W K Gregory, wrote in 1910 that the image of tropical areas propagated by Benjamin Kidd was inaccurate; 'the Australian experiment' was 'the greatest practical attempt yet made to solve the problem whether the waste spaces of the tropics can be developed as white colonies instead of as black dependencies'.[32] With the growth in segregationist ideology in South Africa as well as Australia, segregation in the British Commonwealth was increasing in its appeal the years before the First World War.
the British Commonwealth was increasing in the years before the First World War.

British writers on race in the years after the Anglo-Boer War engaged in an increasingly sharp political debate on the nature and course of British imperialism. A number of liberal "pro-Boers" reacted strongly to the events of the War, arguing for the abandonment of imperial pretensions and greater concentration on the economic development of the British domestic market in order to raise working-class living standards. The argument was most strongly put by J A Hobson in his book *Imperialism* in 1902 which asserted, on the basis of an underconsumptionist thesis, that imperialism was promoted by the urge of finance capitalists to invest in more lucrative overseas markets as opposed to the home one, so increasing economic and class inequalities in the metropolitan society. By 1903 Hobson was depressed by the advance of segregation in the United States, seeing it as a threat to American democracy.[33] Other liberals and some socialists envisaged the British imperial presence in overseas colonies being transformed into a pacific and benevolent one, promoting harmonious relations between races and fostering a "Jamaican" society in contrast to that of America. B Pullen-Bury considers that 'under British rule we have evolved the fact that, with the minimum of education but with the maximum of the white man's guidance, in contrast to the segregation policy of the Americans, a great deal has been done in converting a backward race into helpful members of a civilised community'.[34]

A similar view was expressed by Sydney Olivier who wrote in his book *White Capital and Coloured Labour* in 1906 that Jamaica represented a working model of interracial harmony, in contrast to the more polarised racial societies of the American South or South Africa. Races, Olivier argued, were created by local environments, particularly rural, agrarian ones, for towns tended to destroy racial identities. Deeply hostile to the forces of capitalist industrialisation, Olivier looked to the fostering of peasantries in the colonies as a means of avoiding racial antagonism resulting from the emergence of a black working class.

> *A community of white and black alone is in far greater danger of remaining, so far as the unofficial classes are concerned, a community of employers and serfs, concessionaires and tributaries with, at best, a bureaucracy to keep the peace between them. The graded mixed class in Jamaica helps to make an organic whole of the community and saves it from this distinct cleavage.*[35]

In contrast to this conciliatory social model, Olivier saw the American and South African situations as representing a great political danger in so far as they promoted negrophobia and race prejudice, which was an inherently irrational phenomenon, 'the logic neither of words nor facts'. There was a strong need of mechanisms by which racial polarisation could be defused. The polarised situations in the American South and South Africa represented the danger of aggravating the 'virus' of 'the colour problem' internationally, while the Jamaican model led more to its being ignored, which was the only way the virus could be 'attenuated'.[36]

A similar view was held by H G Wells after he visited the United States. Noting the 'tragedy of colour' in his book *The Future in America* in 1906, Wells was critical of American segregation; while it was true that a 'caste nation' might be 'more various than the whole of a non-caste nation', the separated castes were still more 'monotonous' than in a casteless society. Habits of mind were formed in each caste, 'for all who enter it are taught in one way and trained in the same employment', and Wells probably feared that cultural sterility would arise from this pattern of social evolution.

These fears that segregationism in the American South and South

Africa would develop and possibly attain an international status reflected the defensive nature of British liberal ideas on race in the early years of the century. A conservative counterattack, rooted in an advocacy of segregationism, was mounted against liberals such as Olivier, Hobson and H G Wells. William Archer, in particular, attacked Olivier's view that Southern race prejudice was irrational on the basis of an argument anchored in what would now be termed "culture shock". In 1910, at the time he wrote, one-third of the Southern population was black, in an area for the most part outside the tropical zone. It was, in particular, 'the crowding, *the swamping*, the submerging of the white race by the blacks, that the South cannot reasonably be expected to endure' (emphasis mine).[38] Furthermore, in contrast to Olivier's model of Jamaica, Archer upheld the South as 'the great crucible in which the experiment in inter-racial *chemistry* is working itself out' (emphasis mine). This was of particular importance to English public opinion, he maintained, for the race question in the United States was not an 'abstract one' but one of interest to 'every Englishman who is so far an imperialist as to feel that he cannot simply wash his hands of the problem of Empire.'[39]

Archer proceeded to uphold the Southern segregationist model in terms that could be easily understood by an English audience unfamiliar with the issue of race relations at first hand. Pointing out that in 1910 some 100,000 of Washington's population of 250,000 were black, Archer wrote:

> *Imagine nearly half the population of Nottingham suddenly converted into black and brown people – people different not only in colour but in many other physical characteristics from you and me. Imagine that all the most striking of these differences are in the direction of what our deepest instincts, inherited through a thousand generations, compel us to regard as ugliness – an ugliness often grotesque and simian. Imagine that this horrible metamorphosis...to have taken place as a punishment for certain ancestral crimes and stupidities, of which the living men and women of today are personally innocent. Can you conceive that, after the first shock of surprise was over, Nottingham would take up life again as a mere matter of course, feeling that there was no misfortune in this mingling of incongruities, no problem in the adjustment of the relations?*[40]

With imagery such as this, Archer sought to show the unnaturalness, in scientific terms, of a mixed race society and the inherent reasonableness of "Jim Crow" segregation, which was 'a legitimate measure of defence against constant discomfort'.[41] Furthermore, segregation was seen to reinforce class and racial distinctions which had become embedded in English social thought in the course of the Victorian era. As Douglas

Lorimer has shown, the rise of a professional intelligentsia and middle class by the mid-nineteenth century had contributed to a climate of growing racial exclusiveness from the 1860s onwards, as blacks and colonials were seen as competitors in the upward drive towards respectability and bourgeois gentility.[42] The image of the black person became strongly connected with cultural separateness – an ideal that was further reinforced by Mary Kingsley's emphasis upon the relative rather than absolute differences between European and African cultures after her widely publicised travels in West Africa in the late 1890s.[43]

Archer drew a fine and important distinction between the two dominant black leaders in the United States in the early years of the century. Du Bois was seen as a 'quiet, cultivated, French-looking gentleman' and there was a 'difficulty', Archer felt, in discerning 'any difference of race and tradition, and not to assume, tactlessly, an identical standpoint'. However, while Du Bois led 'from without', Booker T Washington, the founder of the Tuskegee Industrial Training Institute in Alabama and famous for his 1895 Atlanta Exposition Address urging blacks to seek economic rather than political advance, was a leader who led 'from within'. Washington 'could never have been anything else than a negro; he represents all that is best in the race, but nothing that is not in the race. Mr Du Bois is a negro only from outside pressure.'[44] Archer interpreted the different political styles of the two men in terms of class and racial imagery, with a strong emphasis upon the notion that racial dilution connoted an inverse purity of political standpoint; the mixed-race but genteel Du Bois was a 'cloistered intransigent' in comparison to the 'negro' figure of Washington, who was 'an opportunist and a man of action.'[45] This was a political interpretation well in keeping with the sceptical British regard for politicians and the dislike, at the best of times, for political ideologues.

The Development of Segregationism in Britain

In the years after 1910, segregationist ideology enjoyed fairly wide approval amongst sections of the intelligentsia and middle class. In philanthropic and welfare bodies it was seen as a benevolent means of ensuring separate black political advance. At this stage it was not ideologically distinguishable from the cultural relativism of the Kingsleyite school of pioneer anthropologists who centred around the Africa Society founded in her memory in 1900. Edward Dene Morel, of the Congo Reform Association, was a firm believer in the need for the insulation of African cultures from western economic and cultural contact which might threaten their stability. Later, he became a fanatical opponent of the use of black troops by the French forces occupying the Rhineland after the First World War when Germany defaulted on its reparations. With allegations of black troops raping German women, Morel felt the case illustrated the need to keep blacks away from Europe since they were, he believed, so much more sexually developed than whites.[46] The Reverend John Harris, of the Anti-Slavery Society, also believed in segregationism in Southern Africa, and supported the 1913 Natives Land Act on the grounds that it allowed Africans a separate channel of political advance.[47]

After the First World War, a campaign to restrict immigration to the United States from Eastern and Southern Europe led to an upsurge in racist literature which emphasised the theme of "Anglo-Saxon" racial superiority and the benefits of segregation.[48] Allied to the ideology of white supremacy, segregationism also seeped through British political discourse in the early 1920s, and shaped the climate in which the policy of colonial "trusteeship" and "indirect rule" was formulated.

One of the key opinion-formers at this time, Frederick Lugard, favourably reviewed Lothrop Stoddard's *The Rising Tide of Colour* in 1921 on the basis of its opposition to miscegenation, which Lugard agreed enhanced racial deterioration.[49] Lugard emphasised the differing issues of competition from Asian and Chinese people in the Far East, which necessitated 'increased efficiency by the white man and cessation of industrial strife',[50] and the situation in black Africa, where continued white control was necessary through the use of indigenous social institutions.[51] Lugard was no uncritical admirer of the South African model of segregation, feeling the reserves were too small for African needs, although the political implications of this were not yet evident. He was also worried by the challenge to white power being made both in the United States and in South Africa by Marcus Garvey's Universal Negro Improvement Association and the South African "Ethiopian" movement of separatist churches.[52]

Lugard's sentiments were very much part of the post-war climate of opinion on the right, where opposition to interracial liaisons and miscegenation was linked to a campaign for racial "purity" and national homogeneity. Experts such as Sir Arthur Keith saw "nation" and "race" as being the same thing, with war and struggle between races being a process of natural selection.[53] Other race experts such as W R Inge were keen to employ the Anglo-Saxon ideology of Madison Grant, author of *The Passing of the Great Race* (1916), and Lothrop Stoddard as a means of asserting the traditional aristocratic values of the English ruling class against the "Mediterranean race" of Celtic people from Wales, Scotland and Ireland, whom he saw as invading the towns and making the English become 'darker in each generation'.[54] This was an indigenous British, or more specifically English, racism which reinforced a class ideology at a time before significant black immigration.

This more indigenous and parochial debate on race was, however, still overlain by the American segregationist model, which was continually appealed to by experts anxious for a strong support for their arguments. In the case of eugenic hostility to miscegenation, the American parallel was used to buttress a "scientific" argument based upon a theory of inherent racial difference and limits of mental capacity. The eugenicist Reginald Ruggles Gates, for example, argued against miscegenation on the basis of contemporary research in the field of genetics. There were instances, he wrote in *Heredity and Eugenics* in 1923, in which different species of the *Drosophila* fruit fly (frequently used by geneticists due to its rapid reproductive capacity), distinguishable only by experts,[56] produced sterile hybrids, and the evidence from interracial breeding in man seemed to demonstrate similar dangers. Using modern scientific evidence, Gates reinforced the conventional Victorian racial distinction between "advanced" and "backward" races:

> *Where evolution has been going on independently in...races for such long periods, and some races have progressed far beyond others, both mentally and culturally, it is folly to suppose that crosses between a progressive and a primitive race can lead to a desirable result from the point of view of the advanced race, or even of the primitive race.*[57]

Gates also drew upon the US Army intelligence tests of the First World War. These were based upon the intelligence scale invented by Alfred Binet (1857-1911) at the psychology laboratory at the Sorbonne, which in the years after 1918 replaced anthropometric criteria as the means of measuring human mental capacity. Gates used the evidence that only some ten to 25 per cent of black recruits equalled or excelled the white recruits to buttress an hereditarian argument of permanent black mental inferiority.[58] While American blacks might not be a case of 'arrested development', he maintained, they certainly exhibited a 'primitive mentality with less control of the impulses and emotion and less ability to deal with the abstract or symbolic'. Furthermore, the example of Booker T Washington's programme of 'manual education' served as an example of giving education 'most appropriate to his [the black person's] mental status.'[59]

Shifting Criteria for Segregation and White Supremacy

The use of scientific evidence to buttress a racist ideology of segregationism was not resorted to by all the segregationist writers in Britain in the 1920s. Indeed, environmental notions of race differences, based on the idea of separate territorial spheres for races, remained a strong element in British political discourse on race during this period. J W Gregory used further material from Australian racist writers, such as Griffith Taylor, in his book *The Menace of Colour* (1927), to support a case for global segregationism to protect the white race in those territorial spheres where it could flourish behind protective segregationist barriers excluding competition from cheaper black labour.[60] He rejected skull indices and anthropometry as a means for classifying races and instead preferred to rely on a looser colour classification. His main interest was less in establishing a complex scientific hierarchy of races than in identifying the means whereby white supremacy could be maintained in certain areas of the globe.[61] Gregory developed the debate that stretched back to the 1890s with Charles Pearson and Benjamin Kidd; he saw areas such as North America, Australia, South Africa and the southern part of South America as the main loci, outside of Europe, where the white race could hold its own in the coming years. Asia, India, and most of Africa he saw as beyond white rule. The future of the global order depended on the institutionalisation of segregation to ensure world peace:

> *Sympathetic intercourse between selected individuals, combined with the segregation of each race as a whole, may be expected to lead to a happier and more peaceful world than the jarring friction inevitable when dissimilar people meet in competition for their daily bread.*[62]

Unlike earlier segregationist writers such as William Archer, Gregory took a less committed position on the issue of miscegenation, reflecting the upsurge in political debate and social research in this area after 1910. The general consensus amongst British eugenicists, however, was that interracial liaisons produced hereditarily deficient offspring. Major Leonard Darwin, President of the Eugenics Education Society, sent a letter to the premiers of the British Dominions during the 1923 Imperial Conference in London warning that 'interbreeding between widely divergent races' could result in the 'production of types inferior to both parent stocks'.[63] For Gregory, the issue centred around the question that 'if miscegenation between the primary races' was 'undesirable', then 'the co-residence of different races should be avoided in the interest of the future of mankind.'[64]

By the late 1920s, it was becoming clear that, despite the enthusiasm of segregationist ideologues such as Gregory, little co-ordinated action would be taken by the British Commonwealth on the issue. It was South Africa that became the main locus for eugenic social engineering and the 1927 Immorality Act was passed forbidding 'all illicit intercourse' (not marriage) between black Africans and whites. In 1929, the former Union prime minister, General Jan Smuts, in a series of lectures at the newly-opened Rhodes House in Oxford, pleaded for a policy of comprehensive white land settlement in the high veld areas of Eastern and Central Africa, so as to give 'fresh support and stimulus for western civilisation throughout vast surrounding areas.'[65] Furthermore, echoing the arguments of segregationists like Gregory in the Australian context, Smuts pointed out that the tropical areas of Africa were now suitable for white settlement, so that it was

*even possible that, just as in the biological world new types are
evolved in new environments, so a new human type may in time arise
under the unusual climatic conditions of Eastern Africa...The human
laboratory of Africa may yet produce strange results, and time alone
can show whether or not the experiment was worth while in the
interest of humanity.*[66]

However, the collapse of Wall Street in the same year postponed
indefinitely any British governmental support for such a policy and,
although the Colonial Office policy in the 1920s under Lord Milner and
his zealous successor Leo Amery had been strongly supportive of white
settler colonies in Africa, it had not even returned the Protectorate
territories to South Africa, as the latter's policy of territorial segregation
had begun to attract increasing international criticism.[67]

A number of liberal critics of segregation in Britain sought to
disconnect segregation from any scientific pretensions it might have. J H
Oldham, in a critique of Smut's Rhodes House lectures, argued that, not
only could there never be a white "civilisation" in Eastern Africa in the
same sense as in Europe or America, but also that the main creative
forces in Africa came not from white settlement but from the sale of the
continent's tropical products. It was thus not eugenic social engineering
that was needed, but the development of the mineral and agricultural
resources of Africa, together with other parts of the British empire, 'by
the effective imperial organisation of scientific resources'.[68]

A New Climate of Opinion

Oldham's counter-argument reflected a new climate of opinion among
the ruling class in the 1930s. This began moving towards economic and
social colonial development as opposed to a racial mission of white
colonisation, which was increasingly seen as an anachronistic legacy of
Victorian race patriotism of the "Greater Britain" variety. Smut's
lectures set in motion a search for funds by the Rhodes Trust for a survey
of Africa, which reached fruition as the Hailey *African Survey* in 1938.
The racial aspect tended to get lost in a wider analysis of economic and
social development potential in the various African colonies as part of a
process of 'leisurely planning' which would, it was hoped, postpone any
confrontation with critical political issues.[69] This shift towards colonial
development following the 1929 Colonial Development Act was
reinforced by an increasing aversion to Nazi racial ideology in Germany.
This forced the protagonists of eugenics on to the defensive in the 1930s.
Indeed, eugenics came to be seen, even by fairly traditional physical
anthropologists such as George Pitt-Rivers, as transcending the status of
an 'applied science' and becoming a religion.[70] In the light of the
discussions surrounding the joint publication by the Royal
Anthropological Institute and the Institute of Sociology of their report

Race and Culture in 1935, there was a growing resistance to associating national make-ups with races, for Nazi ideology had tried to legitimise German nationalism through Aryan race theories.[71] By the late 1930s eugenics had become more a series of specialised causes, such as the voluntary sterilisation of the mentally "unfit". It was no longer a vision for the complete remodelling of society, as some of the founders had hoped.[72]

Although segregationists such as Gregory continued to make their case before rationalist audiences such as the South Place Ethical Society, [73] the model of racial segregation began to fall outside mainstream establishment discourse in Britain. The policy of "indirect rule" in Africa began to be dissociated from the policy of South African segregation, while social anthropologists trained in the seminars of Malinowski at the London School of Economics began intensive field work, studying African cultures unde the ethos of a "new humanism", one that became increasingly critical of Southern African segregation during the late 1930s and 1940s.[74] It seemed clear to many that British policy should not be identified with that of the white settler South. As one perceptive observer, André Siegfried, wrote in 1931,

> *to determine the frontier between the English and South African policy is, as may be imagined, of vital importance, as vital indeed as was the fixing of the Mason-Dixon line between the Northern and Southern States of America in the last century.*[75]

This growing ideological divergence did not, however, become particularly manifest in terms of government policy until the Second World War. Following the arrival of 2,000 black American troops in Britain by the end of 1942, the British government was forced to make a clear stand in opposition to the importation of segregation from the United States, for fear of antagonising political opinion in the British colonies which were then so crucial to the Allied war effort.[76] This direct confrontation with segregation in the imperial metropolis itself was a clear sign that the previously obfuscatory position on segregation could no longer be maintained. This was reinforced by the rising campaign for civil rights in the United States, and the upsurge of a reform-minded liberalism crystalised by Roosevelt's New Deal programme and the definition of Allied war aims in the 1941 Atlantic Charter.

In 1944, Gunnar Myrdal's *An American Dilemma* envisaged the supersession of Southern segregationism by the "American Creed" of humanist liberalism, based on the Enlightenment ideal of the rights of man. Segregationism as an ideological force for white supremacy in world politics was clearly losing its grip, and by the war's end the bastions of white supremacy in South Africa and the American South were coming under increasing international attack.

In this changing atmosphere, the role of America began to change. Some sections of liberal opinion saw South Africa's policy as doomed for, as the novelist Joyce Cary wrote in *The Case for African Freedom* in 1941, it was no more likely to be able to save itself than the old Confederate South.[77] A Federal Council of Africa in which the United States government could take part would, on the other hand, represent a path for a new and free post-war Africa, which Cary did not yet see as hastening the rise of African nationalist sentiment.[78] Clearly, a shift of perspective had begun to take place, and in the post-war era the struggle for civil rights in the USA was used as a model for encouraging political and civil rights in colonial Africa in order to facilitate the demise of white supremacy in the settler states of the South. By the late 1940s only the extreme right continued to believe in the old pre-war segregationism. Oswald Mosley in *The Alternative* (1947), for example, continued to see the benevolent segregation of Africans from western capitalist and missionary influences as a vital part of a new phase of imperial expansion in an Africa rooted in state corporatist development programmes.[79]

This chapter has focused upon a tradition of ideas favouring segregation and white supremacy rooted in the American South of the "Jim Crow" era but spreading to other white-controlled societies. This tradition influenced the thinking on race by informed and specialist opinion in Britain at a critical phase of its imperial history after the Anglo-Boer War and can be seen as an important factor in the development of racial ideology in Britain before black immigration and the advent of a "race relations" situation. Although the tradition of formal segregation had begun to decline by the time of the arrival of the *Empire Windrush* in 1948, its long-term effects on racial thinking remain a matter for more detailed work in British contemporary history. Certainly it can be counted as an ideological reinforcement of the more amorphous "colonial mentality" which shaped British dealings with non-white communities in its midst though, as chapter eight points out in the case of Birmingham, this interacted with more specific pressures at the local level. Segregationism was a more sophisticated concept than simple racism. The processes of segregationist dispersal, which have been demonstrated in British cities by a number of race relations scholars, need to be understood not simply at the level of the unconscious operation of institutional structures, class and economic interests, but also as a consequence of the operation of a formal political ideology with deep historical roots in British political thought.

NOTES

1. Errol Lawrence, "Just plain common sense: the 'roots' of racism", in CCCS, *The Empire Strikes Back,* Hutchinson, London, 1982, esp. pp. 65-70; Martin Barker, *The New Racism*, Junction Books, London, 1981. For a critique of this thesis see Paul B Rich, "Conservative Ideology and Race in Modern British Politics" in Zig Layton Henry and Paul B Rich (eds), *Race, Government and Politics in Britain,* The Macmillan Press, London and Basingstoke, 1986, pp. 45-72.

2. George M Stocking, "The Limits of 'Presentism' and 'Historicism' in the Historiography of the Behavioural Sciences", in *Race, Culture and Evolution,* Free Press, New York, 1968, pp. 1-12; Michael D Biddiss, "Myths of the Blood", *Patterns of Prejudice,* V, 5 (September-October 1975), pp. 11-19; Michael Banton, "The Idiom of Race: A Critique of Presentism", *Research in Race and Ethnic Relations,* 2, 1980, pp. 21-42; see also chapter two.

3. Michael D Biddiss, "Introduction" in *Images of Race,* Leicester University Press, Leicester, 1979, pp. 11-31.

4. Quoted from Ruth Benedict, *Race and Racism,* Routledge and Kegan Paul, London, 1983 (first ed. 1942), p. 1. See also George L Mosse, *Towards the Final Solution: A History of European Racism,* Dent, London and Fertig, New York, 1979; Michael D Biddiss, "Towards a History of European Racism", *Ethnic and Racial Studies,* 2,4 (October 1979), pp. 508-13.

5. Stuart Anderson, *Race and Rapprochement: Anglo-Saxonism and Anglo-American Relations, 1895-1904,* Associated University Press, London and Toronto, 1981. See also Reginald Horsman, *Race and Manifest Destiny: the Origins of American Racial Anglo-Saxonism,* Harvard University Press, Cambridge, 1981.

6. Alfred Holt Stone, *Studies in the American Race Problem,* Doubleday, Page and Co., London, 1908, pp. 6-7; Kelly Miller, "The American Negro as a Political Factor", *The Nineteenth Century,* LXVII, August 1910, pp. 289-300.

7. Anderson, *op. cit.,* p. 175.

8. Noel Annan, "The Intellectual Aristocracy" in J H Plumb (ed.), *Studies in Social History,* Longman, Green and Co., London, 1955, pp. 243-87.

9. C Vann Woodward, *The Strange Career of Jim Crow* (3 eds), OUP, New York, 1974, p. 69 and *passim.*

10. *Ibid.,* pp. 72-4; I A Newby, *Jim Crow's Defense,* Louisiana State University Press, Baton Rouge, 1973, pp. 19-51; Guion Criffis "The Ideology of White Supremacy, 1876-1910", *The James Sprunt Studies in History and Political Science,* 31, 1946, pp. 124-56.

11. John W Cell, *The Highest State of White Supremacy: The Origins of Segregation in South Africa and the United States,* CUP, Cambridge, 1982, p. 18.

12. V I Lenin, *Leftwing Communism: An Infantile Disorder,* Progress Publishers, Moscow, 1974.

13. Arthur Marwick, "Middle Opinion in the Thirties: Planning, Progress and Political 'Agreement' ",*English Historical Review,* LXXIX (April 1964), pp. 285-98.

14. William Archer, *Through Afro-America,* Chapman and Hall, London, 1910, pp. 237-44. Archer (1856-1924) was born into a Scottish family with strong connections with Norway. He became, after graduating from Edinburgh University, a theatre critic and translater of Ibsen's plays into English. This led to a friendship with George Bernard Shaw. A keen traveller, he visited the United States and Australia and was a strong acolyte of Kipling and the British imperial mission. See Lieut. Col. C Archer, *William Archer,* Allen and Unwin, London, 1931. A biography of Archer is needed.

15. Howard Pim, *Some Aspects of the Native Problem,* Johannesburg, 1905, p. 37.

16. See for example Colin Bundy, *The Rise and Fall of the South African Peasantry,* Heinemann, London, 1979, pp. 221-47.

17. Sol T Plaatje, *Native Life in South Africa* (2 eds), London, n.d. (1971), p. 1.

18. Edward Wilmott Blyden, "West Africa Before Europe", *Journal of the Africa Society,* VIII, July 1903.

19. A B C Merriman-Labor, *Britons Through Negro Spectacles,* The Imperial and

Foreign Co., London, 1909, p. 177.
20. Learie Constantine, *Colour Bar*, Stanley Paul and Co., London, 1954, p. 34.
21. A P Thornton, *Doctrines of Imperialism*, John Wiley, New York, 1965, pp. 2-3.
22. Bernard Semmel, *The Governor Eyre Controversy*, Macgibbon and Kee, London, 1962, pp. 62-85 and *passim*.
23. Professor Cairnes, "The Negro Suffrage", *Macmillans Magazine*, XII, August 1865, p. 335.
24. James Bryce, *The American Commonwealth*, Macmillan, London, 1889, p. 308.
25. James Bryce, *The Relations of the Advanced and Backward Races of Mankind*, Clarendon Press, Oxford, 1902, p. 7.
26. Charles H Pearson, *National Life and Character*, Macmillan, London, p. 72; see also Crauford D Goodwin, "Evolution Theory in Australian Social Thought", *Journal of the History of Ideas*, DDV, 3 (July-September 1965), esp. pp. 402-4.
27. *Ibid.*, pp. 89-90.
28. Benjamin Kidd, *The Control of the Tropics*, Macmillan, New York, 1898; for Kidd's thought see D P Crook, "Was Benjamin Kidd a racist?", *Ethnic and Racial Studies*, 2, 2 (April 1979), pp. 213-21.
29. Bryce, *op. cit.*, p. 15.
30. R A Huttenbach, *Racism and Empire: White Settlers and Coloured Immigrants in the British Self-Governing Colonies, 1830-1910*, Cornell University Press, Ithaca and London, 1976.
31. Bryce, *op. cit.*, p. 44.
32. W K Gregory, "White Labour in Tropical Agriculture", *The Nineteenth Century*, 68, February 1910, p. 368.
33. J A Hobson, "The Negro Problem in the United States", *The Nineteenth Century*, 54, October 1903, pp. 581-94. For more detailed discussions of Hobson's ideas see chapter three.
34. B Pullen-Bury, *Ethiopia in Exile*, London, 1905, pp. 67-8.
35. Sydney Olivier, *White Capital and Coloured Labour*, ILP, London, 1906, pp. 38-9. See also chapter three.
36. *Ibid.*, p. 59.
37. H G Wells, *The Future in America*, Chapman and Hall, London, 1906, p. 149.
38. Archer, *op. cit.*, p. 73.
39. *Ibid.*, pp. x-xiii.
40. *Ibid.*, p. 8.
41. *Ibid.*, p. 72.
42. Douglas A Lorimer, *Colour, Class and the Victorians*, University Press and Holmes and Meier Inc., Leicester, 1978, pp. 203-4.
43. See for example Mary Kingsley, *West African Studies*, Frank Cass, London, 1964 (first ed. 1899); Bernard Porter, *Critics of Empire*, Macmillan, London, 1968, p. 150 and *passim*; J E Flint, "Mary Kingsley – A Reassessment", *Journal of African History*, IV, I, 1963, pp. 95-104.
44. Archer, *op. cit.*, pp. 46-7.
45. *Ibid.*, p. 57.
46. Robert Reinders, "Racialism on the Left: E D Morel and the 'Black Horror on the Rhine' ", *International Journal of Social History*, I, 1968.
47. Brian Willan, "The Anti-Slavery and Aborigines Protection Society and the South African Natives Land Act", *Journal of African History*, XX, 1979, pp. 83-102.
48. John Higham, *Strangers in the Lane: Patterns of American Nativism, 1860-1920*, pp. 155-7, 270-7.
49. F D Lugard, "The Colour Problem", *The Edinburgh Review*, 233, April 1921, p. 268.
50. *Ibid.*, p. 270.
51. *Ibid.*, p. 280.
52. *Ibid.*, pp. 275-6.
53. Arthur Keith, *Nationality and Race From An Anthropologist's Point of View*, Oxford University Press, London, 1919. See also chapter two.

54. W R Inge, "The Future of the English Race", *The Edinburgh Review*, 468, April 1919, p. 84.

55. W R Inge, "The White Man and His Rivals", *Outspoken Essays* (2 Ser.), Longman, Green and Co., London, 1922, p. 226.

56. R Ruggles Gates, *Heredity and Eugenics,* Constable, London, 1923, p. 224.

57. *Ibid.*, p. 225.

58. *Ibid.*, p. 234. For the development of intelligence testing in the United States using the Binet scale and the army tests of the First World War, see Stephen Jay Gould, *The Mismeasurement of Man*, Penguin Books, Harmondsworth, 1981, pp. 146-233.

59. Gates, *op. cit.*, p. 235.

60. J W Gregory, *The Menace of Colour*, Seeley and Co., London, 1925. The author of numerous geographical articles, the Australian Griffith Taylor's *magnum opus* was *Environment and Race*, OUP, London, 1927.

61. Gregory, *op. cit.*, p. 20.

62. *Ibid.*, p. 241.

63. Cited in *ibid.*, p. 232.

64. *Ibid.*, p. 235.

65. General J C Smuts, *Africa and Some World Problems*, Clarendon Press, Oxford, 1930, pp. 42-3.

66. *Ibid.*, p. 63.

67. Martin Channock, *Unconsummated Union: Britain, Rhodesia and South Africa, 1900-1945*, Manchester University Press, Manchester, 1977, pp. 190-210.

68. J H Oldham, *White and Black in Africa: A Critical Examination of the Rhodes Lectures of General Smuts*, Longman, Green and Co., London, 1930, p. 44.

69. Channock, *op. cit.*, p. 258.

70. George Pitt-Rivers, "Anthropological Approach to Ethnogenics: A New Perspective", in E E Evans-Pritchard *et al.*, *Essays Presented to C E Seligman*, Kegan Paul, Trench, Trubner and Co., London, 1934, pp. 246-7.

71. Royal Anthropological Institute and the Institute of Sociology, *Man and Culture*, London, 1935; Lord Raglan, " The Riddle of Race", *The Listener*, 3 October 1934.

72. G R Searle, "Eugenics and Politics in Britain in the 1930s", *Annals of Science*, 36, 1979, p. 163. It was, however, the hope of some experts, including Leo Amery, that eugenics could be included in government planning for a "fitter" population.

73. J W Gregory, *Race As a Political Factor*, Watts and Co., London, 1931.

74. For Malinowski's approach see his "Ethnology and the Study of Society", *Economica*, II, 1922, pp. 208-19; later his view became more critical in the light of the Hailey *African Survey*, as is evidenced by his posthumous *The Dynamics of Culture Contact*, Yale University Press, New Haven and London, 1961 (first ed. 1945).

75. Andre Siegfried, *England's Crisis*, Jonathan Cape, London, 1931, p. 215. See also M A Thomas, "Great Britain and the Coloured Race", *The Contemporary Review*, 147, February 1935, pp. 227-33.

76. Christopher Thorne, "Britain and the Black GIs: Racial Issues and Anglo-American Relations in 1942", *New Community*, Summer 1974; Neil A Wynn, *The Afro-American and the Second World War*, Paul Elek, London, 1976, pp. 32-4.

77. Joyce Cary, *The Case for African Freedom*, Secker and Warburg, London, 1941, p. 66.

78. *Ibid.*, p. 117.

79. Oswald Mosley, *The Alternative*, Mosley Publications, Rawsbury, 1947, pp. 51-4.

Chapter Five

The Impact of South African Segregationist and Apartheid Ideology on British Racial Thought 1945-1960

From Segregation to Apartheid

'The gravest racial crisis in the present generation,' the missionary and friend of Gandhi, C F Andrews, [1] announced in 1932, 'is met with in South Africa.' The impact of South African government policies on racial segregation began to be viewed with considerable alarm by some of the more far-seeing liberals and radical activists in British politics even before the Second World War, despite the growing concentration on Nazism and events in Central Europe. In South Africa the imposition of territorial landholding on racial lines and the reduction of the black Africans to a status which some observers likened to that of an inferior caste [2] appeared increasingly to conflict with the professed ideals of the British Commonwealth, based as it was on equality of status and rights irrespective of colour or creed. Even that ardent advocate of British imperialism, Leo Amery, was driven to declare in 1935 that the South African model of segregation was 'destined sooner or later to break down in the Union itself',[3] an indication that by the 1930s there was little formal British governmental support for South Africa's racial policies.[4]

The important feature of the politics of the British empire/ Commonwealth in the interwar years is that no significant challenge was made to South African domestic policies. Ever since the establishment of the Union in 1910, the British government had refused to intervene on behalf of Africans who were being dispossessed of economic and political rights. In 1914 a deputation from the South

African Native National Congress (later the African National Congress) had been sympathetically received as part of the African protest against the Union government's Natives Land Act the previous year; but no formal government action was taken, on the grounds that South Africa was a self-governing state.[5] Further protests after the First World War and in the late 1920s against the threat to remove African voters in the Cape from the common voters' roll met with a similar response. It was clear by the time of the South African government's 1936 legislation, ending the colour-blind Cape franchise for Africans and further entrenching territorial segregation throughout the Union, that there was little the British government could or would do to check the development of white settler power. There remained only a continuing hope of eventually establishing a British-controlled Central African dominion which could act as a political counterpoise to South African power south of the Limpopo. However, this did not inhibit the development of joint defence plans after South Africa became reconciled to British imperial power in the late 1930s.[6]

By the time of the Second World War, the South African government had been remarkably successful in fending off external intervention, especially from Britain, in its internal politics. This occurred at a time of mounting international concern with the phenomenon of "racism", generally linked with both the horrors of the Nazi persecution of Jews in Central Europe and the violent defence of white privilege in the American South.

The war itself increased the level of active political solidarity between British governing circles and the South African government led by Field-Marshal Smuts, who was seen as a bulwark for British Commonwealth interests against the Afrikaner Nationalists led by Dr D F Malan. A close friend of Winston Churchill, Smuts had had links with the British establishment since being a member of the British War Cabinet under Lloyd George during the First World War. His loyalty to the Allied cause led to a certain underplaying of the continuing extension of racial segregation inside South Africa. The British High Commissioner in Pretoria, Lord Harlech (a former Colonial Under-Secretary of State), wrote to the deputy Prime Minister, Clement Attlee, in 1943 defending the recommendations of the Broome Commission in Natal, 'pegging' Indian settlement in urban areas. Repeating the conventional white Natalian image of the Indian traders as unscrupulous in their activities and failing to keep accounts, he argued:

> *Even when rich they live in appalling squalor and their social and domestic habits make them most unpleasant neighbours. Once a street or neighbourhood becomes Indianised the lot of the remaining Europeans is indeed unenviable, as is that of the white folk in or on the edges of negro Haarlem [sic] in New York...the number of 'educated' or higher class Indians in South Africa is few and far*

between, and many of the Natal Indians appear to have far lower standards of living and of cleanliness than the Native Zulus in spite of their superior wealth and money getting capacity. They are apparently content with and make 'slum' conditions even when they have not the excuse of poverty.[7]

Harlech's outlook was shaped by an intense admiration for Smuts, although he, along with many British government officials, recognised that there was no obvious successor to the ageing leader of the United Party government. The deputy Prime Minister, Jan Hofmeyr, was looked on with distrust, not merely for his "liberal" views on racial issues, but because of his close links with the Chamber of Mines, which Harlech considered made him generally uninterested in South Africa's war effort and more concerned with internal industrialisation.[8]

Given Smut's undoubted political importance for British military and imperial policy during the war, the British government looked to a process of guided internal political reform in order to enhance the political credibility of "moderate" African, Indian and Coloured leadership. At a famous address in Cape Town in 1942, Smuts had declared that segregation had 'fallen on evil days'; and further declarations in favour of reform by his Secretary of Native Affairs, Douglas Smit, led to some hopes in British governing circles that the structures of segregation would at least be modified.[9] In 1944, however, even the true-blue imperial enthusiast and Colonial Secretary, Lord Cranborne (later Lord Salisbury), was driven to declare that 'we are apt to hear admirable statements on this matter (regarding "progress" on the "colour question") in public speeches but they do not seem to be followed up much in practice.'[10] By the later stages of the war, an increasingly realist attitude began to inform British perceptions of South African domestic policy.

A crucial figure in this reappraisal was undoubtedly Sir Evelyn Baring, Lord Harlech's successor as High Commissioner in Pretoria. A scion of the Cromer family, with long imperial connections (he went on in 1951 to become Governor of Kenya on the brink of the Mau Mau emergency), Baring was under no illusions about the basis of South African segregation, which was 'not so much a means of keeping two races apart as of keeping one of them down.'[11] In a series of incisive political reports between 1946 and the 1948 election, in which Smuts was defeated by the Nationalists, Baring analysed the sensitive political balance in white South African politics. The British government received his reports with mounting concern, viewing the 1946 African Mine Strike on the Witwatersrand as Communist-inspired, although also realising that this was a terrain in which the British government could do very little directly.[12] The actual defeat of Smuts was put down, in part, to the decision of Hofmeyr to focus on the political rights of Africans; this Baring considered an evident political error since it played into the hands of Hofmeyr's Nationalist opponents, who lampooned him for wanting to establish a black government. Baring thought he would have done better to have focused on economic issues and to have avoided falling in with 'the wishes of leading educated Africans.'[13]

The years 1946-48 were a political watershed in South Africa. Although the *Financial Times* still tried to defend the system of compound labour at the time of the 1946 strike on the grounds that it was a 'generally accepted principle of civilisation that the standard of living of the backward races should be raised',[14] the tide of opinion amongst liberals and left wingers reflected an increasing concern at the trend of events in South Africa. 'There are limitations to the patience and restraint even of moderate African political leadership,' declared the *Manchester Guardian*[15] on the suspension of the Natives Representative Council in the wake of the strike. At this time evidence began to emerge of growing interest among British trade unions, albeit of a somewhat ill-informed sort. The Secretary of the St Helier Branch of the Amalgamated Union of Building Trade Workers, for example, wrote to the Colonial Secretary, asking him to use his influence 'to try and stop the violence being used against the natives of South Africa.'[16]

After Smuts

The British government studiously sought not to be seen to be intervening in South African affairs. An Afrikaner Nationalist government that was pledged to establish a republic in South Africa, while at the same time showing willingness to continue trading with Britain as well as involving herself in a common western defensive alliance, was seen as a political force to be handled with care. To a number of British observers, it appeared unlikely that the Nationalists could be removed from power by the white opposition, especially after the 1949 riots between Indians and Zulus in Durban, which some civil servants forecast would hasten the break-up of the United Party and encourage defections of conservative English members from Natal to the Nationalists.[17] By the early 1950s, South Africa was emerging as a challenge to the unity of the Commonwealth, and the British government became worried at the campaign mounting in the United Nations against apartheid. Privately, criticism was voiced by some leading Colonial Office officials that the South African apartheid policy diverged radically from that of Britain's own Colonial Development and Welfare programme. Andrew Cohen, the Under-Secretary of State for African Affairs at the Colonial Office, complained that the new South African officials seemed ignorant of developments in West Africa which were breaking down the old structures of government based on hereditary tribal elites.[18]

Not all shared the view that apartheid was necessarily unworkable or politically disastrous, and there were complaints from the UK High Commission in Pretoria that the British press was giving a distorted view of South African affairs.[19] But the government, whether Labour up to 1951 or Conservative thereafter, was unwilling to take a lead in orchestrating a political view on South African affairs, and as far as possible kept a low profile on the issue in the UN. This was particularly the case when it came to formulating a strategy on the South West African (Namibian) issue. The Foreign Office considered it bad tactics to put forward a proposal alongside the South African one, which the General Assembly would later reject. The important thing was to avoid having to hang on South African coat-tails, while at the same time avoiding taking sides with the radical critics of the South African policies. In September 1950, the Cabinet decided on a policy that would mean 'avoiding expression of sympathy with native policy of present Government' but at the same time would 'refrain from openly condemning it.'[20] This lukewarm attempt at political neutrality was partly based on a short-term political perspective, despite the realisation that the Nationalists were unlikely to be defeated. It also reflected a more general hope, in the light of the 1948 Report of the Fagan Commission in South Africa, that government policy there would eventually recognise the permanency of black urbanisation and that ultimately apartheid could not be made to work.[21] As the 1950s progressed, British opinion outside the government realised that a firmer set of policies were required, especially as race relations were becoming an issue of international concern.

The Emergence of Organised Action in Britain

As liberal opinion in Britain became involved with the direction of race relations in Southern Africa in the early 1950s, a number of organisations grew up to initiate more specialised attention. This phenomenon reflected both the general feature in English politics of establishing associations, committees or leagues to focus upon particular issues, and a recognition that "expert" opinion and advice in this area was in quite short supply and could be put to greatest use by establishing a small following around a particular individual or group of concerned activists. *The Round Table*, a normally conservative periodical with an imperial past, captured the mood in this respect when it urged, on the question of South Africa,

....much more thought and experience in the field of race relations and forms of government in the Colonial Empire. Especially is this needed in multi-racial societies, like those of East and Southern Africa where the simple question, 'National self-government or not', at once breaks into the sharp splinters of who is to govern, and how are the rights of the different communities to be balanced.[22]

At the establishment level, this plea found a response in the beginning of study and research on race relations at the Royal Institute of International Affairs at Chatham House in October 1952, leading eventually to the establishment of a separate Institute of Race Relations under the directorship of Philip Mason in 1958. The ethos here was one of a careful weighing of the evidence in a neutral manner for the judgement of the "official mind", and the avoidance wherever possible of strong moral judgements. The chief obstacle to this process was precisely a restrictive and deterministic ideology like racial segregation and, as Philip Mason warned in an important book *An Essay on Racial Tension* (based on a paper given at a Commonwealth Relations Conference in March 1954), the most successful governing classes were those that did not restrict or limit recruitment into their ranks. As a former member of the Indian Civil Service, Mason directed his argument to those concerned with establishing new ruling elites in colonial territories on the brink of independence, and he warned that segregation led to 'perpetual watchfulness ... for the dominant race which is likely to breed tension, irritability and bitterness.'[23] These strictures illustrated a mood of benign paternalism in the last generation of British colonial administrators, who were increasingly anxious to distance themselves from the South African policy, despite efforts by officials in the South African Native Affairs Department to draw on British ideas of colonial administration as articulated in Lord Hailey's *African Survey.*[24]

This establishment concern to separate itself from the Germanic thoroughness of Dr Verwoerd's evolving Department of Native Affairs was not necessarily shared by the more morally engaged liberal activists. The Labour Party seemed unwilling to offer much of a lead on the issue, despite noises from some Labour politicians. Its Advisory Committee on Imperial Affairs, an important forum that had debated South African policy as far back as the early 1930s, was finally wound up in January 1950 on the grounds, wrote the Party's Secretary Morgan Phillips, that preference should be given to 'experts who would be consulted individually on questions in this field.'[25]

Into this vacuum stepped a number of individuals with varying degrees of experience of and commitment to the area of race relations in the colonial context. Between 1952 and 1954 several organisations with an interest in the race field were formed. The most notable were: Racial Unity, founded by a white missionary, Mary Attlee (sister of Labour's leader), who returned from South Africa to be shocked by the ignorance and unconcern of the British public on racial issues; the Africa Bureau, formed around the Reverend Michael Scott, an Anglican priest who had gained considerable publicity in Britain after his attacks on the prison labour system in South Africa and South Africa's occupation of South West Africa under a League of Nations mandate; and Christian Action, under the driving force of the radical Canon John Collins, who operated from Amen Court, close to St Paul's Cathedral, where he preached against the inactivity of the Church of England and its failure to take a lead on social and political issues. Finally, a group of left-wing activists in the Labour Party formed the Movement for Colonial Freedom in 1954, in order to awaken public concern over racism and imperialism.

Racial Unity started as a nonpartisan organisation that was closely linked with the Anti-Slavery Society at its headquarters at Denison House in the Vauxhall Bridge Road. After its launching at a large meeting in Central Hall, Westminster, presided over by Lord Hailsham, Mary Attlee hoped the body would be a source of 'popular information' which would 'enlist the co-operation of all sections of public life', although her hopes for senuring £10,000 from government support were wildly ambitious.[26] The Colonial Office gave only its tacit support and the movement was unable to attract exclusive government interest. In the event, Mary Attlee's own interests centred on South Africa,[27] although the diffuseness of the organisation led Racial Unity to ally itself to a small group of amateur sociologists called the Racial Relations Group (RRG), who had cut adrift from the declining Institute of Sociology. The RRG was led by Frank Norman, a former adviser on labour relations in the Westindies, whose interest in the field of race stretched back to the 1911 Universal Races Congress. This encouraged Racial Unity to drift away from specifically African issues, especially after it received a sharp rebuff from Michael Scott, who saw it as complicating a situation where there were already too many committees. As Scott wrote to Racial Unity's Secretary, Colin Turnbull, in July 1952:

> *As one who was requested by Africans to come to this country to secure support for their case, I feel bound to say that I am very disturbed. The practice of setting up new committees from among the same sort of people to deal with real African issues every time a new one arises is both confusing to the British public and bewildering to Africans who are already uncertain who to turn to for support.*[28]

The competition among the groups for a public hearing reflected a growing urge to shape establishment opinion at a politically fluid time. Missionary groups tried to develop new approaches to an increasingly secular British public, as well as a radicalised black political leadership in Africa that was becoming distrustful of the old-style missionary paternalism. Racial Unity tried to find and identity for itself as a small organisation that put out a series of *Racial Unity Bulletins*, held periodic meetings on international issues dealing with race and colour and promoted a limited amount of fraternising with a small black following through social gatherings.[29] Its political impact was minimal, and it became bogged down in a series of requests to the government for a general enquiry on race and immigration into Britain; a tactic that proved ineffective when it emerged that the government had its own Interdepartmental Committee on Coloured People in the United Kingdom.[30]

While Racial Unity tried to monopolise liberal concern on indigenous British issues, the Africa Bureau concentrated on African issues. Its Executive Committee of Lord Hemingford, Lady Pakenham, and Arthur Creech Jones, together with Michael Scott as Director, left it well placed to influence establishment opinion from outside Colonial Office circles, especially as its Trustees were Margery Perham (the biographer of Lord Lugard), the Rev. Canon Stopford and Lord Noel Buxton. Michael Scott remained the dominant figure. Described by *Picture Post* as a 'quiet, constrained, soft-spoken man who favours understatement',[31] he was able to use the Africa Bureau for the political objective of continuing his campaign in the United Nations against both South Africa's apartheid system and its mandate over South West Africa.

On his return to Britain from the UN in 1950 Scott had become quite a celebrity among reformist circles, especially those of the Quakers, and even in Conservative towns fairly large audiences turned out to hear him speak. In April of that year, for example, 800 turned up in Eastbourne Town Hall and donated £55.[32] In some cases, this interest was a development of an existing concern with race relations, as in Cardiff, where the Secretary of the Colonial Defence Association wrote of the local interest in Scott's activities, which coincided with the Association's aims of exposing 'the inequalities and exploitation of Coloured people both in the colonies and in Britain.'[33] Scott appeared to have struck a deep chord in British liberal circles, one which, in some respects, stretched back unbroken to the anti-slavery impulse of the nineteenth century, as well as representing an ardent faith in African social and economic development which extended far beyond the projects being initiated inside the Colonial Office.[34] 'Michael Scott's mission is a judgement on the British people,' declared the *Christian Messenger*, a Christian journal edited by David Kyley:

> We have too lightly dealt with this tremendous responsibility in days past. Now, we must make up our mind. Our attitude at Lake Success over South West Africa has been decidedly weak. If we surrender to Dr Malan ... what remains of British prestige and authority in the world will be gone for ever. No subtlety, no so-called plebiscites, will save us from this shame.[35]

Similarly, Mrs Bertram Lloyd, a granddaughter of Bishop Colenso, wrote of her 'deep thankfulness' after hearing a speech of Scott's in the Central Hall, Westminster, for 'sometimes it really seemed as if all the self-serving labour of the Colenso family had been completely undone! But with you as the champion of the oppressed there is now renewed hope for the future.'[36]

Radicals, Liberals and Christians at Odds

In the early 1950s, Michael Scott championed a radical application of concepts of social engineering at a time when it seemed as though the liberal tradition inside South Africa itself was faltering. Scott was highly distrustful of the South African liberals organised around the South African Institute of Race Relations, whom he saw as incapable of mounting any strong opposition on the South West Africa issue. He returned to England 'more than ever convinced that England's own house must be put in order both at home and in the Colonies – one has no answer at all when the Colour Bar in N. Rhodesia is pointed to as being far worse than in the Union because it exists under the hypocrisy of "Partnership".'[37] This was not a view shared by all sections of liberal opinion in Britain, some of which were, by 1952, drawn to the partnership ideals of the small multiracial Capricorn Africa Society, covering the British colonies in East and Central Africa and founded by Colonel David Stirling.[38] The Colonial Office sought at an early stage to resist Stirling's campaign for a "two pyramids" policy in Central Africa, in favour of a policy that recognised the emergence of African trade unions on the copper belt.[39] For his part, Scott represented a new breed of politically committed churchmen who had lost faith in the older methods of liberal 'dialogue' and had become openly supportive of more radical action through African nationalist movements such as the African National Congress. This tradition was followed later in the 1950s by Father Trevor Huddleston, author of *Naught For Your Comfort* (1956), and the Anglican Bishop Ambrose Reeves, who was eventually deported from South Africa in 1960.

The crisis of the liberal tradition in South Africa before the emergence of the South African Liberal Party in 1953 was viewed in many quarters in Britain with considerable regret. The Race Relations Committee of the Society of Friends reported an exodus of 'disillusioned liberal whites' from the Union which was seen as undermining the 'welfare and development work' of those who remained.[40] Some observers considered this liberalism as rather anachronistic; Anthony Sampson compared it with that of the British Liberal Party of the 1920s and 1930s as it sought a compromise between Conservatism and socialism.[41]

Meanwhile, the Africa Bureau sought a more long-term reorientation in British thought on South Africa. It published Michael Scott's UN statement of 1952 as a pamphlet entitled *Civilisation Indivisible*, in which Christians worldwide were urged to get directly involved in the South African issue. Apartheid was graphically depicted as threatening the whole basis of "civilisation" in Southern Africa and, unless checked, as leading to the "disintegration" of South African society, despite the forces of industrialisation and economic integration.[42]

This plea for Christian involvement found a ready response from

Canon Collins, who had been an observer at the 1948 Amsterdam Assembly which established the World Council of Churches. Like Scott, Collins had become disillusioned with the role of the Church of England and formed Christian Action with a view to organising a radical Christian voice in British society. Like the founders of Racial Unity, however, Collins soon found himself perceived as a rival and meddler by Michael Scott, who had initially asked for Christian Action's support in 1949.[43] After a meeting in July 1952, Collins sought to promote Christian Action 'to undertake the task of stimulating the Christian conscience throughout the country, and particularly within the churches, on the many practical problems of the moment in Africa.' This especially meant making people realise 'that they must relate their acceptance of the principle of no discrimination to the practical issues at present on the map.'[44] While sharing a similar radical approach, Collins was not seen as having the same detailed knowledge of local conditions in Southern Africa, and Christian Action appeared to be trying to cover the same ground as Scott's own Africa Bureau.[45] Nevertheless the challenge that both groups made to the established church acted as a precursor to the debate in the 1960s and 1970s on issues of immigration and multiculturalism, centred around the question of whether the churches in Britain should simply reflect existing secular liberal opinion or attempt, through a national campaign, to move beyond it.[46]

Collins proceeded to organise Christian Action's involvement in race issues along more popular lines than the Africa Bureau's informational and lobbying methods. The Defiance Campaign in South Africa in 1952 was not perceived in official circles in the Commonwealth Relations Office as being of major political significance, for it was not yet seen as leading to a nationwide passive resistance movement. Some officers interpreted it as confirming the Indian domination of the African organisations centred around the ANC.[47] By contrast, Collins hoped to mobilise British support for the large number of South Africans caught up in the resulting court cases, and this led to Christian Action establishing a defence fund for those in need of legal assistance. Collins hoped that this issue would encourage 'the idea of a comprehensive Christian political programme for a nationwide movement',[48] and the *Christian Action Newsletter* looked for a campaign that would amount to an effective missionary revival amongst British Christians. 'We are conscious of the need,' it proclaimed in December 1952, 'to bring the Christian message of hope and reconciliation to those millions of black people in Africa who may otherwise increasingly lose confidence in white people.' The appeal for involvement overseas did not mean that the British situation could be overlooked and it was important 'to see that no coloured stranger in our midst shall spend this coming Christmastide without being offered hospitality in a Christian home.'[49]

Collins' activities were viewed with some disapproval in the Commonwealth Relations Office and one civil servant, D M Cleary (who had served in the Pretoria High Commission), proposed that the British government should take action to stop the outflow of funds to the defendants in South Africa[50] on the grounds that Christian Action was infringing its charitable status. This idea was rejected on the grounds that there were 'powerful sections of opinion' in Britain which sympathised with the South African passive resisters, and intervention 'would lead to all kinds of difficulties internally in this country, quite apart from what might be felt and said elsewhere in the Commonwealth'.[51] Clearly it would be easier to leave any restrictions to the South African government.

Christian Action was significant for the manner in which it developed a specifically British view of Christian responsibilities on racial questions, free from the usual missionary and colonial background. It welcomed African resistance to white rule all over Africa, and saw South Africa as the key area where the issues surrounding race would be fought out most dramatically and conclusively:

> ...it is in South Africa that there is the best chance to show the 60 million Africans in Africa that we really sympathise with them in their legitimate aspirations.[52]

This view of Africa as a single homogeneous continent, overlooking language, cultural and ethnic differences, still owed much to the traditional imperial stereotype. The analysis of South African politics revealed little understanding of its internal complexities. Furthermore, a ready use was made of the Nazi analogy to explain Malan's policies and, after making a visit to the country in 1954, Collins also warned of the possible emergence not only of 'violence and bloodshed' but also of 'a black Hitler'.[53]

Despite its prognostication in 1954 that white rule in the Union could not last more than a further two years,[54] Christian Action proceeded to establish links with white South African liberals, organised since 1953 through the Liberal Party, as part of its programme of channelling funds for legal expenses to African detainees. In December 1952 a small South African branch of Christian Action had been established, with the Rev. A W Blaxall as convenor and the novelist Alan Paton, author of *Cry, The Beloved Country* (1948), as chairman. Christian Action pledged itself to donate some £5,000 for the detainees. Although the Liberal Party refused to participate in the 1955 Congress of the People at Kliptown, which led to the *Freedom Charter*, Christian Action kept up its links with Paton, who effectively ran the organisation's South African branch until at least 1960. There were, however, complaints that funds from Britain were bypassing the South African organisation.[55]

Christian Action became less respectable in establishment eyes as it swung round behind the African nationalist cause and lost the support of

Conservative members such as Lord Halifax. Collins became something of a *bête noire* in the popular press and was the target of abusive letters and obscene telephone calls. In the 1950s the organisation contributed to the awakening of British public opinion to the issues of racism and apartheid and, in the wake of the Sharpeville episode, the Labour Party felt provoked into organising a boycott of South African goods as a popular means of British moral protest. Although the campaign was ineffective, it laid the foundations for more radical action in the 1960s, led by the Anti-Apartheid Movement, culminating in 1970 in the campaign against the tour of the South African rugby team.

The Politicisation of British Opinion on Apartheid

The growth of public concern over the direction of apartheid in the 1950s acted as an important radicalising force in the middle ground of opinion on racial issues.[56] Although the war years had driven a lot of overt racial prejudice underground, overall British society was still not especially familiar with overseas racial issues, and was probably as well aquainted with the state of affairs in the United States from the fights between white American Southerners and blacks in British pubs and dance halls in the early 1940s, as it was with conditions in Central and Southern Africa.

In intellectual and academic circles there had been a realisation, even before the war, that South African segregation was linked to the dynamics of capitalist industrialisation. The links between economic expansion and racism in the South African system had been studied by some analysts on the left in Britain, for instance Sydney Olivier in *The Anatomy of African Misery* (1927) and Leonard Barnes in *The New Boer War* (1931). These studies emphasised the phenomenon of "white capital", reflected in an alliance of mining and agricultural capitalists organised behind the reactionary ideology of Boer or Afrikaner nationalism. This was a phenomenon which in many respects sought a restoration of the master-servant or *baaskap* relationships of the Trekker Republics of the nineteenth century.[57] During the 1940s, as the Smuts government brought South Africa onto the Allied side during the war, this debate had declined in an atmosphere that confidently looked to the forces of industrialisation and urbanisation to break down the structures of segregation. The long-term implications of territorial segregation in the Union only became visible again in the late 1940s, in the wake of Smut's defeat in 1948 and India's criticism in the United Nations of South African treatment of its Indian population. The logic of segregationism conflicted more and more with the liberal Commonwealth ideal. The differing internal policies of the Commonwealth had been successfully reconciled in the pre-war years (though not without some difficulty), but it was clear that the climate of the post-war international arena made the former political balancing-trick effectively impossible.[58]

The Conservative press in Britain tried to play down the analogy, frequently made in the left-wing press, between Malan's policies and those of Hitler. As G H Calpin wrote in *The Spectator*, 'democracy takes many shapes and forms, as witness its practice in America and Britain, and there is nothing to forbid a contribution to democratic life in South Africa through the principles which imbue Dr Malan's philosophy.'[59] For sections of the left and the Labour Party, however, the threat of apartheid was too immediate for action to be delayed any longer, despite the fact that the Fabian Colonial Bureau had for most of the 1940s refused to discuss South African affairs on the grounds that the country was no longer a colonial responsibility of the British government.[60] The decision in 1950 by Patrick Gordon-Walker, the Secretary for Commonwealth Relations, to prohibit the African chief Seretse Khama from returning to the British Protectorate of Bechuanaland (Botswana) after he married a white woman, Ruth Williams, was sharply condemned by the *New Statesman* as 'appeasement' of South Africa and as undermining the post-war Colonial Development and Welfare Programme under pressure from Smuts and the South African government.[61] Rita Hinden, now awakened to the threat posed by apartheid, also warned of the dangers of a possible 'race war' in Africa, in which the Commonwealth 'would go down in ruins.' This outcome could not be avoided by 'appeasement' and it was necessary for Britain to 'take an absolutely firm and unshakeable stand', which might mean calling South Africa's bluff:

> *Isolation will perhaps create more problems for her than for us, partly as she will have the whole of world opinion against her, whereas we shall be in an impregnable moral position, rallying behind us all the colonial races as well.*[62]

The Seretse Khama issue reinforced the climate of moral concern in Britain over race relations in Southern Africa and the apparent dangers of a revival of fascism and *Herrenvolkism*.[63] South Africa, and to a lesser extent the colonies in Central Africa, now represented Britain's "Deep South" in liberal and radical opinion. Despite the warnings of Michael Scott, many observers continued to argue that apartheid, as an ideology, was still too weak to halt the forces of capitalist industrialisation, which were seen as leading inexorably towards racial integration in the urban context. Thus Basil Davidson commented, after a visit to the region in 1951, that apartheid was 'a tattered little ideology whose rays are too poor and thin to hide the moral and intellectual wretchedness of White thought in South Africa'. Apartheid, or segregation, was seen as acting in opposition to the worldwide trend towards "racial equality", while

...the irresistible force of economic integration is opposed to the immovable object of White prejudice. **Eppure si muove:** *it is the irresistible force which wins and must win, although no more than a handful of people in South Africa seem to realise this ... the integration of Black and White society is taking place, through industrialisation, under their very eyes; and yet they and most South African whites continue to babble forth the old myths and slogans as if the world had stopped with Rhodes and Kruger.*[64]

With the hindsight of three decades, which have seen the emergence of a formidable South African military and state apparatus, it is possible to conclude that such observations were naïve in the extreme in the faith they placed on the logic of market forces and the processes of industrialisation.[65] In part these ideas reflected both a wider failure within an insulated society such as Britain to understand the logic and power of a nationalist and racist ideology like apartheid, and an historical failure to perceive that racial segregation was generally compatible with capitalist industrialisation. Segregation on territorial lines facilitated the release of pools of cheap African labour from the pre-capitalist reserve economies which served as reservoirs for the control of black labour mobility and a deflection of the political aspirations of the educated African political elite. In the absence, however, of such an understanding of South African apartheid ideology[66] both liberal and radical discourse in Britain focused on apartheid as a moral issue which challenged Britain's claim to be leading a multiracial Commonwealth.

The Focus on Attitudes and Prejudice

The general effect of this moral engagement was to focus on racism in Southern and Central Africa at the attitudinal level rather than seeing it as the product of a set of social and economic structures. For some analysts who employed psychological methods in order to understand the phenomenon of race prejudice, the levels of attitudes and the underlying social structures were interlinked. This was exemplified by the pioneering study by Eric John Dingwall, *Racial Pride and Prejudice*, in 1946. This did much to popularise the study of racial psychology in the post-war years; while noting the seeming irrationality of the South African system, which was 'being rent by a series of fantastic experiences which satisfy nobody',[67] the author went on to acknowledge that 'the whole question of a colour bar in Africa is so closely linked up with the economics of private enterprise, and its relation to public duty and administration, that it would be a mistake to separate them.'[68] On the other hand, in South Africa there had by this time developed a body of literature centred around the work of Professor

I D MacCrone at the University of the Witwatersrand, whose study *Race Attitudes in South Africa* (1938) stressed the atavistic nature of racism as a product of the pre-industrial frontier society. The racial attitudes of contemporary whites in South Africa were interpreted as a long-term legacy of colonial conflict with African tribes, and were perceived as irrational phenomena, standing in contradiction to the logic of the industrial system and its general tendency towards racial integration.[69] Some of these ideas became popularised in novel form by Alan Paton. In *Too Late the Phalarope* (1953) he depicted his central character, Pieter Van Vlaanderen, as being the emotionally crippled product of traditional Afrikaner society, rooted in the past and the days of the frontier and burdened by psychological neuroses of race.[70]

MacCrone's thesis had a significant impact on race relations theories in the 1940s and 1950s, although more detailed intellectual historiography is needed to trace his overall influence on academic thought. In general, his line of argument did much to reinforce the general perception among liberal thinkers that racial segregation in South Africa was both produced and sustained in good measure by the irrational phenomenon of white colour prejudice. This view also accorded with the prevailing climate of moral aversion to racial ideology generally in the light of both the experiences of Nazism in Central Europe and the interpretation of "racism" given in Ruth Benedict's classic text *Race and Racism*, which was published in the early 1940s. Benedict, too, had in large measure accepted the frontier thesis to explain racist ideology in the colonial context, despite the advent of industrialisation in such a society as South Africa.[71] Her general depiction of "racism" as 'the new Calvinism which asserts that one group has the stigmata of superiority and the other has those of inferiority' was generally true as far as it went, as was her observation that it was a danger which could affect the entire globe.[72]

Such general interpretations of the nature of racism did not, however, lead to the development of a more systematic analysis of the comparative dynamics of racist politics and ideology. This approach would have been untypical of the American anthropological tradition, which was more concerned with delineating the patterns of different cultures without seeking a more systematic understanding of their history from a non-Eurocentric perspective.[73] In the case of racism in South Africa, this reinforced the belief that white-racial ideology, especially after the Nationalist defeat of Smuts in 1948, was a new version of Nazism which could lead to the creation of a white *Herrenvolk* on the tip of Africa.[74] It failed to ask whether the dynamics of South African capitalist industrialisation were different in kind from the ideological crisis in the mature German industrial society of the early 1930s which had led to the rise of Hitler. In many respects, we still lack an adequate historical comparison of the two kinds of racism. It has been observed recently, however, that in an oversimplified sense the essential dynamics of European fascist and Nazi ideology were pre-capitalist in orientation and reflective of political struggles in relatively industrialised societies. In the colonial context, on the other hand, racism generally reinforced capitalist expansion and, in the case of South Africa, capitalist industrialisation.[75]

The argument that apartheid was a result of white racial prejudice was fairly common in British liberal circles in the late 1940s and 1950s. C W W Greenidge, President of the Anti-Slavery Society, saw South Africa as unfit to keep its South West African mandate because 'it maintains that Africans are an inferior race designed to serve the superior white race and have never been capable of reaching equality with the white race.'[76] In addition, Mary Benson, Secretary of the Africa Bureau, interpreted apartheid in terms of a political strategy by the South African government, using 'race prejudice as a political weapon very successfully.'[77] This was a more politically conscious liberalism compared to the more mechanistic arguments centred upon market forces and industrialisation which defensive liberals in South Africa were espousing at this time. For example, J D Rheinallt-Jones, the former Director of the South African Institute of Race Relations, maintained in 1950 that 'social and economic forces' were 'driving' the South African government to recognise that 'economic apartheid' was 'impracticable' and that in a few years 'progressive forces' would gain sufficient ground to ensure the 'full integration of the African people in the economic and political life of the country.'[78]

The liberal groups in Britain, together with several more radical South Africans such as Donald Molteno, tended to emphasise not economic forces, but political ones.[79] Some even went as far as to foretell a mass uprising which would quickly demolish apartheid and white rule, although most observers were unable to predict exactly when. 'Though still many years off,' Anthony Sampson, the former editor of *Drum* magazine, wrote in 1959, the year before Sharpeville, 'there seems little hope of averting an eventual head-on clash between the two competing nationalisms, African and Afrikaner.'[80]

In many respects, this tradition of engaged moral and political concern would have benefited considerably from more formal social science analysis, especially of the dynamics of the South African political economy. There were hints of the beginnings of such an analysis at a "Crisis in Africa Conference" organised by the Union of Democratic Control (UDC) in September 1950. This organisation had a long history of opposition to imperialism and had had close links with the Independent Labour Party in the interwar years. In essence it provided a forum for radical opinion, though it failed to develop a strong enough body of analysis to challenge the prevailing wisdom on the inherent dynamics of industrialisation. At the conference Thomas Hodgkin argued, in a paper entitled "The Crisis in International Relations", that the South African régime appeared to be strengthening white rule by the expansion of its industrial and military base in alliance with Britain and the west. This he saw as a development that could conceivably extend to Central Africa if the three territories became merged in a Central African Federation.[81]

These arguments came to be used in the campaign against Central African Federation by the UDC, and also by the left-leaning Movement for Colonial Freedom (MCF) after it was launched in April 1954.[82] It was, in particular, the fear of the possible spread of the South African system of segregation to the protectorate territories of Lesotho, Swaziland and Botswana in Southern Africa and to Central Africa which stimulated the MCF to embark on a public campaign in Britain in the 1950s. It warned of the dangers of apartheid and pressed for legislation to outlaw colour discrimination in both Britain and the colonial territories, so as to strengthen the liberal opposition inside South Africa.[83]

Some sociologists did develop the concept of "race prejudice" into a more complex and resilient analytical term by linking it to the wider study of ethnic and racial groups. One of the key popular works in this respect was Anthony Richmond's study, *The Colour Problem*, published by Penguin in 1955 and reprinted and revised in 1961. While still being 'irrational,' Richmond argued, 'race consciousness' and the belief in racial superiority and inferiority had become a powerful social force. The operation of this 'race consciousness' needed to be understood in a wider framework than that of the conventional term "colour bar", for it embraced three separate elements: colour prejudice, racial discrimination and social separation.[84] By applying this conception to apartheid itself, Richmond concluded that it was not simply the operation of 'colour' or of whites prejudiced into believing they were racially superior to blacks, but the reflection of a more general process of ethnic or racial group domination. 'Apartheid,' he concluded, 'is not merely an instrument for the separation of various ethnic groups, but for the continued domination of the African, Coloured and Asian communities by the European.'[85]

In many respects, Richmond's analysis synthesised the folk wisdom on apartheid generated by liberal and missionary bodies, although he sought to differentiate his approach as an objective sociological analysis, distinct from the 'alternative one' in which whites in South Africa would have eventually to 'face the moral issues involved, which cannot be evaded for ever' (a rather paternalistic view of South African political change which excluded all non-whites from the ethical debate, conceiving them as passive recipients of white moral decision-making).[86] His analysis of South Africa drew on quotations from *Cry, The Beloved Country* to describe South African society, from Michael Scott on the forced labour system and the Passive Resistance Campaign, and from Leo Marquard on United Party policy. He saw the Liberal Party as the 'only really radical party in South Africa', excluding the small, white, left-wing Congress of Democrats whose members attended the Congress of the People at Kliptown, and also the African National Congress, on the grounds that it did not participate in the white party political system.[87] The analysis subordinated class dynamics to group ones, although there was some confusion over the terms "ethnic" and "racial", which appeared at some points to merge into each other:

> *Partial separation combined with discrimination will never achieve its alleged object, which is the maintenance of racial* harmony and cultural autonomy, because the subordinate *ethnic* groups will not tolerate their role indefinitely.[88] (emphasis mine)

Nevertheless, Richmond's work was an important sociological reformulation of liberal discourse surrounding the apartheid issue both in Britain and South Africa.

Apartheid, the Central African Federation and Britain: Overlooked Linkages

In Britain, public opposition to apartheid developed only slowly during the 1950s. In the period before Sharpeville, it appeared to many observers of South African politics that black resistance was still of a relatively weak nature. Julius Lewin, for instance, argued in a famous paper in 1958 that there was not going to be an immediate revolution in South Africa, despite continued predictions of impending catastrophe.[89] Meanwhile, with the riots in Nyasaland in 1959, the heart began to go out of the multiracial ideal of "partnership" in Central Africa, and this was reflected in the warnings of the Monckton Commission the following year that its future depended upon the 'goodwill' of both black and white races.[90] In 1958 the Institute of Race Relations in London saw Central Africa as an area of especial interest, especially as its Director, Philip Mason, had in the early 1950s been a prominent advocate of the "partnership" idea on the grounds that it might modify South African policy.[91]

However, 1960, as Michael Banton has pointed out, was an *annus mirabilis* for the development of race relations research in general. The attainment of independence by a number of black African states, the growth in the American Civil Rights movement, and the crisis in South Africa following the Sharpeville shootings made 1960 a turning point in which· the emergence of black political movements internationally 'upset the deterministic streak in the sociology of race relations, showing that the behaviour of the subordinated is not completely determined by the social structure, for they have some power to choose the sort of group they will be.'[92] In many respects the mobilisation of black nationalism shifted the crisis of group identity from blacks to whites, the former bearers of "western civilisation". As Philip Mason pointed out in *Year of Decision*, a critical impasse confronted the whites in Southern Rhodesia; they faced a choice of either becoming an economically productive minority in a black-run state (a similar position, he thought, to that of the Jews in Britain or the Parsees in India) or else going 'the South African way, which must surely mean, sooner or later, change even more violent and catastrophic.'[93]

In 1961 an important phase in British relations with South Africa came to an end, as the latter country became a republic after a referendum among white voters and left the Commonwealth. For a large section of British opinion in the post-war years it had been the continued hope that, through the exercise of reasoned pressure, political dialogue and the counterpoise of the Central African Federation after 1953, the South African government could be shifted from its commitment to the apartheid doctrine and adopt a programme more in accord with contemporary concepts of "pluralism" or "partnership" between races. While these ideas had gripped a considerable section of "middle opinion" in Britain, it was also clear that they were not strongly held by many members of the British government, and Harold Macmillan later confessed to thinking partnership an 'idealistic but perhaps impracticable concept'.[94] The Monckton Commission in 1960, for example, indicated growing doubts in the British official mind on the worth of continuing "partnership" concepts, despite the fact that the admittance of failure would imply that there was 'no hope of survival for any multi-racial society in the African continent and that differences of colour and race are irreconcilable.'[95] For those activists on the left who were involved in movements like Christian Action and the MCF, the weakness of the ideal lay precisely in its failure to recognise the claims of African nationalism and majority rule. With the failure of the Central African Federation in 1963, British involvement on the issue shifted irreparably as the policy of decolonisation escalated and the African states, with the exception of Southern Rhodesia, achieved majority rule in the next few years. After 1963, British policy could no longer be guided in opposition to apartheid by the alternative mode of "partnership", and the more radical critique of white settler rule based on the claims of African nationalism and black majority began to gain increasing ground in the centre of British opinion.

The period from 1945 to the early 1960s was marked by a rising concern in Britain over the trajectory of South African politics and the use of apartheid. This concern occurred alongside a growing sociological interest in race relations generally, though at the level of government policy this tended to be focused towards the ideal of producing a harmonious political system based on the sharing of power between different racial groups on the "partnership" model. The collapse of the Central African Federation and the resurgence of black nationalism in the early 1960s transformed the ideological anchorage of race relations research as the subject area became increasingly politicised. The growing international abhorrence of apartheid led to a more sophisticated analysis of the workings of South African society and politics, especially as a new generation of South African political exiles began to settle in Britain as a result of the political bannings and arrests in the early 1960s.

The ideological and political impact of these new trends on the British debate on race needs more detailed research. This chapter has sought to demonstrate the importance of analysing the international linkages of political ideas and ideology. The crystallisation of British race relations research in the 1960s around the distinct issues of black immigration and settlement in Britain and external "colonial" and "post-colonial" issues of race in areas such as Southern Africa has generally led to these linkages being overlooked by researchers at a time when a wide body of social theory on race was being developed. The close historical ties between Britain and South Africa indicate that a considerable body of British thought on race has been shaped by the South African example. This needs, along with that for Latin political sociology of "race relations" needs, along with that for Latin America, to be incorporated into an international body of theory.[96] It is very likely that, from the stand-point of the history of contemporary British thought on race, South Africa has played almost as significant a catalysing role as the United States, despite the greater sophistication of formal race relations sociology in the latter society. With the emergent political and economic crisis in South Africa at the present time, this is an issue not merely of historical curiosity but of fundamental contemporary importance for the politics of race.

NOTES

1. C F Andrews, "Racial Influences", in Sir Arthur Salter *et al., The Causes of War,* Macmillan, London, 1932, p. 84.
2. See, for example, R F A Hoernlé, *South African Native Policy and the Liberal Spirit,* The University of Cape Town on behalf of the Phelps-Stokes Fund, Cape Town, 1939, p. 4. For a discussion of this debate in South Africa on the problem of "caste" see Paul B Rich, *White Power and the Liberal Conscience: Racial Segregation and South African Liberalism, 1921-1960,* Manchester University Press, 1984, pp. 75-6.
3. L S Amery, *The Forward View,* Geoffrey Bles, London, 1935, p. 253.
4. See chapter four.
5. Peter Walshe, *The Rise of African Nationalism in South Africa,* C. Hurst and Co., London, 1970, p. 51.
6. Martin Chanock, *Unconsummated Union: Britain, Rhodesia and South Africa,* Manchester University Press, Manchester, 1977, p.204.
7. DO 35/1284. Lord Harlech to C R Attlee, 28 April 1943. See also DO 35/1122/G899/1. Lord Harlech to C R Attlee, 22 February 1943.
8. DO 35/1639. Lord Harlech to S of S Dominions Affairs, 13 September 1943. Harlech's views were discussed by Churchill with the S of S. W S Churchill, handwritten note, 6 October 1943.
9. DO 35/1122/G899/1. Address by D L Smit, Secretary of Native Affairs, at a meeting arranged by Pretoria Ministers Fraternal, 24 November 1942, and minute by Emrys Evans, 13 January 1943.
10. DO 35/1122/G689/15. Lord Cranborne to Lord Swindon (draft), May 1944.
11. DO 35/1122/G699/35. E Baring to Lord Addison, 12 September 1946. See also Charles Douglas-Home, *Evelyn Baring: The Last Proconsul,* Collins, London, 1978, esp. pp. 139-50.
12. *Ibid.,* minute by Sir C Dixon n.d.
13. DO 35/3139. Sir E Baring to Rt Hon P Noel-Baker, 12 June 1948.
14. *Financial Times,* 8 November 1946.
15. *Manchester Guardian,* 13 September 1946.
16. DO 35/1122/G689/34. F Allen, Branch Sec., St Helier Branch, Amalgamated Union of Building Trade Workers to The Secretary, Colonial Office, 17 August 1946.
17. DO 35/3256. I MacLennan, memorandum on Durban Riots, 17 January 1949.
18. DO 35/3148. A Cohen to G L Clutton, 6 July 1949.
19. DO 35/31514. H A F Rumbold to E R Sudbury, 18 November 1950.
20. DO 35/3839. C P Hope (FO) to G E Crombie, 14 September 1950; extract from CM (50). Conclusions of a Cabinet Meeting held on Thursday 28 September 1950.
21. DO 35/3255. E Baring to P N I Baker, 22 May 1948.
22. *The Round Table,* 164, September 1951, p. 223.
23. Philip Mason, *An Essay on Racial Tension,* RIIA, London and New York, 1954, pp. 131-2.
24. This was especially true of Douglas Smit, Secretary of Native Affairs and later a member of the Native Affairs Commission in the last Smuts government. See Rich, *White Power and the Liberal Conscience,* Manchester, 1984, pp. 100-1.
25. *C W W Greenidge Papers,* Rhodes House, Oxford, 12/1, F M Phillips to CWWG, 3 January 1950.
26. *The Friend,* 22 February 1952; CO 876/272. M Attlee to J Griffiths, 15 August 1951. One official considered the organisation would be likely to be stillborn, I Cummings, minute n.d.
27. *Africa Bureau Papers,* Rhodes House, Oxford, MSS Afr S1681. M Attlee to Lady Pakenham, 2 April 1952.
28. *Ibid.,* M Scott to C T Turnbull, July 1952.
29. For a more detailed description of Racial Unity see Paul B Rich, *Race and Empire in British Politics,* esp. chapter eight.
30. CO 876/273. F Norman to J Griffiths, 30 September 1951; B G Smallman to F

Norman, 11 February 1952; F Norman to Smallman, 14 February 1952; Smallman to Norman, 28 February 1952.

31. *Picture Post*, 24 December 1949; Adamastor, *op. cit.*, pp. 110-1.

32. *John Fletcher Papers*, Society of Friends, Euston Road, London, John (?) to J Fletcher, 8 June 1950.

33. *Ibid.*, Harry O'Connor to J Fletcher, 8 June 1950.

34. See, for example, L Arthur Lewis, Michael Scott, Martin Wight and Colin Legum, *Attitude to Africa*, Penguin Books, Harmondsworth, 1951.

35. *The Christian Messenger*, 98, 6 June 1950.

36. MSS Afr S1681. Mrs B Lloyd to M Scott, 18 April 1950.

37. *John Fletcher Papers*, M Scott, and J Fletcher, 30 August 1949 and 9 January 1952; M Scott, "A Practical Hope for Africa", *The Observer*, 9 March 1952.

38. David Stirling and A N Wilson, *A Native Policy for Africa*, Salisbury (Rhodesia), 1950; Capricorn Africa Society, *Greater Rhodesia*, Salisbury (Rhodesia), 1952.

39. CO 1915/70. Andrew Cohen, minute, 23 November 1951.

40. MSS Afr S1681 30/4. Report to Meeting for Sufferings from the Race Relations Committee, June 1952.

41. Anthony Sampson, *Common Sense About Africa*, Victor Gollancz, London, 1960, pp. 54-5.

42. Africa Bureau, London, 1953, p. 2.

43. MSS Afr S1681 29/7. J Collins to M Scott, 2 March and 24 March 1949; M Scott to J Collins, 25 March 1949. Canon John Collins, *Faith Under Fire*, London, p. 186.

44. *Ibid.*, J Collins, 10 July 1952.

45. M Scott to J Collins, 18 July 1952.

46. Stephen Deakin, "The Churches, Immigration and Race Relations", *New Community*, Vol. XII, No. 1 (Winter 1984-85), pp. 101-15.

47. DO 35/3259. F W Aston, minute, 3 October 1952.

48. Collins, *op. cit.*, p. 186.

49. *Christian Action Newsletter*, December 1952.

50. DO 35/3137. D M Cleary, minute, 27 November 1952.

51. *Ibid.*, C Costley-White, minute, 1 December 1952.

52. Christian Action leaflet for meeting at Central Hall, Westminster, 22 February 1953.

53. *Christian Action Newsletter*, September 1954. For the development of the imperial view of Africa in the nineteenth century see H Alan and C Cairns, *Prelude to Imperialism*, Routledge and Kegan Paul, London, 1965.

54. *Christian Action Newsletter*, September 1954.

55. *Alan Paton Papers*, Church of the Province Archives, University of the Witwatersrand, 8(i), A Paton to Bishop of Johannesburg, 9 June 1960.

56. Arthur Marwick, "Middle Opinion in the Thirties: Planning, Progress and Political 'Agreement' ", *English Historical Review*, Vol. LXXIX (April 1964), pp. 285-98.

57. For an analysis of this debate see Paul B Rich, "Industrialisation, Fabianism and Race: Sydney Olivier and the liberal critique of South African segregation", Institute of Commonwealth Studies (ICS) seminar paper, London, 1984; "W M Macmillan, South African segregation and Commonwealth race relations 1919-1938" in Hugh Macmillan and Shula Marks (eds), *Africa and Empire: W.M. Macmillan, Historian and Social Critic*, Temple Smith, London, 1989, pp. 192-211.

58. Hugh Tinker, "Colour and Colonisation: A Study in Rival Commonwealth Ideals of Human Settlement", *The Round Table*, 240 (November 1979), pp. 405-16.

59. G H Calpin, "South African Janus", *The Spectator*, 15 April 1949.

60. C J Samson, "The Fabian Colonial Bureau and Southern Africa, 1950-55", in Institute of Commonwealth Studies, Collected Seminar Papers, *The Societies of Southern Africa in the Nineteenth and Twentieth Centuries*, Vol. 10, ICS, London, 1981, pp. 103-11.

61. *New Statesman*, 18 March 1950.

62. Rita Hinden, "Seretse: The Red Issue", *New Statesman*, 1 April 1950; Arthur Creech-Jones, "Black and White in Southern Africa", *The Spectator*, 7 April 1950.

63. E S Sachs, "The Answer to Malan", *New Statesman*, 26 August 1950; Adamastor, *White Man Boss*, Victor Gollancz, London, 1951. Reginald Reynolds, however, considered South Africa's rulers 'too essentially feudal to be fascist', *Beware of Africans*, Jarrolds, London, 1955, p. 349.

64. Basil Davidson, "Prisoners of Prejudice", *New Statesman*, 28 July 1951; "The Hope for Black and White", *ibid.*, 4 August 1951; *Report on Southern Africa*, Jonathan Cape, London, 1952, p. 142. More recently, Davidson has admitted the weakness of the industrialisation thesis and that the South African economy could expand on the basis of apartheid and racial segregation. *Southern Africa: Progress or Disaster?*, Canon Collins Memorial Lecture, 1984. International Defence and Aid, London, 1984, p. 28.

65. For an analysis of the growth in South African military power since the 1950s, see Kenneth W Grundy, *Soldiers Without Politics*, University of California Press, Berkeley and Los Angeles, 1983.

66. John W Cell, *The Highest Stage of White Supremacy: The Origins of Segregation in South Africa and the United States*, CUP, Cambridge, 1982.

67. Eric John Dingwall, *Racial Pride and Prejudice*, Watts and Co., London, 1946, p. 125.

68. *Ibid.*, p. 160.

69. I D MacCrone, *Race Attitudes in South Africa*, OUP, London, 1937.

70. For an analysis of this novel in the context of English language fiction in South Africa see Paul B Rich, "Liberal Realism in South African Fiction, 1948-1966", *English in Africa*, Vol. 12, No. 1 (May 1985), pp. 47-81.

71. Ruth Benedict, *Race and Racism*, Routledge and Kegan Paul, London, 1983 (first ed. 1942), p. 109.

72. *Ibid.*, p. 2.

73. Ruth Benedict, *Patterns of Culture*, Routledge and Kegan Paul, London, 1968 (first ed. 1935). For a recent critique of the ahistorical nature of this tradition of American cultural anthropology see Eric R Wolf, *Europe and the People Without History*, University of California Press, Berkeley and Los Angeles, 1982.

74. See, for example, Jan H Hofmeyr, *Christian Principles and Race Problems*, SAIRR, Johannesburg, 1945, p. 11.

75. D Van Arkel, "Racism in Europe", in R Ross (ed.), *Racism and Colonialism*, Martinus Hijhoff Pub., The Hague, Boston and London, 1982, p. 31.

76. *Anti-Slavery Papers*, Rhodes House, Oxford, MSS Brit Emp S19 D10/9 f1. C W W Greenidge to David Astor, 17 December 1951.

77. MSS Afr 1681. M Benson to M Webb, 1 February 1954; Mary Benson, *The Tragedy of Apartheid*, Christian Action, 1954: 'Granted that to some extent history has led to the policy of segregation that exists in South Africa, it is fear which adds fuel to the fire of racialism.'

78. *Rheinallt-Jones Papers*, Church of the Province Archives, University of the Witwatersrand, G26/15. J D R-J to Ralph Bunche, 20 November 1950. For an analysis of the South African debate at this time see Martin Legassick, "Legislation, Ideology and Economy in Post-1948 South Africa", *Journal of Southern Africa Studies*, 1, 1 October 1974, pp. 5-35.

79. Donald Molteno, *Towards a Democratic South Africa*, SAIRR, Johannesburg, 1959.

80. Samson, *op. cit.*, p. 153.

81. Thomas Hodgkin, "The Crisis in International Relations", mimeoed paper given at UDC "Crisis in Africa Conference", 21-22 September 1950, p. 11.

82. See, for example, Reverend George Norton, *Should South Africa Expand?*, UDC, London, 1951; Julius Lewin, *Britain's Colour Bar in Africa*, UDC, London, 1952. Fenner Brockway later argued that it was 'doubtful' if South Africa could maintain apartheid 'in the long run', since its philosophy contained a contradiction in that, 'whilst the mingling of whites and blacks is abhorrent to them, the Europeans want Africans to do all the hard manual labour.' He recognised though the nature of the urban locations and the exclusion of blacks from skilled work but 'no prohibition can permanently prevent the African workers from demanding fuller opportunities', *British Protectorates – Key to South African Freedom*, UDC, London, 1958. This was a more

cautious assessment, compared with the South African liberals' vulgar marxist mechanism, and also avoided the opposite apocalypic scenario of a grand revolutionary overthrow in favour of a more protracted struggle through organised labour.

83. Movement for Colonial Freedom, leaflet dated 10 October 1956; Fenner Brockway, *Towards Tomorrow*, Hart Davis MacGibbon, London, 1977, pp. 64-5.

84. Anthony H Richmond, *The Colour Problem*, Penguin Books, Harmondsworth, 1961, pp. 18-19.

85. *Ibid.*, p. 111.

86. *Ibid.*, p. 104. Trevor Huddleston, however, argued that the South African whites could have 'no justifiable claim to moral leadership', *Naught For Your Comfort*, Collins, London, 1956, p. 250.

87. *Ibid.*, p. 131.

88. *Ibid.*, pp. 113, 122.

89. Julius Lewin, "No Revolution Round the Corner", *Africa South*, 1958, reprinted in *Politics and Law in South Africa*, Merlin Press, London, 1963, pp. 107-15.

90. *Report of the Advisory Commission on the Review of the Constitution of Rhodesia and Nyasaland*, Cmnd. 1148, HMSO, London, para. 84.

91. Philip Mason, "Partnership in Central Africa", *International Affairs*, Vol. 33, No. 2 (April 1951), pp. 150-64.

92. Michael Banton, "1960: A Turning Point in the Study of Race Relations", *Daedalus*, 2 (Spring 1974), p. 36.

93. Philip Mason, *Year of Decision*, OUP, for the IRR, London, p. 254.

94. Harold Macmillan, *Pointing the Way, 1959-1961*, Macmillan, London, 1972, p. 132.

95. *Report of the Advisory Commission on the Review of the Constitution of Rhodesia and Nyasaland*, Cmnd. 1148, HMSO, London, 1960, para. 71.

96. Michael Banton, *The Idea of Race*, London, 1977, p. 9.

Chapter Six

The Black Diaspora in Britain: Afro-Caribbean Students and the Struggle for a Political Identity 1900-1950

The history of black student politics is another neglected aspect of British race relations. At one level, the emergence of an Afro-Caribbean student population in such university cities as London, Edinburgh and Bristol has been perceived as part of the establishment of a militant intelligentsia within the "black diaspora", anchored around an ideology of Pan-Africanism.[1] At another level, it has been seen by some black intellectuals as part of a history of intellectual and cultural rootlessness in which the 'coloured intellectual' who has been 'thrown up by a specific history ... remains stranded on its shores even as it recedes. And what he comes into is not so much a twilight world, as the world of false shadows and false light.'[2] Neither of these views, however, takes account of the specific history of the black student population within British society and the nature of the social and political relationships which were forged.

Afro-Caribbean student politics in Britain have, furthermore, been subsumed into a discussion of the nature and role of Harold Moody's League of Coloured People (LCP), as in Peter Fryer's study of black people's history in Britain. African students, and the West African Students Union especially, have been marginalised as part of the nationalist history of Nigeria and West Africa. In contrast, Moody's LCP has been seen as a prototypical political party for a specifically black British population.[3] This view overlooks the complexities of the black student population and its history. It was not merely a temporary and itinerant population whose politics focused entirely on colonial territories, but was an important dimension in the emergence of a black population within the British imperial metropolis itself.

The growth of the African and Westindian student population in Britain, and in London in particular, did not occur by chance. It was an inexorable accompaniment to an imperial process whose liberal tenets of bringing "freedom" and "justice" to "backward races" did lead to the creation of certain avenues of social mobility within the parameters of the British racial and class system. Many of the black students who came to Britain did so to gain professional qualifications in areas such as law and medicine, and while many stayed only temporarily, others remained and formed part of the small black British population. Many of those who returned home established a pattern of family and kinship links with relatives who remained, perpetuated by sons and daughters repeating their parents' footsteps and coming to British universities and polytechnics in pursuit of higher education.

This chapter focuses on the emergence of this black student community in Britain from the early twentieth century up to the Second World War, and discusses the significance of the political traditions it established. While a less cohesive and more socially volatile entity than the communities of working-class black people in seaports such as Liverpool and Cardiff, Afro-Caribbean and Asian students were closer to the central structures of political power in the metropolis, a position that frequently led to the exposure of contradictions within the imperial rule itself. While imperialism, as A P Thornton has suggested, confers on the imperial authority the power to release the dynamic forces of will, room, time and money in the areas under its control, its ultimate essence is not motion but control. The continuation of empire depended upon the acceptance of this control.[4] The presence of a growing black student population in the heart of the imperial metropolis revealed this essential contradiction in an especially acute form long before the emergence of larger numbers of black settlers after the Second World War. The manner in which imperial authority and allied colonial administration reacted to this paradox makes the study of black students especially important and interesting.

The Early Phase

One of the most significant features of the initial pattern of Afro-Caribbean student migration to Britain is that it came slightly later than that of Indian students and confronted a government and its allies among missionaries and concerned "friends of the native" who had already developed an apparatus of control to meet the Indian student "problem".

There had been Indian students in Britain since at least the 1850s and in 1871 the first Indian had graduated from Oxford. The previous year the National Indian Association had been founded in Bristol 'to promote by voluntary effort the enlightenment and improvement of our fellow Indian subjects' and a similar body was founded in Edinburgh in 1881. By 1894 there were some 308 Indian students in Britain and nationalist ideas started to gain ground, especially through the activities of a radical barrister, Shyami Krishnavarma. He had been at Balliol College, Oxford, from 1879 to 1883 and started a newssheet at "Indian House" in Highgate. Krishnavarma's open support for political assassination led to his disbarment from the Inner Temple in May 1909. In the following July the Assistant District Commissioner to the Secretary of State for India, one Colonel Sir Curzon Wyllie, was shot dead by a Punjabi student at a reception of the Indian National Association. The resulting government investigation instigated by the Indian Secretary, John Morley, awakened political opinion to the whole black student issue. By the time the question of facilities and hospitality for the growing number of African students in Britain arose, there was a sharper political response.[5]

Small numbers of students from West Africa had been coming to Britain for higher education since at least the 1850s. The West African, Joseph Renner Maxwell, for example, graduated from Oxford in the 1870s and proceeded to study law at the Inns of Court.[6] By the Edwardian period a small trickle of African students was coming to Britain, especially from West Africa, as the demise of the older African mercantile class resulted in a growing desire by several chiefs for their sons to receive a European education in order to succeed in an increasingly competitive colonial society.[7]

The Edwardian society to which these Africans came was one basking in the arrogance of empire. London represented the quintessence of urban and metropolitan values in contrast to colonial "provincial" ones. 'What the British Empire has been to that World,' one New Zealand commentator, Edith Grossmann, wrote in 1907, ' London now is to the Empire.'[8] This imperial arrogance was not an all-enveloping creed, despite the jingoist euphoria which had momentarily overtaken British society in the 1890s through the yellow press and the eventual victory against the Boers at Mafeking. By the 1880s an Oxbridge intelligentsia had emerged which was anchored around liberal political and social values, and these continued to survive through the imperialist interlude of the next two decades, receiving a considerable injection of new life with the victory of the Liberal Party in the general election of 1906.[9] For the liberal intelligentsia the question of colour and racial prejudice became an increasingly important one both politically and ethically, especially as the British victory over the Boers in South Africa had raised the issue of racial segregation as a model of colonial control, and the practice of the American South had a considerable appeal to some "race experts" in Britain.[10] Some liberals condemned segregationist practices in South Africa and the system of compound labour while also rejecting the idea that blacks could ever come and live permanently in Britain. 'We do not attempt to import blacks, coolies and Polynesians into Great Britain,' wrote the classical scholar Gilbert Murray, who was a strong critic of the war, in 1900. 'The opposition of the working classes at home would be furious; and even if that obstacle were overcome, the coloured men would die too fast in our climate.'[11] Colour and race continued to be seen by most as remote issues and attitudes at this time tended, as in the mid-Victorian period, to be formed in a vacuum.[12]

However, on occasions race did demand an immediate political or moral stand. In 1907 the scholar A V Dicey turned down an invitation to dine at the American Club at Balliol when he heard that a black Rhodes scholar from Pennsylvania was to be refused admission; he also tried to act on the refusal of the university volunteer corps to admit a black British student.[13] The growing climate of liberal concern impressed some black Anglophile observers, such as the Sierra Leone lawyer A B C Merriman-Labor, who wrote enthusiastically in his book *Britons Through Negro Spectacles* in 1909: 'Take it from me, that here, in Britain, we have already justice for the Blacks, and equally for Blacks and Whites. We shall have equality and justice ourselves some day.'[14] At the same time he was careful to point out that the black person in Britain remained forever a stranger, for the country was itself 'the land of the stranger who cannot find a home in his own country'. But for the 'foreigner', white or black, Merriman-Labor considered that 'a stranger of *respect* will, as a rule, receive amongst liberal-minded people, any position that his ability merits.'[15] (emphasis mine)

The position and relation of the black 'foreigner' in Britain hinged on his ability to find a niche within the tight British class system, anchored as it was around a strongly defined bourgeois concept of gentility and respectability.[16] This was a reflection of the centrality of the metropolitan capital in an imperial system that was strongly rooted in a class hierarchy. As Edith Grossmann pointed out:

> ...the best blood and brains of the unleisured workers are constantly drawn off to renew the vitality of the aristocracy of All the Talents, just as the Empire replenishes itself from the lower races, and London replenishes itself from the whole of the Empire. The English instinct for governing and managing – that silent, intangible, irresistible power of absorbing and suppressing – is concentrated in every part of its system; in the dominance of class as much as race.[17]

As long as the black students coming to Britain represented the cream of their countrymen and were destined simply to gain qualifications and then return to senior positions within the colonial system of the country of origin, things went well. But, as the numbers of students grew, a racial situation was produced in Britain as black students struggled to find accommodation and friends in a lonely and indifferent society. By the time of the First World War, the situation had been compounded by stresses within the imperial system itself. Nationalism began to emerge in many parts of an empire that was starting to suffer a crisis of faith as so much of its life blood was spilled in the trenches of France and Flanders. By the early 1930s this crisis had become evident to some of the radical black intellectuals who had come to reside in Britain. George Padmore wrote of a broad British colonial strategy of creating an 'upper stratum of petty bourgeois intellectuals' who were alienated from the 'broad masses' and amenable to the dictates of imperial policy. The success of this policy hinged to a considerable degree on maintaining the idea that British society represented justice and fair play for all, irrespective of colour. This Padmore denounced as a myth for 'the British bourgeoisie is shrewd and cunning, they are not of yesterday. They are one of the oldest ruling classes in the world, with centuries of colonial experience.'[18] This argument depended on a conception of the African "petty bourgeois" student population as entirely pliable and passive in the hands of British colonial policy makers. The events of the 1930s and 1940s tended to refute this monolithic conception of empire.

The Question of Control

Despite Merriman-Labor's optimistic view of a beneficent and liberal English society, the experience of many black students was considerably different. The hopes of many for an education in middle-class values that would ensure rapid social mobility and acceptance became complicated by racial prejudice which produced social marginalisation. Forced, very often, to take the cheapest accommodation in the poorer areas of London and other cities, black students found themselves amidst working-class communities which were often hostile or suspicious and where prostitutes were the only female contact. Purchasing sexual favours was a common enough occupation of the Victorian and Edwardian middle-class male, but the position of the black students highlighted class polarities at this time in a particularly acute form. 'It is no use pretending that a cheap lodging house in Bayswater or Earls Court affords opportunities of learning English ways and customs,' wrote an Indian student, K Choudray, in 1910. 'On the contrary, many a young fellow has picked up bad manners and the slang of cheap diggings' and ended up contacting prostitutes. The need was for a 'well organised hostel' where such 'troubles' would not occur and where 'arrangements for social intercourse with English people of good stock could easily be made.'[19]

This question of accommodation and social facilities was taken up by organised ethical and welfare bodies, especially after the 1911 Universal Races Congress highlighted the issue of race for many members of the liberal middle class.[20] After the Congress, the Egyptian nationalist Duse

Mohammed Ali began editing *The African Times and Orient Review*. In 1912, there were calls in the paper's columns for a Universal Races Club to be formed in London 'free from the domination by any kind of clique, official or otherwise, where students of all races may meet for social intercourse and for free discussion, and where Europeans who are willing to associate on equal terms may freely do so.'[21] As a response to such calls, the Anti-Slavery Society (APS) helped to organise a new London University Club where such social intercourse could take place. However, the venture met with the paper's scorn for it 'turned out to be something in the nature of a "rounding up" place for West Africans with a nice respectable sprinkling of ex-West African and ex-Colonial Office officials thrown in as patrons to give weight to the scheme.'[22] Organised philanthropic opinion was not going to avoid the issue and the call for both hostel accommodation and a social centre was one that it took up with increasing interest by the time of the First World War.

Public attitudes had been stirred by growing concern about possible "threats" to the nation's health and morals by the "amateur" female prostitute, who was seen as a potential carrier of venereal disease and a corrupter of the morals of the young men fighting in the First World War. The racist sexual imagery that was associated with this discourse linked the "problems" of prostitution, and greater freedom and mobility for women emancipated by the war, with the "problem" of race and moral corruption by the intrusion of different races into English society.[23] The black conveyers of this perceived moral corruption were usually jazz musicians, cabaret artistes and actresses, together with groups of gangland leaders and pimps of an international underworld that formed the basis for thrillers like John Buchan's *The Three Hostages* (1924). Black students, for the most part, were seen as a bourgeois group who could be either "rescued" or "protected" from such dangers if enough facilities were provided to ease their stay in Britain.

It was in this context that the Student Christian Movement (SCM) became drawn into the black student welfare issue, leading to the establishment in November 1917 of Student Movement House, an international student centre in the heartland of the capital. SCM grew up in the early years of the century as a focus for Christian proselytisation amongst young people in Britain and its daily affairs were handled by an Irishman, Reverend Tissington Tatlow. A residential centre for Chinese students was established by the Movement in Holford Road, north Hampstead in 1913 and Tatlow was keen to see further facilities for black students.[24] The response from within colonial circles for such ventures was not particularly encouraging. At a conference at the Westminster Palace Hotel in June 1913, called jointly by the African Society and the Anti-Slavery Society, there were calls by a number of interested observers on race issues for a 'friendly recognition in this country' of the nature of the problems confronting African students and a committee was established to take the matter further.[25]

West African governments remained opposed to the scheme and their view was well summarised by Frederick Lugard who wrote that 'Africans should as far as possible be educated in Africa, and ... nothing should be done to attract them to England'. His support for the scheme extended only as far as those Africans who were 'necessarily' in Britain. Furthermore, if a hostel was established it should be run on fairly strict lines, 'with the power to inflict punishment in case of insubordination' and the constant threat of expulsion should be a strong deterrent since it would 'militate against their employment in their colony'.[26]

SCM tended to take a broader view of the issue and tried to avoid seeing it as a paternalist extension of African colonial policy. Tatlow was able to secure the backing of several wealthy sponsors for the proposed international student centre, a nonracial venture catering for the needs of all students in London (some 30,000) who were scattered in all parts of the city. The dedication of the centre to the nation's fallen probably helped to stimulate interest and, on the basis of some £1200, Tatlow secured the lease on 32 Russell Square, right in the heart of London student and university life. A further £3,870 was raised to equip it.[27]

The ethos of the Movement was one of avoiding politics and seeking as far as possible the ideal of promoting 'agreement' or 'order'. The objective was to focus on the 'common ground' of 'games and acting, ... things serious and things trivial' which would make the respective participants 'happy and efficient as members of one club'.[28] To this extent, SCM was both typical of a more general English approach to clubs and societies and an innovative attempt to extend a model that had firm roots within English culture on to an international plane. These ideals were a fairly common reflection of "internationalist" liberal opinion at this time, though SCM was soon forced to confront the mood of growing nationalism among many black students in Britain.

The Foreign Student Committee of SCM submitted a general statement of principle at the end of 1919 which argued that it was necessary to recognise important limitations in the internationalist ideal in terms of racial attitudes and prejudice. The Committee began by seeing the issue in terms of the 'position and outlook' of women which had 'changed so rapidly during the last few years that there is at the present time in the minds of many of them a conflict between new and old ideals and an uncertainty as to the true principles which should guide future development.' While the 'present situation' was 'undoubtedly difficult and uncertain' it was 'impossible for women to go back to an old conception which is felt by many to be unsound.'[29] Nevertheless, intermarriage between white women and 'foreign' students would be 'unwise and harmful' for there was a 'strong feeling' against it 'not only on the British but also on the Foreign side.' The ideal of international friendship it defended as important precisely because it was a 'real safeguard against immorality and undesirable relationships which are often the outcome of loneliness and acquaintance with none but a lower type of woman.' The 'difficulty' could also be 'met if British men will trust their women more fully, and show it by readiness to discuss the points at issue more frankly and honestly.'[30]

This statement of the "friendship" ideal was important for the manner in which it was developed beyond a race relations theme of black-white relations to include a re-examination of the relationships between white men and women. It tended, however, to be eclipsed by a more basic concern to ensure that potential black nationalist leaders did not leave Britain politically embittered by the racial prejudice they had encountered. To some extent this was recognised in SCM by those of its workers who had fairly extensive contact with African and Asian students in London. The Foreign Student Secretary, R Brewster, worked amongst the 1600 students from Africa and Asia in London between 1921 and 1923 and warned of a 'growing tendency to look on missions as de-nationalising influences'.[31] 'We have ... in London today,' he continued, 'the future leaders of the East living lives of lonely study, longing to see what is best in English life and unable to see it, trying to avoid what is worst and unable to escape.' There was thus an 'outstanding need' for 'friendship based on understanding. Colour prejudice, popular ignorance, mutual suspicion, have erected barriers which have to be removed before friendship is possible.'[32] This simply restated the existing international friendship ideal that had defined SCM's approach and it was by no means clear that it was going to be universally successful for all the students in London at this time. For some Asian students it was not a particular problem anyway, since a strong assertion of Indian or Chinese cultural identity was sufficient to cope with both the supposed strains of London life and the appeals of missionary proselytisation. One Indian student wrote in 1920 that, given that Indian students in Britain found 'few friendships of the best and highest sort', they did not confront any real challenges to their faith and were 'never seriously tempted to consider Christianity, much less accept it'.[33]

In the case of African students, a more paternalistic approach was developed after the First World War that avoided the extreme authoritarianism of the pre-war years while as far as possible eschewing the international friendship ideal of SCM. Foremost in the formulation of this new approach was the Reverend John Harris of the Anti-Slavery Society. Harris had been a missionary in the Congo before returning to England where he worked for E D Morel's Congo Reform Association. In 1910 he became Secretary of the newly amalgamated Anti-Slavery and Aborigines Protection Society and was soon drawn into the politics of Central and Southern Africa. As a benevolent paternalist, Harris favoured a form of liberal racial segregation as a means of perpetuating African social and tribal institutions, for he doubted the African's ability to survive in western industrial society. His ideas were generally in accordance with post-Versailles notions of colonial "trusteeship" in Africa, but stopped short of the more radical segregationism of J A Hobson and E D Morel. Their views amounted to a form of romantic anticapitalism, which attacked the materialism of western and white settler capitalism in Africa from an ethical perspective and doubted the fitness of western industrial societies to carry out any sort of civilising mission in its colonial possessions.[34] Both schools of thought agreed on the idea of maintaining a rural peasantry and the fostering of its folk values. The net result was that Harris became deeply suspicious of African students coming to study in Britain and was anxious for the imposition of control and supervision. 'The moral dangers of London life,' he wrote to Lord Cromer in 1919, 'are too obvious and experience seems to show that certain political influences are too often brought to bear tending to undermine the loyalty of these men and women at their most impressionable age.'[35]

Harris was increasingly distrustful of African political leadership. The South African ANC, for example, when it came to London in 1914 to protest against the South African government's Native Affairs Act of 1913, borrowed money from funds gathered by the APS which it failed to return. Further money was lost after African students failed to repay loans from a fund managed by Harris to help provide welfare facilities for the African labour contingent that was brought to Europe to assist the allied forces during the First World War.[36] By the end of the war Harris was profoundly disillusioned by his dealings with African students and political leaders. 'The thing which disappoints so many of us,' he wrote to the South African J T Gumede, 'is our almost invariable experience, that in money matters you cannot trust the African.'[37]

Harris' attitudes were a reflection of the ideological stresses that were occurring within free trade liberalism. In its classical form, this was an ideology of "possessory individualism" in which money was the source of value in a property-owning society. For the system to work, certain commonly acknowledged patterns of behaviour were essential, including the idea that money that was loaned had to be repaid. For African students migrating to the centre of the British empire the significance of this concept was not immediately apparent and Harris' disillusion was a reflection both of a profound clash of values towards goods and property, as well as the fact that for African political leaders the financial loans were simply the benefit derived from a temporary alliance with missionary and welfare bodies. For many African politicians the development of nationalist consciousness by the end of the First World War meant that the welfare bodies were a means towards a long-term nationalist objective, and many African and Caribbean students were often deeply critical of what appeared to them to be a harsh materialism in British society. As the Guyanese writer Ayube M Edun observed in London in the 1930s, 'in this scramble to go on and on, in this hubbub of ceaseless traffic, life seems to be nothing else than a lunatic wave of haste and flutter'.[38] Harris' hopes for establishing control over African

students and intellectuals were thus part of a wider ideological struggle
occurring within British imperialism in which ostensibly "welfare"
objectives had a far wider political resonance.

Growing African Resistance

By the time Harris began planning, in mid 1919, the establishment of a
hostel for Africans in London, the political climate had changed
dramatically from the more paternalistic days before 1914, and African
students were less willing to accept missionary guidance and paternal
control. Some black political leaders in Britain, like the Trinidadian
Felix Hercules, had by then become disillusioned with the
internationalist liberal "friendship" ideal and began to establish roots in
their own countries.[39] As the editor of the paper *African Telegraph*,
founded by J Eldred Taylor in late 1918, Hercules was in an important
position to shape black political thinking in Britain. This was reinforced
by his posts of General Secretary of the Society of People's of African
Origin and Associate Secretary of the African Progress Union (APU). A
tentative amalgamation of the two organisations occurred in the spring
of 1919, but they still tended to work separately, despite hopes for the
development of a more united African student position in London.
Writing from the Student Movement House at the end of 1918, Hercules
reassured Harris of his intentions to promote 'good relations between
Africa and England',[40] but by the middle of the following year events
occurred which nullified this ideal.

Hercules became the target of political hostility in colonial circles due
to a controversial article entitled "The African Nationalism" which he
wrote in the *African Telegraph* in December 1918.[41] During the same
month, at an inaugural dinner of the APU at the Great Eastern Hotel,
Liverpool Street, he attacked the materialism of western civilisation and
defined the destiny of the African race as lying in 'the domain of lofty
ideals in the sphere of the intellect, in the field of high endeavour, in the
province of the spiritual, in the realm of noble achievements. For herein
alone are to be found permanency and security.'[42] Hercules' speech
resulted in a split between moderate and radical factions among the
small black intelligentsia. Hercules continued to hope that the fostering
of ties with Harris and the Anti-Slavery lobby could be useful in order to
gain funds to launch a new African paper. In 1919 Hercules became
estranged from Taylor and the *African Telegraph*, as his speech had led
him to be accused of 'holding up [his] race to ridicule'. Since he could no
longer depend on the support of the editor John Archer, he turned
momentarily to Harris in an endeavour 'to start a genuine African paper
in England' which would be 'clear and while avoiding personalities, fight
for the highest interest of Africa and the West Indies'.[43] Harris failed to
respond to this olive branch, seeing his role, at this stage at least, strictly
in welfare terms.

Hercules' hopes for a Pan-Africanist revival accorded with the post-war international political climate,[44] but the upsurge of racial riots in British seaports, such as Liverpool and Cardiff, in June 1919 put a damper on these more ambitious political goals. The leadership in the APU tried to revive the idea of an African hostel as a place of refuge in a society that appeared increasingly hostile and racist.[45] Harris was not especially encouraging, arguing that the riots made the establishment of the hostel difficult since landlords would be unwilling to let property for such a purpose except at high prices.[46] The accommodative political stance of the mainstream APU leadership prevailed over the coming months as Hercules became increasingly isolated from his former London base. Touring Liverpool and Cardiff in June he made a number of speeches in support of the black seamen caught up in the riots and finally left for the Caribbean early in July to commence a new phase of his career as a politician in Jamaica.[47] In the more placid political climate of London, Harris hoped it would be possible, in the latter half of 1919, to forge around the hostel scheme closer ties with the volatile and divisive APU.

It had been recognised fairly early on in Anti-Slavery circles that the cooperation of the APU was essential for the hostel proposal to gain any widespread acceptance among the small African student population in London.[48] In April 1919 Hercules deliberately dropped out of the whole scheme so as not to oppose Harris directly, and some of the more Anglophile APU members, such as the Ghanaian merchant Robert Broadhurst, opposed it on the grounds that the money needed for it would be better spent erecting a monument to Britain's war dead, so creating a 'feeling which would minimise the various inconveniences hitherto and now being experienced by Africans in England'.[49] There were also continuing political divisions, despite the amalgamation of the APU with the Society of People's of African Origin to form the Union of African Peoples,[50] for some African students saw the project as a covert means by the APU to increase its membership as well as a form of segregation which would insulate them from wider student life in London.[51] The APU leadership, however, saw the riots as necessitating a separate hostel for African students in such a hostile society[52] and met and discussed the idea with Harris as well as agreeing, by the end of 1921, to cooperate with the Welfare of Africans in Europe War Fund (Surplus) Committee, which had money left over from its welfare work during the war.[53]

The early 1920s proved a politically quiescent time among the 100 or so African students in London and most activities continued to be centred around Student Movement House which had, by 1920, some 100 members of differing nationalities (although approximately half were British). The Pan-Africanist theme temporarily declined and Harris concentrated his efforts on welfare work for African sailors who had been left stranded in Britain when their jobs were taken by white seamen.

Collaborating with the Colonial Office and individuals of political influence such as Sir Harry Johnston, Harris concentrated mainly on repatriating the seamen, since the funds of his own Welfare of Africans in Europe Committee were limited. This welfare work reinforced the view that Africans really had no place in European industrial society and Harris was critical of organisations like the YMCA getting involved since they did not 'possess the particular knowledge and experience of the African which is essential to successful work'.[54]

Harris' moral position was fortified by the effect of a new paternalist liberalism that was establishing itself in South Africa at this time, centred especially on the Witwatersrand. He was especially impressed by the work of the Quaker accountant, Howard Pim, who took charge of the Ohlange Institute in Natal which had been established on industrial training lines by the African leader John Dube. The slender resources of the Institute led to growing indebtedness and Harris saw the issue as confirming that 'the native community in South Africa cannot produce, unaided, men with the ability required to consolidate and extend the existing work' thus requiring additional white 'supervision'.[55] The same approach tended to underpin Harris' attitude to the hostel issue in London as it resurfaced in the late 1920s after a renewal of political activity by African students, this time from West Africa.

The West African Students Union

While a number of African student societies continued to exist in London in the early 1920s, a strong fillip came with the establishment in 1924 of the Nigerian Progress Union by a young Nigerian law student, Ladipo Solanke. Coming to England in 1922, Solanke had studied at Fourah Bay College and was called to the Bar in 1926. Solanke's dream was a united West Africa and, after obtaining the support of the President of the West African National Congress, Casely Hayford, he went on to establish the West African Students Union (WASU) in August 1925.[56]

The emergence of WASU sharpened and clarified African political objectives, in contrast with the more eclectic goals and ambitions of the APU and the Society of People's of African Origin. While the latter groups had sought to unite students from various parts of Africa and the Westindies, WASU focused on the rights of Africans in West Africa, especially in terms of the conventional liberal goals of the rights of the individual and equality before the law.[57] The leadership of the Union saw their role as the political vanguard for a nationalist movement in the British colonies of West Africa centred around the West African National Congress. The Union was far less concerned about the question of segregation from other students, for the political value of a separate area of residence in a hostel lay in the provision of the right atmosphere for the sharpening of nationalist thought. As the Secretary of WASU wrote in 1929, a 'hostel in the very heart of the Empire' was 'one of the necessary factors' if 'rapid progress' was to be made by 'the West African nations with the British Empire'.[58] Solanke conceived this in terms of demonstrating the cultural worth of African cuisine for 'West African students want a hostel in London where West African delicious and most palatable dishes may be served, not only to West African children but to all Londoners and other races in this country and to compete side by side with those of the Indian, Chinese and other Oriental hostels.'[59]

In his search to establish such a hostel Solanke initially looked, not to John Harris and the Anti-Slavery Society, but to the Fabian critic of imperialism, Sydney Olivier, who had recognised in a speech in 1919 the capacity of Africans for 'self-government'. Solanke saw such support as reason enough for the release of the £2000 in a trust fund administered by the APS, which he felt was probably in the 'custody' of the Colonial Office.[60] Olivier was not an effective ally since his main political activities were centred on East Africa, settler rule in Kenya and the discussions of the Labour Party Advisory Committee on Imperial Affairs. Although a former governor of Jamaica, he had no knowledge of or connections with West Africa.[61] Solanke toured West Africa in 1929 and 1931 raising some funds for the hostel, and a house was found in Camden Road, north London.

The WASU funds could only cover the expenses for a few months and Solanke was forced to turn to the body with both funds and an interest in the field, Harris' Welfare in Africa War Funds (Surplus) Committee. Under its President, Sir Thomas Fowell Buxton, this committee met another interested party, the African Club Organising Committee, in July 1931 at a joint conference in the Colonial Office. The latter committee was under the chairmanship of Sir Percy Nunn, who sought to play down any direct ties with the CO. It had, however, Hanns Vischer OBE among its members. He was Joint Secretary to the Advisory Committee on Education in the Colonies as well as a prominent figure in the recently formed International African Institute under the presidency of Lord Lugard.[62]

The conference reflected a widening of interest in the hostel idea among colonial circles as African students in London were recognised as an increasingly important political grouping with long-term ramifications for colonial policy in Africa itself. Sir Percy Nunn, in opening the proceedings, noted 'the treatment which natives of Africa received in London frequently caused them to go back to Africa embittered in their feelings towards Great Britain and the Empire' such that it was necessary to obtain 'the goodwill of the Africans themselves.'[63] The African Club Organising Committee sought the cooperation of the Anti-Slavery Committee since it controlled funds which were then estimated at £2,200. Alternative funds had not been forthcoming for the project.[64] To some extent, there was a difference of approach between the two committees since, as the Chairman of the conference, Drummond Shiels, pointed out, the Anti-Slavery Committee was mainly engaged in 'rescue work' for working-class African seamen as opposed to the essentially middle-class African student population.[65]

The failure at this stage to secure a united CO/APS policy behind the hostel scheme meant that in January 1933 WASU went ahead unilaterally and opened its hostel in Camden Road on the basis of some £1386 collected by Solanke. It soon found the rent for the property too heavy and began seeking the ownership of a freehold property. Donations from West Africa were forthcoming and the Nigerian government gave £250 'for a freehold permanent house for WASU hostel'. After 1936 further financial support was obtained by Hanns Vischer from West African trading interests such as the United Africa Company (£200), Cadbury Brothers (£50) and Barclays Bank (£50). After 1934 WASU became embroiled in competition with another hostel in London, Aggrey House, which had been opened in 1932 for both African and Westindian students after recommendations from a Colonial Office conference. Although it had close links with the CO, funds for it came from West African governments and commercial interests after appeals from Hanns Vischer and a £2,500 grant from the Carnegie corporation.[66] WASU accused its rival hostel of being a tool of the Colonial Office, which in turn concluded that WASU 'Could not be used in its scheme to bring African students in London under its control' and so had resorted to Harold Moody of the LCP.[67]

To gain the funds necessary for the purchase of a property, Solanke was forced to gain the support of Harris, who was not involved in the Aggrey House scheme. Harris obtained a building society mortgage and this led to the eventual purchase of a freehold property, 1 South Villas, Camden Square, in early 1938. Harris and General Grey, the Chairman of the Welfare of Africans in Europe Committee, completed the conveyancing and the new hostel opened on 7 July of the same year under the title "African House". Although the WASU leadership believed they had gained control of a freehold property, the actual title deed left them as tenants of the trustees, Harris and Grey, acting in the name of the Welfare of Africans in Europe War Fund Committee.

Harris' ability to maintain some financial control over WASU was aided by the split among African student opinion engendered by the rival Aggrey House. The Warden of the latter was the Sierra Leonian Ivor Cummings, who worked for the Colonial Office in the 1940s, while Harold Moody was one of the trustees. Although Moody was seen in some quarters of WASU as a sellout to the Colonial Office,[68] Harris was probably not especially anxious for this split to be reconciled since he had already encountered political opposition from the LCP over his campaign for the repatriation of black seamen from Britain following the Fletcher Report in Liverpool in 1930.[69] At a time when he was planning a deputation to the Home Office on the issue, Harris wrote to Vischer saying that there would be 'a difficulty about getting the two sections to unite and keep in harmony, anyhow while Moody is believed to be having anything to do with it'.[70] Vischer tended to perceive the issue in less personal terms, seeing no objection to a 'political club' or to WASU working with Aggrey House, which had 'been opened as a social centre irrespective of creed or politics'.[71] Vischer's open-minded liberal approach provided a useful brokerage role when it came to trying to resolve the deepening conflict between the APS and WASU.

The dispute had come to a head by 1939 as WASU drew up a memorandum outlining their complaints regarding their status as tenants of the South Villas property. Although the original Trust deed had been rejected by the Union, a new draft to alter their status had not been shown to them, despite the fact that the Union had agreed to appointing four white members of the management committee of the hostel.[72] Harris' response at this point was to announce that since 'amicable arrangements' were no longer possible the Welfare Committee should itself take over the management of the hostel.[73] It proved difficult for Harris to gain unanimous support for this proposal. Vischer, in particular, continued to defend Solanke's management of African House and hoped for some form of reconciliation with the rival Aggrey House through a joint board of management.[74] In so far as he had been instrumental in gaining further funding from West African interests in the late 1930s his opinion carried considerable weight. Harris threatened that the withdrawal of the African Welfare Committee from supporting the hostel would leave WASU having to pay off the mortgage on African House, which amounted to some £45 a year, and tried to caste the whole blame for the split onto Solanke personally. 'If there had been only reasonable treatment of the Committee by Solanke,' he angrily wrote to Vischer, 'we could have raised the balance remaining. Now there is no "spirit" in anybody to attempt it, thus by his folly and absurdity he has prejudiced, for many years to come, a project which promises so well.'[75]

Harris' anger was a reflection of an old style paternalism that could not really adapt to the changing political climate in London in the late 1930s. 'I expect you and I have decided,' he wrote to Vischer, 'that we will never, if we live a thousand years, undertake helping Africans in this way again.'[76] He accused Solanke of 'trying to drive people to "eat dirt" at his feet';[77] but the Anti-Slavery Society desisted from involving itself in a costly legal wrangle to repossess African House. Harris was bitter at what appeared to him to be a betrayal by Vischer, whom he considered 'not the kind of man with whom I would like to go tiger hunting.'[78] Colonial Office pressure and the support of Vischer ensured the appointment of a new management committee early in 1940 consisting of the right-wing Labour MP Dr L Haden-Guest, the Reverend Reginald Sorensen (who later became Labour MP for Leyton), Hanns Vischer and Solanke.[79]

The exigencies of war meant that WASU was afforded greater political leeway. The Colonial Office was anxious to appease nationalist opinion in colonial territories so as to secure continued supplies of raw materials for the war effort. Periodic threats of legal action against WASU were made by the Anti-Slavery Society and General Grey tried to get African students living on public assistance in Britain deported, claiming many were 'agitators'.[80] However, the death of Harris in 1940 took the heart out of the APS campaign and Harris' successor, the Westindian sugar planter C W W Greenidge, was less anxious to be embroiled in controversy. A new approach to the African student issue began as the Colonial Office, in particular, was anxious not to repeat the errors of Harris and the Anti-Slavery Society.

The Second World War and the Emergence of a Welfare Approach

The war years saw not only a dramatic decline in the position of Britain as a major world power, especially after the defeats at the hands of the Japanese in Asia in 1942, but also the growing recognition among prominent sections of educated opinion that racism was politically and morally unacceptable. Although this often led only to racist prejudices being driven out of public discourse into the privacy of the home and personal diaries, it did encourage a new political climate in which the British colonial doctrine of partnership, announced in 1942, led to a growing belief that black student opinion should not be antagonised by incidents of racial discrimination. This was reflected in the attitude to 12,000 black American troops being stationed in Britain at the end of 1942. The Churchill cabinet, after pressure from the Colonial Office and the minister, Lord Cranborne, rejected proposals by the Secretary of War, James Grigg, for the voluntary segregation of the black troops to isolate them from British dance halls, public houses and women.[81]

The war atmosphere helped to reduce the level of racial prejudice encountered by black students in Britain, especially in London. The pressure on accommodation was relieved as a large number of black students moved out of the capital. Prior to the outbreak of hostilities in 1939 a small survey conducted by Kenneth Little revealed widespread prejudice among landladies and guesthouse proprietors; of some 560 covered in the survey, 44.2 per cent of those in London and 37.3 per cent elsewhere revealed an 'aversion' to blacks, with attitudes ranging from 'Europeans Only' to 'No Niggers'.[82]

By the middle of June 1941, however, following the students' evacuation, Ladipo Solanke confirmed only irregular student attendance at African House, which was then charging 22/6 a week bed and breakfast, with less than half of the 12 places in the hostel occupied.[83] The survival of the hostel depended increasingly on grants from West African governments, of which only a £250 per annum grant from Nigeria had been consistently paid since 1937. There was not only a strong financial incentive for Solanke to pressurise the CO to provide financial assistance, but also the long-standing political motive of trying to broaden the department's interest away from its Aggrey House protégé. The WASU hostel, he claimed in a letter to Reginald Sorensen, one of the trustees, 'is the People's Institution as against Aggrey House the Government Institution for Imperial Colonial policy.'[84]

Aggrey House had, in fact, been closed temporarily in May 1940 after a refusal by the hostel's management committee to support the trustees in their barring a member for 'immoral conduct'. The club reopened in September the same year after a purge of a 'clique of senior members' whom the CO charged with 'using the House for their own purposes'.[85] The wartime requirements for accommodation for both black servicemen and war workers increased government pressure on the Colonial Office to step up its control of Aggrey House and expand its facilities. A Treasury grant of £1000 led to a second house being purchased as an annex, while the main source of funding for the hostel remained some £900 from colonial governments.

In the autumn of 1940 a Colonial Office committee proposed a new organisation which would be financed entirely by sources within Britain, leading to the establishment of a non-residential social and cultural centre for both Africans and Westindians.[86] This policy was reinforced by a report of the West African Governors Conference in 1939 which urged closer cooperation between Aggrey House and WASU and the possible amalgamation of the two hostels.[87]

By mid-1941, therefore, Solanke and WASU were confronting not only growing financial restrictions but also increasing pressure for uniformity and tidiness in British colonial policy which would restrict the autonomy of the institution. Despite Keith's view of Solanke as a 'difficult and contentious person',[88] the CO was anxious to bring the WASU hostel 'within the framework of our scheme'.[89] In August the deputy Prime Minister, Clement Attlee, visited the Union and the CO paid off its outstanding mortgage. By December of 1942 it had also paid for repairs to the WASU hostel costing £200, together with a further grant of £100. The CO was especially anxious to furnish accommodation for Westindian war workers who often came to London during the war on recreational visits arranged in collaboration with Moody's League of Coloured Peoples. The WASU hostel was probably felt to be too West African in orientation to provide the suitable facilities. The CO concern stemmed too from fears of further political unrest in the Westindies following the riots of 1936-37. The resulting report of the Moyne Commission was not published for the duration of the war through fear that it could be of use to enemy propaganda.

The proposed multinational non-residential centre in London never came to fruition and it was ultimately the reputation of Aggrey House upon which the CO relied, seeing it, as J L Keith minuted in October 1942, as 'of interest throughout the whole of the Colonial Empire'.[90] By March 1944 the non-residential centre idea had been transposed into

Harold Moody's scheme for a colonial cultural centre in London, although he was unable to gain the sufficient funds to establish this before his death in 1947.[91] Despite these problems, WASU managed to survive the war and continued into the 1950s as both a student centre and a hostel for the growing number of black settlers in Britain in the late 1940s. In the post-war years the Union became an important centre for African nationalist hostility to the Colonial Development and Welfare Programme. As early as June 1946 the Labour Colonial Secretary, Arthur Creech Jones, hoping to bring the Workers Education Association into black student training, wrote of his 'distress' at the 'mounting estrangement of Colonial students in this country from British thought and life, and the increasing bitterness of their attitude towards Britain and the British tradition.'[92] It was undoubtedly the black students' acute colour and racial awareness which made both Keith and his deputy, Ivor Cummings, immediately conscious of the wider political ramifications of the barring of Cummings from the Bristol Hotel on racial grounds in Lagos in 1947.[93] By then political events had already begun to pass out of the British government's control. The 1948 Accra riots initiated the process of decolonisation in West Africa which led also to the progressive abandonment of Colonial Office control in the field of student management. In 1950 the control of the student facilities was handed over to the British Council as an attempt was made to 'bring coloured students into intimate touch with the British people'.[94]

In the years between the establishment of Student Movement House in 1917 and the takeover of student affairs by the British Council in 1950, a three-fold process of control over black student bodies in Britain can be observed: missionary and philanthropic concern such as that of SCM and the Anti-Slavery Society, followed by more formal Colonial Office control during the 1940s and then a more informal governmental interest via the British Council. The pattern resembled, somewhat paradoxically, the very process of British imperial intrusion, colonisation and neo-colonial withdrawal from Africa itself from the early nineteenth century to the 1950s and early 1960s, though contracted into a short period in the closing phase of empire. Perhaps this indicates the saliency of black student politics in Britain, at least for a short time, and its wider significance both in the withdrawal from empire and the settlement of a permanent black population in Britain.

Ladipo Solanke lived in Britain through most of this period, and became drawn into establishing WASU, so he wrote to the sociologist Violaine Junod in 1953, due to the operation of the pre-war 'colour bar'. He still did not feel 'a full member of British society' and, though there had been 'improvements' so far as his personal relationships with white people in Britain were concerned, the 'colour bar' was now 'being practised by certain politicians including some non-political but highly diplomatic persons among the white elements in this country'.[95] Despite this renewal and indeed intensification of racism in British society as the withdrawal from empire began to take place, the issue of black students in Britain was seen by the 1950s in terms of their incorporation and acceptance by the white liberal educational institutions. Disproving the theory of Padmore in the early 1930s that British universities, like other institutions, were becoming increasingly racially discriminatory,[96] by the 1950s the emergence of an assimilationist ethos led, in elite institutions such as Oxford and Cambridge, to the active seeking out of black students. However, as the sociologist Sheila Kitzinger observed, this raised the problems of black identity in an integrated society in an acute form, for 'the Negro' becomes 'divested of social personality by those people who go out of their way to befriend him'.[97] Once more the black student issue highlighted a wider social process and raised the issue of assimilationist ideology which was to hit British society in a more far-reaching manner in the following two decades.

NOTES

1. George Shepperson, "Introduction" in Martin L Kilson and Robert I Rotberg (eds), *The African Diaspora: Interpretative Essays*, Harvard University Press, Cambridge (Mass), 1976, pp. 1-10; Immanuel Geiss, *The Pan African Movement*, Methuen, London, 1974, pp. 340-62.
2. A Sivanandan, "The Liberation of the Black Intellectual" in *A Different Kind of Hunger*, Pluto Press, London, 1982, p. 82; see also Chris Mullard, *Black Britain*, Allen and Unwin, London, 1973.
3. Peter Fryer, *Staying Power: The History of Black People in Britain*, Pluto Press, London, 1984, esp. pp. 324-6.
4. A P Thornton, *Imperialism in the Twentieth Century*, Macmillan Press, London, 1977, pp. 32-51.
5. Much of the previous paragraph is based on F H Brown, "Indian Students in Britain", *The Edinburgh Review*, 217, 443 (January 1913), pp. 138-56.
6. Joseph Renner Maxwell, *Advantages and Disadvantages of European Intercourse with the West Coast of Africa*, Swart and Allen, London, 1881.
7. Susan B Kaplow, "The Mudfish and the Crocodile: Underdevelopment of a West African Bourgeoisie", *Science and Society*, 41, 1977-78, pp. 317-33; Hans Werner Debrunner, *Presence and Prestige: Africans in Europe*, Basler Afrikaner Bibliographienm, Basel, 1979, pp. 368-9.
8. Edith Searle Grossmann, "A Colonial Study of London Civilisation", *The Nineteenth Century*, LXI (April 1907), pp. 560-1.
9. J P C Roach, "Victorian Universities and the National Intelligentsia", *Victorian Studies*, II, 2 (December 1959), pp. 131-50; see also John Roach, "Liberalism and the Victorian Intelligentsia", *The Cambridge Historical Journal*, XIII, i, 1957, pp. 58-81. This argument has been questioned by Christopher Harvie, "Ideology and Home Rule: James Bryce, A V Dicey and Ireland, 1880-1887", *The English Historical Review*, XCI (April 1976), pp. 298-314.
10. See chapter four.
11. Gilbert Murray, "The Exploitation of Inferior Races in Ancient and Modern Times" in Francis W Hurst *et al.*, *Liberalism and the Empire*, R Briarly Johnson, London, 1900, p. 141.
12. James Walvin, *Passage to Britain*, Penguin Books, Harmondsworth, 1984, p. 42.
13. *Bryce MSS*, Bodleian Library, Oxford, A V Dicey to J Bryce, 23 December 1907.
14. A B C Merriman-Labor, *Britons Through Negro Spectacles or A Negro in Britain*, Imperial and Foreign Co., London, 1909, p. 138.
15. *Ibid.*, pp. 149-50.
16. N G Annan, "The Intellectual Aristocracy" in J H Plumb (ed), *Studies in Social History*, Longmans, London, 1955, pp. 243-87.
17. Grossmann, *op. cit.*, p. 566.
18. George Padmore, "How Britain Governs the Blacks" in Nancy Cunard (ed), *Negro: An Anthropology*, Wishart, London, 1934, pp. 811-12.
19. K Choudray, "The Indian Student in England", *The Student Movement*, XII (January 1910).
20. See chapter three.
21. William H Seed, "The Need for Inter-Racial Unity", *Afr. Times and Or. Rev.*, November 1912.
22. *Afr. Times and Or. Rev.*, 21 April 1914.
23. Lucy Bland and Frank Mort, "Look Out For The Good Time Girl: Dangerous Sexualities as a Threat to National Health" in Bill Schwartz *et al.*, *Formations of Nation and People*, Routledge and Kegan Paul, London, 1984, pp. 142-5.
24. Jeffrey P Green, "Caribbean students in London 1917-1920 and their international connection through the Student Movement House, 32, Russell Square, London", unpublished paper, n.d., p. 1.
25. *Nathan MSS*, Rhodes House, Oxford, Circular dated 20 June 1913 outlining

Conference at Westminster Palace Hotel, 18 April 1913; Geiss, *op. cit.*, pp. 294-5.

26. *Ibid.*, F V Lugard to Watson, 27 June 1913. See also MSS British Empire 522-431, C Harcourt to Watson, 20 July 1914. Lugard continued to have doubts on the role of educated African class workers in Colonial development well into the 1930s, see Lord Lugard, "Colonial Administration", *Economics*, August 1933, p. 251.

27. Green, *op. cit.*, pp. 2-3.

28. *SCM Archives*, Selly Oak Colleges, Birmingham S17. Leaflet entitled *Student Movement House*, n.p., n.d., p. 4.

29. *SCM Archives*, Memorandum from the Foreign Student Committee to be submitted to the General Committee of the Student Christian Movement, p. 1.

30. *Ibid.*, p. 2.

31. *SCM Arch.*, R Brewster, report entitled "Work Among Foreign Students", June 1923, p. 4.

32. *Ibid.*, p. 5.

33. K Zentariah, "An Indian in England", *The Student Movement*, XXIII, I (October 1920).

34. Preben Kaarsholm, "Imperialist Ideology, Romantic Anti Capitalism and J A Hobson", unpublished paper, African Studies Institute, University of the Witwatersrand, July 1982. For E D Morel see Paul B Rich, *Race and Empire in British Politics*, CUP, Cambridge, 1986, pp. 35-7.

35. *Anti-Slavery MSS*, Rhodes House, Oxford, MSS Brit. Emp. S23 H2/57, John Harris to Lord Cromer, 10 September 1919.

36. *Race and Empire in British Politics*, esp. chapter two.

37. MSS Brit. Emp. S23 H2/57, J Harris to J T Gumede, 24 May 1921.

38. Ayube M Edun, *London's Heart Probe and Britain's Destiny*, Arthur H Stockwell, London, 1935, p. 15.

39. W F Elkins, "Hercules and the Society of People of African Origin", *Caribbean Studies*, 2, 4 (January 1972), pp. 47-8: Jeffrey P Green, *Edmund Thornton Jenkins*, Greenwood Press, Westport, 1982, pp. 64-6; Jeffrey P Green, *A Black Community?: London, 1919*.

40. MSS Brit. Emp. S22 G432, F E M Hercules to J Harris, 25 December 1918.

41. F E M Hercules, "The African and Nationalism", *The African Telegraph*, December 1918.

42. *The African Telegraph*, January – February 1919.

43. MSS Brit. Emp. S22 G432, F E M Hercules to J Harris, 24 May, 11 June 1919.

44. Geiss, *op. cit.*, esp. pp. 283-93.

45. For the riots see Elkins, *op. cit.*, pp. 49-50; Fryer, *op. cit.*, pp. 298-313.

46. MSS Brit. Emp. S23 H2/57, J Harris to J W Taylor, 16 June 1919.

47. Elkins, *op. cit.*, p. 54.

48. MSS Brit. Emp. S23 H2/57, T Buxton to J Harris, 30 April 1919.

49. *Ibid.*, F E M Hercules to J Harris, 29 April 1919; R Broadhurst to J Harris, 23 April 1919.

50. *Ibid.*, R Broadhurst to J Harris, 17 July 1919.

51. *Ibid.*, F A Cockin to J Harris, 13 May 1919.

52. *Ibid.*, J W Taylor to J Harris, 15 June 1919.

53. *Ibid.*, R Broadhurst to J Harris, 29 December 1921.

54. *Ibid.*, J Harris to R Miller, 1 December 1919. In 1919 SCM had discussed with the YMCA the possibility of joint action to provide a hostel for African students. *SCM Arch.*, A69, Tissington Tatlow to Temple, 3 February and 4 June 1919; Tissington Tatlow to R Miller, 3 July 1919.

55. MSS Brit. Emp. S22 191, J Harris to T Buxton, 9 March 1922. See also Paul B Rich, *White Power and the Liberal Conscience: Racial Segregation and South African Liberalism, 1921-1960*, Manchester University Press, Manchester, 1984, esp. pp. 11-32, 63-4.

56. Philip Garigue, "The West African Students Union: A Study in Culture Contact", *Africa*, XXIII, 1953, p. 56; Geiss, *op. cit.*, pp. 297-8.

57. Garigue, *op. cit.*, p. 57.

58. WASU, 8 January 1929.

59. Ladipo Solanke, *United West Africa at the Bar of the Family of Nations*, London, 1927, p. 66.

60. *Ibid.*, citing *West Africa*, 31 May 1919.

61. For an assessment of Olivier see Paul B Rich, "Industrialisation, Fabianism and Race: Sydney Olivier and the liberal critique of South African segregation", ICS, *Collected Seminar Papers*, vol. 14, no. 37 (1988), pp. 64-74, London; Mohammed Nun El-Amin, "Sydney Olivier on Socialism and Colonies", *The Review of Politics*, 39 (1977), pp. 521-39; Richard A Lobdell, "Socialism, Imperialism and Sydney Olivier", unpublished paper, University of Manitoba, 1984.

62. MSS Brit. Emp. S23 H1/17, Note of proceedings of a joint conference between the Welfare of Africans in Europe War Fund (surplus) Committee and the African Club Organising Committee, under the Chairmanship of Dr Drummond Shiels, held in the Colonial Office at 11.30 am, Monday 27 July 1931.

63. *Ibid.*, p. 2.

64. *Ibid.*, p. 2.

65. *Ibid.*, p. 3.

66. *Reginald Sorensen Papers*, House of Lords Library, SOR/168, report on WASU Hostel submitted by Dr R B Wellesley Cole from Data Supplied by Mr Ladipo Solanke, n.d.

67. WASU, *The Truth About Aggrey House*, London, 1934, pp. 4-5.

68. MSS Brit. Emp. S23 H1/21, L Odunsi (Secretary, African Hostel Defence Committee) to J Harris, 3 April 1934, J Harris to Odunsi, 24 April 1934.

69. Paul B Rich, "Philanthropic Racism in Britain: The Liverpool University Settlement, The Anti-Slavery Society and the issue of 'half caste' children, 1919-1951", *Immigrants and Minorities*, 3, 1 (March 1984), esp. pp. 79-82.

70. MSS Brit. Emp. S23 H/21, J Harris to H Vischer, 3 December 1935.

71. *Ibid.*, H Vischer to J Harris, 5 December 1935.

72. MSS Brit. Emp. S23 H1/27, Memorandum of the claim of the West African Students Union to the Hostel Known as African House at No. 1, South Villas, Camden Square, NW1, 24 February 1939, p. 6.

73. *Ibid.*, Notes by Sir John Harris on Memorandum Submitted from the West African Students Union Through Solicitors, pp. 1-2.

74. MSS Brit. Emp. S23 H1/26, H Vischer to J Harris, 28 July and 1 August 1939.

75. *Ibid.*, J Harris to H Vischer, 10 August 1939.

76. *Ibid.*, J Harris to H Vischer, 5 March 1940.

77. *Ibid.*, J Harris to H Vischer, 2 April 1940.

78. *Ibid.*, J Harris to Drake-Brockman, 13 February 1940.

79. *Ibid.*, W H Grey, *Circular to Members of the Welfare Committee*, 21 February 1940.

80. *Ibid.*, W H Grey to Rt Hon Sir John Anderson, 10 July 1940.

81. Christopher Thorne, "Britain and the Black GIs: Racial Issues and Anglo-American Relations in 1942", *New Community*, 3 (Summer 1974). Thorne's assessment of the Churchill cabinet's response to the issue has been partly challenged by Graham Smith, *When Jim Crow Met John Bull*, London, 1987, who points out that segregation occurred in practice at the local level.

82. Kenneth Little, *Negroes in Britain*, Routledge and Kegan Paul, London, 1972 (first ed. 1948), p. 294.

83. SOR/168, Notes of an interview between the Rt Hon Mr George Hall MP (Under Secretary of State for the Colonies) and Mr Ladipo Solanke (Warden WASU), Wednesday 11 June 1941.

84. *Ibid.*, L Solanke to R Sorensen, 12 May 1941.

85. *Ibid.*, J L Maloney, Memorandum on Aggrey House for Advisory Committee on the Welfare of Coloured People in the United Kingdom (ACWUK), no. 9, 16 September 1942, p. 1.

86. *Ibid.*, p. 2.

87. *Ibid.*, J L Maloney, Memorandum on African House for ACWUK, 10 October 1942, p. 1.

88. CO 876/56, J L Keith, minute, 19 June 1942.

89. *Ibid.*, J L Maloney to Sir Sidney Abrahams, 9 October 1942; minute, 13 November 1942. Hanns Vischer pointed out that Solanke 'in his strange way' was 'fighting for exactly what we want him to have', MSS Brit. Emp. S23 H1/26, H Vischer to C W W Greenidge, 31 July 1941.

90. CO 876/20, J L Keith, minute, 24 October 1942.

91. David A Vaughan, *Negro Victory: The Life of Dr Harold Moody*, Independent Press, London, 1950, p. 133.

92. CO 876/72, Arthur Creech Jones, minute, 26 June 1946.

93. J E Flint, "Scandal at the Bristol Hotel: Some Thoughts on Racial Discrimination in Britain and West Africa and its Relationship to the Planning of Decolonisation, 1937-47", *Journal of Imperial and Commonwealth History*, XII, 1 (October 1983), pp. 74-93.

94. *News Chronicle*, 30 December 1949; "Political and Economic Planning", *Colonial Students in Britain*, P.E.P., London, 1955, p. 51. The British Council called a conference of interested welfare organisations and this led, from 1950, to a Standing Committee that co-ordinated the work of 44 organisations.

95. Ladipo Solanke to Violaine Junod, 2 February 1953, encl. questionnaire. I am grateful to Miss V Junod for this document.

96. "Race Prejudice in England" (*The Negro Worker*, March 1932), reproduced in Cunard, *op. cit.*, pp. 553-5. The author was almost certainly Padmore.

97. Sheila Kitzinger, "Conditional Philanthropy Towards Coloured Students in Britain", *Phylon*, 21, 1960, p. 172; see also Sheila Webster, "Negros in Bluebrick: An Analysis of the Assimilation of African and West Indian Students in the Universities of Oxford and Cambridge", MS, University of Edinburgh, n.d.

Chapter Seven

Blacks in Britain: Response and Reaction 1945-62

The settlers from the Westindies and South Asia who arrived in Britain between the late 1940s and the 1960s found a society remarkably unprepared for their incorporation into its elaborate class and cultural networks. From the very start of this post-war migration, when the *SS Empire Windrush* docked at Tilbury in June 1948 with 492 passengers from the Westindies, there was a mixture, in governmental circles, of fear of impending racial conflict and a more detached dismissal of the whole issue as a storm in a teacup. For example, one Home Office civil servant minuted that 'sooner or later action must be taken to keep out the undesirable elements of our colonial population', for their presence in Britain would present 'a formidable problem' to the various government departments concerned.[1] Some government ministers, including the Prime Minister, Clement Attlee, refused to take the 'Jamaican party' to the United Kingdom 'too seriously',[2] although anxiety in official circles increased over the following years. It was pointed out to the Colonial Secretary, Arthur Creech Jones, as early as 1948 that any attempt to restrict this immigration through legislation would have to come from Britain itself rather than the colonies, otherwise there would be massive opportunities for evasion. 'In the case of Jamaica,' some ministerial notes pointed out, 'the next country would be Cuba, and obviously we cannot control the Government of Cuba.'[3]

In the initial stages of the immigration, therefore, the Colonial Office, which was seen as the department most responsible for the issue, sought a tightening up of informal controls. Guidelines were issued to Colonial governors for informing would-be immigrants of the problems they would face in terms of jobs and accommodation in post-war Britain. There was a particular concern that the pattern of pre-war race relations in the seaport towns of Cardiff and Liverpool, where there had been rioting and attacks on black seamen by white mobs in 1919, might be repeated on a larger scale. Given the problems of accommodation shortages and discrimination against blacks in employment, the new black settlers were seen as likely to drift to the dockland areas and reinforce the existing black communities that had grown up there.[4]

The main experience of the Colonial Office lay in promoting economic development in the colonial context through funds released via the 1940 and 1945 Colonial Development and Welfare Acts, and the immigration from the Caribbean to the "mother country" was seen as a nuisance that was, by and large, outside its area of experience or function.[5] It was believed

> *That it is very greatly to the detriment of the Colonial peoples themselves that this influx should continue. We see no prospect that if it does continue we can avoid the creation of serious social problems such as the growth of depressed coloured quarters in English cities and a considerable increase in colour feeling on the part of the general population.*[6]

But continue the 'influx' did, so that by 1953 the numbers of black immigrants were some 3,000 a year. Other government departments, such as the Ministry of Labour and the Home Office, were forced to formulate a policy in response to the migration, for it was recognised, in almost all sections of official opinion, that racial segregation was politically and socially undesirable. The victory of the Allies in the war had been over Nazi "racism", an increasingly incendiary political term and one that was coming to be employed by nationalist movements in the colonies. The main government emphasis became one of trying to encourage educational and industrial training programmes for the immigrants to fit them for industrial employment. This was also a means for dispersing the immigrants to different towns and cities and became a favourite option of the Inter-Departmental Committee on Colonial People in the United Kingdom, which was chaired by a Colonial Office official, J L Keith. He had had considerable experience during the war with problems confronting black students and seamen in Britain. The Committee acted as an important forum for the emergence of a common official attitude in the late 1940s.

By June 1950 the Labour cabinet recognised that the "colour problem" presented by the black settlers was of sufficient magnitude to necessitate the appointment of a cabinet sub-committee to look into the question of immigration control. One memorandum submitted jointly by the Home Office, Ministry of Labour, Colonial Office and Ministry of Transport estimated the black population in Britain to be 30,000 and urged that any proposed law restricting immigration would have to be 'of general application irrespective of race or colour'.[7] In its conclusion, the sub-committee, while not ruling out the possibility of immigration control in the future, rejected the idea for the present, due to the 'comparatively small scale of immigration into this country', and 'the important and controversial issues of policy involved in legislation to control it'.[8] With legislation rejected as a means for managing the emergent "colour problem", the policy of successive governments, both Labour and Conservative, over the following decade was one of benign neglect and a shifting of responsibility for the immigrants' reception and eventual assimilation onto the voluntary sector and local authorities.

It was the hope of some researchers and investigators at this time that more government involvement in facilitating racial assimilation could be encouraged. An East African student, Derek Bamuta, conducted a six-week survey into conditions in Stepney, in London's dockland, in 1949 where an identifiable "coloured quarter" was emerging. Bamuta noted the racial discrimination against West Africans trying to settle in the area and the difficulties in finding accommodation. He recommended the establishment of 'some organisation that will help these people to become full members of the country with a sense of responsibility towards the country as a whole.'[9]

The response of Arthur Creech Jones, the Colonial Secretary, in January 1950 was, however, half-hearted. Reflecting the general reluctance of the Colonial Office to get involved in any direct welfare effort, Creech's secretary, N D Watson, wrote in response to an enquiry from Downing Street that such efforts should be made on a local basis for 'experience shows that many of these people are virtually unemployable in this country and are a source of a good deal of racial friction.'[10]

This policy, as Lord Listowel, a Labour junior minister at the Colonial Office, outlined in an address to the London Council of Social Service in July 1949, meant the use of local voluntary bodies so as to prevent 'the creation of specific coloured areas in this country'. For the most part the policy was continued by the Conservative government after its return to office in 1951. While there was a suggestion from Winston Churchill in cabinet for a "keep Britain white" campaign in the 1955 general election, [12] the Conservatives eschewed making immigration a party political issue during this period and continued to hope, at least until the riots in Nottingham and Notting Dale in 1958, that the voluntary sector would be capable of handling the issue, thereby keeping it out of politics.

The local councils of social service up and down the country approached the area of black immigration with very limited experience. The idea of "social service" had quite a long tradition in British philanthropy and can be traced back to the rise of a secularised Anglican conscience at the end of the nineteenth century centred around the notion of "duty". The National Council of Social Service was established in 1919 and had developed the notion of "community service" in response to growing patterns of suburbanisation around housing estates. Local councils of social service had concerned themselves with local community centres, clubs for the unemployed and rural community councils in villages. They had not been concerned with "multiracial" issues, which had been confined mainly to the seaport towns. In Liverpool, the university community had been involved in the issue in the late 1920s and 1930s through the Liverpool Association for the Welfare of Half-Caste Children.[13] Other issues surrounding colour, like the problems confronting black students in Britain, had been taken up either by activist bodies like the West African Students Union (WASU) in London, run by Ladipo Solanke, or the various universities concerned.[14] In addition, the Colonial Office had taken a welfare interest in students during the war years through fear of rising colonial nationalism, but by the early 1950s it had devolved its responsibility to the British Council. Thus, the councils of social service approached the issue of post-war black immigration with few clear guidelines and tended to resort to whatever "expert" advice there was available, whether from missionaries with a colonial experience, a small number of interested social workers or from social anthropologists and sociologists who were by this time becoming interested in the new subject area of "race relations".

Expert and specialised opinion on race and immigration was scarce in Britain at this time and could do little to prevent the emergence of a popular stereotype of racial catastrophe and conflict deeply shaped by the colonial experience. The very process of withdrawal from empire in the 1950s exacerbated the traditional images in the popular mind. In Kenya, for example, the Mau Mau movement reinforced existing stereotypes of blacks as bloodthirsty savages in the tradition of Rider Haggard and John Buchan. However, the fact that black immigrants to Britain were settling in urban localities meant, for the most part, that African bush images or the exotic Asian settings of Kipling's Indian stories needed to be supplemented by urban landscapes to have greater credibility. One obvious parallel was that of the United States and particularly Harlem, in New York, which by this time had been fairly well established in the public mind through films, black singers, musicians and popular novels with a Harlem background. As early as 1951 one writer, Mervyn Jones, warned in the *New Statesman* that 'distinctively Negro quarters, on the American model, are coming into existence to replace the old cosmopolitan neighbourhoods normal before the war.' Citing the pattern of black settlement in Stepney, Camden Town, Paddington and North Kensington, with a "spill" area off

Tottenham Court Road, Jones saw a pattern similar to New York and the way Harlem was created.[15] This image of seediness and of blacks linked to gangsterism and prostitution deepened during the 1950s as the shortage of accommodation drove black immigrants into the cheapest housing available, often at the mercy of unscrupulous rack-renting landlords.

Given these doubts in even mainstream liberal circles on the future of race relations, the efforts of voluntary bodies had a somewhat inauspicious start. The local social services journal, *Social Service Quarterly*, displayed a naive optimism in the early 1950s with its hope that the black immigrants could be fairly easily assimilated into its more general scheme of flourishing local communities. The language that was used, even into the early 1960s, was derived from American race relations sociology and the tradition of the Chicago school of social science, which had perceived a "race relations cycle" of contact, confrontation, accommodation and eventual assimilation. This mode of thought owed much to biological metaphors derived from Darwinism, and tended to reduce the political dynamics involved in black-white relationships to a series of technical "problems" of mutual understanding and adjustment. In early 1962, Joan Maizels wrote in the *Social Service Quarterly* that 'assimilation' in Britain would be 'facilitated by the growth of social relationships and by the spread of mutual understanding between host and immigrant communities. To break down the barriers which impede these developments is now essential.'[16] The ultimate state of 'assimilation' tended to remain unquestioned. In the 1950s not only white race relations experts but some black political spokesmen, such as Learie Constantine, had spoken of assimilation in a period before the rise of the Black Power Movement in the United States and the renewed emphasis upon independent black political and cultural assertion.[17]

During the mid-1950s a number of associations were established by both local authorities and the voluntary associations in order to promote the ideals of interracial understanding. This was a time of growing labour shortages and Westindian workers were sought by various employers, such as London Transport, to do jobs for which white workers could not be found. In the Midlands a Commonwealth Welfare Council was founded by 14 West Midland local authorities, while in Willesden an International Friendship Council was formed. The foundation of a Brotherhood Association in Lambeth in March 1956, however, gave vent to divisions in the ruling Labour group, for some critics argued that there had not been such an association for early immigrants, such as the Eastern European Jews. The friendship councils, nevertheless, did act as a forum for discussion for small groups of concerned blacks and whites on what was becoming commonly known as "the colour problem". Some of these councils were willing to confront the political issues surrounding immigration. This was in contrast to Mary Attlee's Racial Unity

Movement,[18] which hoped that the whole issue of immigration could be satisfactorily dealt with through a government enquiry.

Beyond the more general discussion of race matters and the establishment of social links through the interracial councils, the question of overt racial discrimination gradually gained a tighter political focus. As early as 1950 a bill to outlaw racial discrimination had been introduced into Parliament by Reginald Sorensen, Labour MP for Leyton, who had long had links with black groups in Britain, such as WASU. Although this bill was thrown out, as were succeeding bills introduced throughout the 1950s by Fenner Brockway, the matter was seen as of crucial importance by civil libertarians. Discrimination against blacks in employment and housing had a long history; Harold Moody's League of Coloured Peoples had fought for black nurses to get jobs in hospitals in the 1930s. In 1944 the cricketer Learie Constantine won a court case against the Imperial Hotel in Russell Square which had refused him admittance due to the supposed hostility of white American officers staying there. Brockway saw the issue as of great moral significance at a time when Britain's liberal reputation was seen to count for something abroad. For the National Council for Civil Liberties, too, with a tradition of fighting against fascism and anti-Semitism going back to the 1930s, racial discrimination was of great importance and one of its leaflets in 1956, *It isn't Colour bar but...*, stated that the period was now a testing time, for:

> *All over the world the eyes of coloured people – and of colour conscious whites too – are on Britain. Are we to become the laughing stock of all the negro baiters everywhere, because we who were once bold and high principled in our condemnation of them now crudely submit to their dogmas and imitate their practices?*[19]

This shows the rather exaggerated self-importance which was attached to British liberal principles and indicates that progressive opinion still upheld the idea of a British "civilising mission", despite the actual decline of British imperial power. Certainly, the humanitarians tended to overlook the tradition of British racism that stemmed from Carlyle, Governor Eyre and the Victorian imperialists who had by no means always resisted the 'negro baiters'. This misreading of history was, part of a much wider body of opinion which had emerged during the interwar years, championing the Commonwealth ideal and a pacific conception of the former British empire, couched in terms of bringing Whig ideals of freedom and justice to colonial territories now demanding independence.

The academic study of race and immigration at this time tended to avoid historical issues in favour of more detailed local and community studies. The School of Anthropology at the University of Edinburgh in the early 1950s, for example, saw the main issue as that of sociological obstacles to the assimilation of the black "newcomers" due to racial values entrenched in British society. Research by a number of students at Edinburgh gathered by Dr Kenneth Little (who had himself published a study of the black community in Cardiff in 1948 under the title *Negroes in Britain*) made it clear that the black population was not a single community. It was sharply divided on class, religious and cultural grounds. There was resistance to assimilation from some of the black communities themselves, such as the Moslem community on Tyneside, which the black sociologist, Sydney Collins, described in *Coloured Minorities in Britain* in 1957.[20] Michael Banton, in a study of the black population in Stepney that was published as *The Coloured Quarter* in 1955, wrote of the structural and cultural divisions between different groups of settlers, especially between Westindians, West Africans and Pakistanis, so that some groups became 'accommodating' to the dominant British society, others 'adapting'.[21] Given this pattern of sociological research, which was to grow voluminously in the years ahead, it was clear even at this early stage that coordinated black politics would be difficult to establish in Britain and it was not going to be easy to form one dominant black political body like the NAACP in the United States.

Kenneth Little had been impressed by some aspects of the US pattern after a year at Fisk University in 1949-50. In 1953 he submitted a memorandum to the Labour Party's National Executive Committee that argued for legislation modelled on the Fair Employment Practices legislation of the United States, as well as 'colour bar legislation' that could be a means of 'stirring the national conscience and of creating a new standard of public behaviour in relation to coloured people'.[22] The Commonwealth Sub-Committee of the Labour Party National Executive Committee, however, was persuaded against any legislation 'for a purely propaganda value', and focused instead on specific discriminatory abuses in leases, inns and public houses, lodging houses and dance halls and in employment.[23] The campaign slowly gained momentum and won over wavering opinion in the political centre after the 1958 Notting Dale and Nottingham riots.[24] A number of critics on the left saw the riots as the product of social tensions that required more radical action than the moral appeals to a common human brotherhood from the interracial councils. Norman Manley, who had written a doctoral thesis on race relations in Liverpool, appealed for a mobilisation of 'the solid traditional and powerful British opinion which sets its face against colour prejudice and all forms of intolerance.'[25] The Labour Party was seen as a focus of mainstream liberal resistance to racial intolerance. In the period after 1958 there was a growing politicisation of British race relations, which had the additional effect of increasing pressure for immigration control.

While some Labour activists, such as the Party's Commonwealth

Officer, John Hatch, were keen to formulate a strong political response to the events of the summer of 1958, there were worries even at this stage that race and immigration were issues that might lose the Party the support of white working-class voters. Kenneth Little wrote to the Party's leader, Hugh Gaitskell, warning that mere 'book knowledge' of the issue was not enough and it was necessary to have a sociological knowledge of the audience to whom one was appealing.[26] Some recent converts to anti-discrimination legislation, such as the Welfare Liaison Officer of the British Caribbean Welfare Service and the Jamaican civil servant Ivo de Souza, were optimistic that it would not be difficult for the Party to gain public support for the measure. But the reports that came in from various constituencies in which black immigrants had settled were not auspicious. The Secretary of the Vauxhall Labour Party, for example, wrote that 'the coloured people who come to live in this borough appear to have no desire whatever to be clasped to our white bosom, nor to be welcomed with open arms to either our family or social life.' The immigrants were, she noted, 'completely indifferent to efforts made to absorb them or to make them feel at home', and that 'not only should sympathy and understanding be extended to coloured immigrants, but that attention should be paid to the natural reactions of working-class white people under present circumstances.'[27]

The phenomenon of white working-class nativism was by no means new in British politics for it had surfaced at the time of agitation against the immigration of Jews from Eastern Europe at the turn of the century and later during the attempts by the British Union of Fascists to mobilise working-class support against Jews in the 1930s. Anti-black nativism in the 1950s came in the wake of the shock to national prestige in the Suez debacle of 1956 and became part of a conservative and more introverted nationalism anchored around an increasingly self-conscious conception of Britishness.[28] There was sometimes a class definition to this racial nationalism. One angry correspondent wrote to the Secretary of the Labour Party that 'many older men and not so old have been forced on the scrap heap by the cheap unskilled labour market... I'm all for the betterment of the Coloureds in their *own lands*. Not the betterment of the rich classes of this land who send them here to keep us in fear of work and future employment.'[29] This working-class racism buttressed an increasingly vocal Conservative and right-wing hostility to black immigration by the end of the 1950s as disillusion with the notion of the Commonwealth began.

There had been calls for immigration control from the Conservative back benches, but as the immigration figures rose to some 58,000 in 1960 the pressures became more vocal. Black immigration, argued *The Spectator* following the 1958 riots, was contributing to a 'ghetto style of living', for the immigrants 'flood into a few slum and near slum areas, creating antagonisms among the poor whites already installed there, and providing the kind of community where crime and gangsterism can easily breed.'[30] This imagery of a dehumanised 'flood' creating pathological social conditions of crime and gangsterism became increasingly popular in informed discussion and in its most extreme form led to a racism that vehemently opposed black-white relationships and marriage on the eugenic grounds of social health. G C L Bertram (a Fellow of St John's College, Cambridge) warned, in a pamphlet published by the Eugenics Society in 1958, that the miscegenation of black immigrants with whites was socially deleterious since they brought 'measurable and largely inheritable physical attributes below the average for the United Kingdom'.[31] But this argument was based on the increasingly obsolescent pseudoscience of anthropometry and the measurement of physical types by physical anthropologists, though it was persuasive enough to be used by Lord Elton in a book against black immigration published in 1965 entitled *The Unarmed Invasion*.[32] For the most part, mainstream political opinion that favoured immigration control did not use explicitly racist arguments to support their case, but a more ambiguous set of assertions based on fears for the future and a vision of the breakdown of social and moral order. The involvement of teenage "Teddy Boys" in the 1958 riots was an important theme in this respect, and one writer in *The Contemporary Review*, Esme Wynne-Tyson, saw the 'enforced intermingling' of black and white races in Britain as threatening the nation's youth:

> *The 'hot' music, primitive dances, and other sensual practices of the coloured races, have permeated with their devolutionary influences every corner of a once proud civilization, debasing and obstructing the process of an originally highly ethical people.*[33]

This association of the black presence with moral decline became popularised through the media; the 1959 film *Sapphire* linked the mixed race "half-caste" with prostitution and the underworld (although this film did contain many useful documentary aspects which pointed out the social diversity of the immigrants and the problems of white racism). The National Council of Social Service tried to defend the immigrants, especially the Westindians, from charges of "loose living" in its circular, *Nacoss News*, but nevertheless admitted 'of all the possible causes of difficulty and tension ... differences of outlook and ways of living remain the most intractable', and noted the charges of some whites concerning 'the noisy social habits' of some immigrants.[34]

"Race relations" became a serious industry as growing ties were forged with the newly established Institute of Race Relations in London, which had hived off from the Royal Institute of International Affairs in 1958 under the directorship of Philip Mason, and had developed a British interest as well as a wider international one. The recognition that social work and the easing of racial tensions in many inner cities required increasingly specialised expertise encouraged a climate favouring immigration control in order that resources could be geared to coping with those immigrants who had already settled in Britain. There was a concern over the ability of the social services to maintain an adequate level of social control in the inner city areas. This enhanced the back-bench Conservative and constituency pressure in favour of legislative restriction. After years of resisting these appeals through fear of antagonising opinion in the Westindies and India, the Conservative government finally decided to introduce a bill in the autumn of 1961. Speaking in support of the measure, the Home Secretary, R A Butler, noted that the essence of the bill was 'control', for the voluntary sector could 'deal with limited numbers only, and, if the numbers of new entrants are excessive, their assimilation into our society presents the gravest difficulty.'[35]

The 1962 Commonwealth Immigrants Act was the result of a new determination to intervene in this area and initiate a measure of restriction on the numbers of black immigrants. There had been measures to control immigration through the 1905 and 1914 Alien Acts, and in 1925 the Special Restriction (Coloured Alien Seamen) Order had been passed to restrict the entry of black "alien" seamen, some of whom claimed British citizenship but were unable to produce the necessary documentation. There had traditionally been powerful political pressures inhibiting the restriction of Commonwealth immigrants, and it was this concern for the Commonwealth connection which the 1962 Act overrode. Initiating a new pattern of restriction of immigrants from the Caribbean and South Asia, the legislation brought Britain, as the former imperial mother country, into line with her more racially conscious ex-colonial daughters. Restriction of black immigration had first been initiated in Australia and New Zealand in 1901 to exclude Asian and Chinese immigrants and prevent competition with white labour. Based on an education test developed in Natal, these restrictions had been introduced in a climate of militant Anglo-Saxonism and belief in the inherent superiority of white racial stocks.[36] Although the supporters of the 1962 legislation (apart from an extreme right-wing fringe) desisted from justifying it in such terms, the measure did echo some of the previous patterns of restriction in the white dominions, even though the criterion of admittance was through a voucher system gearing numbers of likely "newcomers" to the likely jobs available for them.

Furthermore, the Act marked an important shift away from notions of a benign "civilising" mission behind the Commonwealth ideal. The 1960s saw increasing reference to the "integration" rather than the "assimilation" of black immigrants and there was a growing awareness among welfare bodies and those in the "race industry" that Britain was becoming an ethnically and culturally plural society. The establishment of identifiable ethnic communities in many inner cities led to the new field of "community relations" which began to replace the earlier discussion of "race relations" in official parlance. The impact of the change on wider public discussion was not immediately apparent. By the time of the general election in 1964, race had become an increasingly important issue in electoral politics. Far from putting a damper on racial issues in British politics by tightening up government control over the numbers of black immigrants, the Commonwealth Immigrants Act marked the emergence of race as a national political issue. In the case of cities like Birmingham, as the next chapter shows, this led to a pattern of partial residential segregation of ethnic minority communities in metropolitan suburbs.

NOTES

1. HO 213/714, S E Dadley, minute, 28 May 1948.
2. HO 213/715, C R Attlee to J D Murray MP, 5 July 1948.
3. *Arthur Creech Jones Papers*, Rhodes House, Oxford, ACJ 56/4, Jamaicans Arriving at Tilbury, Supp. Notes for Sec. of State, n.d.
4. MT 9/5463, W H Hardman (Minister of Labour) to J L Keith, 22 June 1949. Keith was also anxious to avoid the establishment of permanently segregated black communities in inner city areas, *ibid.*, J L Keith to Under Sec. of State, HO, 3 September 1948.
5. *Ibid.*, J L Keith to Under Sec. of State, HO, 3 September 1948.
6. CO 876/234, J B Wilson, minute, 2 September 1950.
7. CAB 130/61 Gen 325/2, Memo by the Home Office, Min. of Labour and Nat. Serv., Commonwealth Rel. Office, Col. Office and Min. of Transport, 17 July 1950.
8. CAB 130/6/27215 Gen 325, second meeting on Immigration of British subjects into the United Kingdom, minutes of meeting held on 10 January 1951. For further discussion of this policy see Paul B Rich, *Race and Empire in British Politics*, CUP, Cambridge, pp. 182-91.
9. CO 876/231, Derek Bamuta, *Report of an investigation into conditions of the coloured People in Stepney, E.I.*, 1950.
10. *Ibid.*, N D Watson to E G Cass, 18 January 1950.
11. CO 876/231, Address by Lord Listowel to the London Council of Social Service, 6 July 1949.
12. Harold Macmillan, *At The End Of the Day, 1961-1963*, The Macmillan Press, London and Basingstoke, 1973, pp. 73-4.
13. *Race and Empire in British Politics*, pp. 130-44.
14. See chapter six.
15. M Jones, "A Question of Gloom", *New Statesman*, 11 August 1951.
16. Joan Maizels, "A Local Survey of Racial Attitudes", *Social Service Quarterly*, XXXV, 3 (December 1961–February 1962), p. 116.
17. Learie Constantine, *Colour Bar*, S. Paul and Co., London 1954, 1956.
18. See chapter five.
19. NCCL, *It isn't Colour Bar but...*, in NCCL collection, Hull University Library.
20. Sydney Collins, *Coloured Minorities in Britain*, Lutterworth, London, 1957.
21. Michael Banton, *The Coloured Quarter*, Jonathan Cape, London, 1955, pp. 214-15.
22. K Little, memo entitled "Colour Bar Legislation", submitted to Commonwealth Sub Cte of the Labour Party National Executive Cte, p. 6. I am grateful to Professor Michael Banton for this document.
23. Keith Hindell, "The Genesis of the Race Relations Bill", *Political Quarterly*, 4 (October-December 1961), p. 391; Cedric Thornberry, "Commitment to withdrawal? The place of law in race relations in Britain", *Race*, 1 (1969), pp. 76-7.
24. The NCCL, for instance, considered by October 1959 that 'positive measures' to overcome colour prejudice were essential, DCL 93/2a, Hon Sec to David Pitt 7 October 1959. One undated memo pointed out that the NCCL, in taking up the immigration issue, was 'merely carrying out its mandate to defend and extend the civil liberties of the individual throughout the Commonwealth and, in this case, the United Kingdom itself.' See also *Labour Party Archives*, Walworth Road, London, Race Relations File, Ivo de Souza to J T Callaghan, 25 June 1958.
25. Norman Manley, "A Challenge to Britain", *New Statesman*, 20 September 1958.
26. *Labour Party Archives*, Race Relations File, K Little to H Gaitskell, 4 September 1958.
27. *Ibid.*, Mrs Elsie L Boltz, Gen Secretary, Vauxhall Labour Party, to Eric Whittle, 26 February 1957.
28. See chapter one. The history of this patriotism forms part of a longer study in which I am engaged entitled *Ruined Eden: The Politics of British Patriotism*.
29. *Labour Party Archives*, Race Relations File, Bernard Rainsford to the Secretary, The Labour Party, 3 September 1958.

30. *Spectator*, 5 September 1958.

31. *The Times*, 30 September 1958. The pamphlet also warned that 'outbreaks of reactionary distaste and race violence' would be 'all too probable in the United Kingdom as at intervals elsewhere in the world.'

32. Lord Elton, *The Unarmed Invasion*, G Bles, London, 1965. See also Paul B Rich, "Conservative Ideology and Race in Modern British Politics" in Zig Layton Henry and Paul B Rich (eds), *Race, Government and Politics in Britain*, The Macmillan Press, London and Basingstoke, 1986, pp. 45-72.

33. Esme Wynne-Tyson, "Thoughts on the Colour Problem", *Contemporary Review*, January 1959, p. 43.

34. *Nacoss News*, 63 (December 1961-January 1962).

35. *Parliamentary Debate*, House of Commons, 16 November 1961, col. 649.

36. Charles Price, " 'White' Restrictions on 'Coloured' Immigration", *Race*, VII, 3 (1966), pp. 217-34.

Chapter Eight

The Politics of Race and Segregation in British Cities: The Case of Birmingham, 1945-1976

The Problem of 'Segregation'

The establishment of ethnic minority settlements in a number of British towns and cities in the years since 1945 has led a number of social analysts to make comparisons with other patterns of urban race relations, such as those in the United States and South Africa. In part, this can be seen as the result of a comparatively provincial society such as Britain struggling to acquaint itself with the complexities of "race issues" which hitherto had tended to be the preserve of a small coterie of specialists who had been involved in colonial race relations.[1] There was an additional tendency, though, of seeking to warn and alert the British public of the possible social dangers involved in the establishment of black communities in urban locales. Here situations might emerge resembling those of the United States, and especially its large black area of Harlem, New York, which connoted both the exotic and a threat to conventional morals. Indeed, from an early stage of New Commonwealth immigration, it seemed that ethnic minority settlement would pose major challenges to the conventional wisdom of urban and town planning (inherited to a large degree from the Progressivist movement in both Britain and the United States earlier in the century) which emphasised the city as a coherent moral entity with a cohesive set of values integrated into a common national culture.[2]

This ideological dilemma in city planning was compounded by the late 1950s by the increasing political unacceptability of any strategy of conscious racial segregation. The international climate veered sharply away from such a doctrine in the light of both the American Supreme Court decision in 1954 (in *Brown v Board of Education*) that separate educational facilities for blacks and whites could not be equal, and the growing hostility towards the South African government's policy of apartheid. While it remained possible for social analysts and geographers to seek to measure the degree of social "segregation" that had occurred in the urban context, politically the term "segregation" had become anathema. The term denoted the continuation of older modes of white political and economic supremacy that were inherited from nineteenth-century imperial expansion and from the failure of Radical Reconstruction in the American South.[3] The experience of fighting against Nazism in the Second World War, as well as the political intricacies involved in completing a decolonisation programme from the late 1940s onwards, made successive British governments aware that it was politically impossible to accede to any requests for formal segregation of the black communities. Much of the political thinking in the Westminster–Whitehall centre was thoroughly attuned to international attitudes to race in the post-war years and, as the centre of an emerging "Commonwealth of Nations", the British government could not afford to be subject to charges of racial discrimination. In May 1950 the Colonial Secretary, James Griffiths, noted in a departmental memorandum that 'it would ... be a wrong policy to treat the colonial residents as a class apart from the community in general, though it must be recognised that they do need special guidance.'[4] In general, it was hoped that through a version of enlightened "trusteeship" the British government could ensure the absorption of the black settlers into British society without too much friction as a consequence of mounting racial prejudice.[5]

By the mid-to-late 1960s, however, there was growing anxiety in a number of race relations circles that discrimination against black immigrants in the housing market was forcing a concentration into the cheaper and more run-down areas of British inner cities, where black ghettoes might be established. In effect, a British version of racial segregation seemed likely to be created, more through unintentional neglect than conscious design. Even the strongest proponents of the idea of the pluralistic integration of the immigrant communities warned that if policies were not adopted to reverse the process there was a danger of the inner city areas becoming the repositaries of black communities who would be both divorced and alienated from mainstream British society. In 1971, Sheila Patterson argued that while the existing pattern of "segregation" had occurred on a class or colour-class basis, there was still a possibility that it could become permanent such that 'a rigid and fairly visible under-class may evolve in certain urban areas that are heavily settled by coloured immigrants, if special measures are not taken' while 'self-segregating groups can evolve out of rejection and alienation.'[6]

These doubts among the liberal school of race relations were compounded by various attempts at more radical and structural explanations of the process of immigration and settlement in Britain which saw the pattern of segregation as a consequence of an emulation of the model of colonial rule in the former imperial periphery. One of the most prominent of such explanations has been by John Rex, who has argued that black immigrants in Britain are essentially 'colonial immigrants', subject to the same kind of treatment that had formerly been meted out to both themselves and their fellow townspeople and villagers in their places of colonial origin. The assertion is frequently guarded and tentative, with little concrete evidence to back it up, but, for example, in *Race Relations in Sociological Theory* we read:

> *What* seems *to happen is that colour is taken as the indication that a man is only entitled to colonial status, and this means that he has to be placed outside the normal stratification system. The stratification system thus becomes extended to take account of additional social positions marked by a degree of rightlessness not to be found amongst the incorporated workers.*[7] (emphasis mine)

The relationship between the 'stratification system' and the operation of values is often unclear in Rex's work. In a study of Sparkbrook with Robert Moore, *Race, Community and Conflict*, 1967, Rex argues that the segregation of black immigrants was a product of the struggle between different 'housing classes' defined in Weberian terms, that is, not with reference to the means of production but as a consequence of differential access to the housing market.[8] The discrimination observed in the method of allocation of council houses by local authorities was a result of pressure from long-established residents who formed a 'housing class' separate from that constituted by the recently arrived black colonial immigrants. As a result, a basic sociological distinction can be drawn 'between local people and immigrants, and between those with normal family situations and isolates and deviants. These will live in the lodging houses.'[9]

The Rex and Moore thesis has undoubtedly been a compelling one and has done much to reinforce an analogy with the situation in South Africa where, during the mid-1920s, the white working class became drawn into an apparatus of racial segregation which blunted its potential radicalism in return for a privileged social position considerably superior to the black proletariat. The structural orientation of the approach tended to relegate the role of subjective values to comparatively marginal positions, despite the fact that, as subsequent research has indicated, they have a critical role in the operation of the housing market. Jon Gower Davies, for example, has argued, on the basis of research in Newcastle, that the Rex-Moore thesis overlooked the degree to which black, and especially Asian, immigrants chose not to apply for council houses. Many Asians were small entrepreneurs with strong values of home ownership and profit-making.[10] Similar evidence emerged from a survey conducted by Martin Plant in the Handsworth and Balsall Heath areas of Birmingham. It revealed that the high incidence of Asian home ownership in the city – 74 per cent on the basis of the 1966 census – was to a considerable degree through choice, especially as nearly all the Asian respondents did not wish to move, compared to half the whites and Westindians.[11] The Rex-Moore thesis, therefore, could be subject to the charge that, in its commitment to the values of the British welfare state and the ideal of public housing, it ignored the dimension of ethnic exclusivity which made home ownership a vital component of Asian communal identity.

A considerable number of the single immigrant men who Rex and Moore investigated in the Sparkbrook lodging houses in the "twilight zones" of the Birmingham middle ring were really on their way towards sorting themselves out into ethnic communities as their wives and children joined them from India and Pakistan. Badr Dahya has argued, on the basis of research into Pakistani communities in Bradford, Birmingham and other British locations, that there was not only a strong prevalence of the 'myth of return', but also a more general fission and fragmentation of the 'Asian community' into subgroups such as Mirpuris, Chhachhis, Pathans and Punjabis in order to maintain the kin groups of their villages of origin. In this context, 'ethnic preference' was seen to be interacting with the urban housing market in order to explain the desire of Asian ethnic communities to establish neighbourhoods where small businesses could flourish.[12] Such evidence seems to back the conclusions drawn from anthropological research which indicate a distinct cycle of ethnic minority settlement in Britain: from the early pioneer phase, to the lodging house era, the period of consolidation or family reunion, and finally a trend towards suburbanisation which could take the form of either private home ownership or residence on council estates.[13] It would be foolish to conclude that all Asian communities would necessarily wish to buy their houses. Some, especially the Asian refugees from East Africa with no 'myth of return', clearly wished to apply for council-owned property. However, the more complex pattern of Asian settlement in Britain since the early 1960s reveals no simple process of segregation, as the Rex-Moore thesis had imagined, and more complex modes of explanation are necessary.

These methodological doubts about the Rex-Moore thesis were reinforced by evidence at the subjective level of discriminatory practice which the original Sparkbrook investigation assumed was a natural derivation of the housing classes and colonial immigration hypotheses.

Anthony Richmond, for example, pointed out, on the basis of a survey conducted in Bristol, that position in the housing market has no significant correlation with attitudes towards immigration, which tend to be uniformally hostile. Eighty per cent favoured further restrictions on immigration while 60 per cent considered black immigrants had made the Bristol housing shortage worse.[14] Despite this evidence of widespread colour prejudice, the findings of Richmond's Bristol survey, published as *Migration and Race Relations in an English City*, suggest that Westindian and Asian immigrants were by no means uniquely discriminated against on grounds of colour in the housing market, but experienced discrimination as part of the wider conflict over housing as a symbol of social status. The area surveyed in Bristol, St Paul-Montpelier, was characterised by a deteriorating housing stock in which a generally high value was placed on private housing. Asians and Westindians were not alone in experiencing difficulties in obtaining housing, for 32 per cent of the Irish surveyed complained of such difficulties, compared to 40 per cent of those foreign born, although 23 per cent of the Irish and 14 per cent of other immigrants considered their present house better than the one in their home country.[15]

The focus of Richmond's research indicates that a wider framework is needed which places less emphasis on a narrowly defined conflict of 'housing classes' interpreted in generally racial terms. Rather, more significance should be attached to the general areal status of the urban zones in which immigrants, both black and white, come to reside. Clearly race is an important factor in such work, but its role needs to be tested rather than taken as a given. In the Bristol situation, even the lodging house zone was not one in which black immigrants were over-represented.[16]

In Sparkbrook a reworking of the Rex-Moore data by Valerie Karn has shown that the preponderance of immigrants in the lodging house areas was due in part to the sample chosen. It was not weighted to account for the fact that 38 per cent of Sparkbrook's houses were located in 'Sparkbrook I' instead of the 23 per cent from the 1961 census. As a consequence the proportion of the total Sparkbrook population in 'Sparkbrook I' rose from 35 per cent in the census to 56 per cent in 1964 at the time of the study, so leading to an estimated 77 per cent of the immigrants surveyed as living in the same 'lodging house zone'.[17] The distortion so produced could hardly be justified by Rex's claim that 'had we taken a random sample of all the houses in Sparkbrook we would have had such small numbers in these groups that we would not have been able to generalise about them.'[18] A spurious conventional wisdom has been built up in the wake of the book's publication which more careful empirical research has done little to dispel.[19]

The distortions produced by *Race, Community and Conflict*, however, were part of a more general attempt by certain sociologists to isolate black-white relationships in the inner cities, to the exclusion of other social processes, and relate them to a wider set of issues linked to Third World political struggles. In this endeavour, any attempt to link the sociological relationships observed in Sparkbrook to an historical process in the city of Birmingham was ignored. Indeed, Rex tried to distinguish the work of historians from sociologists by claiming that historical research was only interested in discovering 'explanatory laws as a secondary matter to the concern for assessing the evidence'.[20] The effect of this emphasis upon a generally ahistorical sociology was both to divorce the pattern of Birmingham's race relations from any systematic connection with the city's previous history and to make the case for a pattern of racial segregation in Britain that had strong resemblances to that in the American Deep South or settler Africa.[21]

The problem with analogies is that they are often empirically irrefutable; the work of Rex contains no criteria by which it can be falsified. So long as a massive generalisation regarding the nature of "colonialism" and its linkage to racism is made, "colonial immigrants" will always be the victims of an apparently malevolent British racism. There is here a sociology of guilt concerning the history of British imperialism, though in avoiding any careful attention to the historical process Rex has effectively allowed a surrogate theory of history in by the back door – one based upon the premise that a former colonial power such as Britain is in some manner bound to reproduce the pattern of power relations seen in the colonial periphery. In more recent work, Rex has consciously stressed the ideological aspects of this process, perhaps in reaction to the earlier criticisms of his reliance on structures in the Sparkbrook study. Colonials entering British society are constrained, he has argued, by a set of stereotypes suggesting low status (though the evidence of the marginality of the Irish in Sparkbrook might have indicated that this did not necessarily imply a direct connection with race). Nevertheless, a 'sociology of knowledge' is offered as a means of unravelling this 'stock of typifications', suggesting that the issues are far more concerned with a set of subjective perceptions and attitudes than was previously imagined.[22]

The new emphasis on analysing a stock of racial beliefs and typologies in the urban situation indicates that more attention might be paid to what Hazel McFerson, in a rather neglected article, has termed a 'racial tradition' in comparative political analysis. This 'tradition' denotes the set of beliefs, attitudes, ideologies and social customs which actors adopt with respect to race, and can be used to pinpoint the degree to which ascriptive as opposed to non-ascriptive criteria are employed in a particular social situation. Such traditions can be either 'flexible' or 'rigid' and these in turn can shape the degree to which race becomes structured in a particular society:

> *Race is a variable of societal organisation which cuts across and interacts with more conventional factors. Racial tradition is relevant*

for understanding social and political processes not only in societies which have recently experienced institutionalised inequalities such as slavery and colonialism, but also in societies which long ago passed those phases. The racial tradition approach does not overlook class and culture as elements of mobility and stratification, but seeks to analyze the mode and extent by which cultural and economic factors are modified by the characteristics of the prevailing structure and ideology of race relations.[23]

The emphasis upon a 'tradition' of racial beliefs also indicates the need for more detailed historical analysis of racial thought and action in order to generate distinct historical hypotheses in race relations that can be subject to empirical testing. Such an historical approach is useful not only for historians of race, but for sociologists too, for a sociology sensitive to the nuances of historical process is essential for relating structure to action.[25] It is within such an approach that the next section of this chapter will examine the role of race in Birmingham in the post-war period in order to test the work of Rex and Moore against the prevailing trends of the urban and regional process.

Race and Politics in Birmingham

Despite having a strong local identity, it is both economically and politically misleading to isolate Birmingham's historical development from wider regional movements in the West Midlands. Some recent historical writing has cast doubt on the whole notion of the city as a distinct agent of modernisation and industrialisation separated from the apparently backward rural hinterland.[26] This appears to be the case with Birmingham which, from the middle nineteenth century, was crucial as the economic and industrial hub of a Midlands region which enjoyed close links with both London and a wider set of imperial connections.[27] It was within this context that a distinctive Birmingham tradition of municipal politics emerged by the late nineteenth century, symptomatic of a cohesive civil structure that had been forged in relationship with a wider national and imperial identity in late-Victorian Britain. Joseph Chamberlain, a former mayor and prominent politician from the city, was remarkable for forging such links between an older municipal radicalism (that was sceptical of entirely *laissez faire* market processes) and a new imperial enthusiasm (seeking economic consolidation in a colonial empire that stretched from the Caribbean through Africa to India).

The attempt during the first half of the twentieth century to consolidate the British empire as a "Commonwealth of Nations" (aided by Imperial Preference after 1931) formed the immediate background to

Birmingham's acquaintance with black immigration from the former colonies. The Commonwealth ideal enabled the Birmingham political establishment to forge close ties with the Westminster-Whitehall centre of power. Both of Joseph Chamberlain's sons, Austen and Neville, became senior cabinet ministers in the interwar Conservative administrations, Neville succeeding the Bewdley iron master Stanley Baldwin as Prime Minister in 1937. The Edgbaston MP and ardent imperialist, Leo Amery, was Colonial Secretary from 1924-29 and Secretary of State for India during the Second World War. With these links the Birmingham elite felt sure that some of the older industries which had aided the empire, such as the Birmingham Small Arms Company established in Small Heath in 1861, could be superseded by newer industries. In fact, the growth of the motor vehicle and engineering trades bypassed the older Victorian suburbs such as Perry Barr, Aston, Saltley and Small Heath; these now formed the nucleus of a middle band of suburbs as railways and ribbon development drove urban expansion further outwards from the city centre.[28]

The advent of New Commonwealth immigration coincided with a political crisis as the set of links enjoyed by the Birmingham elite before the war failed to be restored in the post-war years. The growth in central government control over Birmingham's affairs during the war continued in the late 1940s, while many of the older elite in the Birmingham Unionist Association started to disappear from the scene. The President, Geoffrey Lloyd, who had come to office under Baldwin, remained in a back seat, while in 1947 a local solicitor, Sir Theodore Pritchett, succeeded one of the older grandees, Byng Kenrick, as leader of the party. A more petty bourgeois element was emerging which indicated a decline in the older families' involvement in municipal affairs and a certain professionalisation of local party politics.[29] The Conservatives, furthermore, were out of power in the Birmingham Council from 1952 to 1966. The Labour administration was keen to try and use whatever influence it could on the political centre in an attempt to make up the drastic shortage of acceptable housing. Visionaries during the war (such as the Bournville Village Trust and the City Engineer, Herbert Manzoni) had hoped that a higher standard of housing would characterise the post-war reconstruction.[30] Despite a Public Health Department survey in 1946 which revealed 81,000 houses without baths, 35,000 without separate WCs and 29,000 built back-to-back, a small-minded conservatism tended to prevail until the later 1940s. It resented cooperation with a wider regional authority on suburban planning and evinced a general belief that the city would stop growing of its own accord.

During the 1950s, the Birmingham Corporation began to recondition large numbers of run-down inner city areas in order to meet the demand for homes. The 1954 Housing Repairs and Rents Act enabled local authorities to acquire and recondition slum properties, and between

1951 and 1966 the city achieved an impressive record in demolishing or putting to alternative use 11.9 per cent of the 1951 housing stock. The overall slum clearance programme between 1945 and 1966 demolished 24,000 to 36,000 of the city's worst houses, ensuring that some of the city's working-class native inhabitants were able to move into better accommodation.[31] From 1949 onwards the local authority reflected the outlook of a number of local Labour Party groups by ensuring that new immigrants were prevented from immediate access to council housing through a five year residence rule.[32]

In many ways, the outlook conditioning Birmingham's housing policy during the first phase of the slum clearance programme of the 1950s was one of rising political nativism as the city retreated from its former status as a centre of imperial trade relationships. The cultural dimensions of this process need extensive analysis by social and cultural historians who can relate it to the debate concerning the pursuit of gentility in English culture and the resistance this engendered both to industrialisation and to the realities of urban modernism.[33] While there had been an expanding pattern of overseas imperial networks in Birmingham, the pursuit of pastoralism had been to some degree shaped by the desire to expand the city's industrial environs in order to serve the empire, where, in imperial theory at least, there lay the clean pastoral terrains of colonial possessions in Africa and Australia. This myth of the "brave new world" in the colonies, however, always had to interact with a second and more indigenous myth; the myth of "Merrie England", made visible by Shakespeare's Warwickshire, the Malvern Hills of Elgar and a gentle pastoral landscape only a short bus or car ride away.[34] After the First World War the older Chamberlainite dream of the imperial "brave new world" gave way to the "Merrie England" myth as provincial English writers such as H V Morton and J B Priestley started to castigate the ugliness of Birmingham's industrial culture. Catching a bus from Coventry to Birmingham in 1933, for example, Priestley noted on the city's outskirts:

> *In the midst of a russet solitude, we came upon a notice board saying,* **This is the City of Birmingham.** *There was nothing in sight but hedgerows, glittering fields and the mist of the autumn morning. For a moment I entertained a wild hope that this really was the City of Birmingham, that the town had been pulled down and carted away.*[35]

Birmingham, indeed, on being experienced at first hand was possibly the personification of Britain's 'urban and industrial civilisation' but, whatever the case, 'it was beastly. It was so many miles of ugliness, squalor and the wrong kind of vulgarity, the decayed anaemic kind.'[36]

Such a rejection of the city was compounded by an attempt, even after the Second World War, to try to pastoralise what was the heart of the city and, in effect, to deny its urbanity. Thus S P G Mais, writing of 'The

English Scene' in 1948, considered that 'the people of Birmingham come in the main from Shakespeare's England. They are still members of small, happy communities. In spite of its enormous size there is always a country atmosphere about the Bull Ring which is nearly the centre of the old town.'[37] This idea of the city being formed from cohesive "communities" continued to haunt discussion and analysis until at least the 1960s; it underpins Rex and Moore's Sparkbrook study. The discussion of 'the English' in the district is anchored in the idea that a cohesive working-class 'community' existed before the onslaught of economic, social and demographic change.[38] The dominance of norms of gentility from the surrounding splendour of rural Warwickshire considerably affected both the shape of the city's politics and the pursuit of further suburbanisation in the post-war years. The Labour Party leaders in control of the City Council throughout the 1950s and the newer, petty bourgeois Conservative political figures had a common interest in trying, as far as resources allowed, to transform the character and pattern of the city's housing to accord with middle-class norms. The problem with cleansing such an Augean stable, however, was that it stretched far beyond simple slum clearance. As Priestley had noted, slums could simply be pulled down; the point about Birmingham's industrial greyness was that it was 'the common stuff out of which most of our big industrial towns are made'.[39]

The significance of much of Birmingham's post-war planning lay in the fact that this "commonness" was to be transcended through a technocratic restructuring which would transform the centre of the city into one of the most modern and dynamic in Europe. The older norms of pastoral gentility would be banished from the transformed city centre, though the hope for the suburbs remained rather more limited; keeping the best, transforming the 'blight' of others[40] and pushing outwards into newer pastures through industrialised building processes. There was an overall design of trying to achieve a reasonable balance between public and private dwellings from a City Council that was distinguished in the post-war period by a remarkably high two-party control of local politics. Between 1945 and 1972, for instance, the Labour and Conservative parties controlled 98 per cent of the Council seats and 95 per cent of the total vote in a line-up that all but excluded the Liberals, who were relegated to one per cent of the seats and four per cent of the vote.[41]

It is probable that this two-party domination of local politics exacerbated the saliency of a distinction between public and private housing, defined not simply in terms of housing classes and domestic property ownership but also in terms of what Dunleavy has called 'consumption sectors'. Here, domestic property ownership becomes one of a number of variables underlying a structural model of voting in which economic, ideological and political structures shape political alignment.[42] The operation of a high degree of political consensus in the post-war years ensured that domestic property ownership could not entirely predict voting intentions, and additional factors came into play, most notably the ideological variable of "race", by the mid to late 1950s.

The 'racial tradition' in Birmingham performed a considerable role in shaping voters' perceptions of political issues, and it is by no means certain that before the advent of black immigration racial or colonial issues had no significance for long-standing Birmingham residents such as those in Sparkbrook.[43] As a city with a strong imperial past, Birmingham had a history of inculcating nationalist and imperialist values into the working class, especially in the years before the First World War.[44] While in general this declined in the interwar years, the experience of belonging to patriotic groups of boy scouts, girl guides and boys' clubs had shaped the perceptions of many middle-aged residents by the time black immigration began, and to a considerable degree a reworking of conventional imperial images occurred to fit the changing city situation.[45] As one cleric, Rev R D Jennings, pointed out in 1960, in the case of Handsworth, English people were 'clearing out' of the area such that 'the vicar's job is primarily to be a missionary and when he moves around some of these roads nearby and sees not a person with a white skin, he begins to think he ought to be paid by the SPG and not by the Ecclesiastical Commissioners.'[46]

The significance of this nativist racial consciousness in Birmingham was that it coincided with an increasing transformation of the city and the dislocation of older patterns of settlement in the areas of the middle ring wards. For the City Council, the issue by the middle 1950s was seen as one they could not easily control, with a housing waiting list of 60,000. Leading a delegation of Council members to the Home Office in January 1955, a former Lord Mayor, Alderman William Bowen, urged the government to focus on economic development programmes in the Westindies in order to try and prevent further immigration.[47] From this time onwards, a campaign was mounted by anti-immigration activists in Birmingham, such as the Conservative Councillor Charles Collett, to oppose further black immigration; and the issue of race became increasingly defined in terms of an immigration problem.[48] As long as the government rejected the city's requests, the movement appeared irresistable, and Birmingham began to set the pace for anti-immigration feeling, though a further politicisation of the issue occurred in the aftermath of the 1958 Notting Dale and Nottingham riots. While Studlar has questioned whether social environment has any effect on racial attitudes in Britain, his argument for the existence of a mass rather than regionally distinctive perception of the immigration issue is qualified by the fact that residence in the West Midlands maintained a statistically significant positive relationship with anti-immigrant opinion in both the 1964 and 1966 general elections.[49] This supports the argument that Birmingham and the West Midlands, along with London, were forerunners of a wider set of national attitudes which came to prevail by the late 1960s following a more populist mobilisation of electoral opinion by Enoch Powell and his supporters in the Conservative Party.[50]

The mobilisation of anti-immigrant opinion in Birmingham during the late 1950s had important long-term implications for wider national political debate, and it is therefore essential to understand the context in which it was allowed to develop. The significant point about the role of race in Birmingham's politics is that it occurred at a time when there was no tradition of black political organisation in the city. New Commonwealth immigrants had been encouraged to move to the West Midlands by various government ministeries, including the Ministry of Labour and the Colonial Office, from the late 1940s onwards, not simply because there was employment available in the industries developing there in the post-war boom (such as engineering and vehicle manufacture), but also because they would avoid concentration in the potential ghetto areas in seaport towns such as Liverpool and Cardiff. Thus the immigrants came to a city which had a long imperial understanding of race, but only weak black community links. The situation in Birmingham in the 1950s, therefore, exemplified what some black observers saw as the disappearance of a black political identity in Britain. This was associated with the decline of earlier activity, such as that of the League of Coloured Peoples in the 1930s and 1940s, and with the depersonalisation of cultural minorities into the collective term "immigrants".[51]

This absence of cohesive communal or political consciousness amongst the first generation of black immigrants was not altogether surprising. Many settlers, especially those of Westindian origin, expected to be absorbed into what they hoped was a colour-blind British society. They only developed at a later date, in the 1960s and 1970s, a group identity in reaction to anti-black prejudice. In the case of Asian immigrants, the pioneer generation had one link with the local political structure through the figure of Dr Dhani Prem, who had been involved in Birmingham politics from 1945 onwards and had been elected as a Labour councillor for the Great Barr ward. After having little success in getting the local Labour Party to adopt black candidates, Prem decided to try and neutralise the anti-immigrant lobby by urging the Indian Prime Minister, Pandit Nehru, to restrict the number of Indian immigrants leaving India. In August 1955, he began to establish a Commonwealth Welfare Council for the West Midlands. He hoped to widen the existing welfare work which had begun with the Co-ordinating Committee for Overseas Nationals, established by some Protestant churches under the Chairmanship of the Archdeacon of Birmingham, Ven S Harvie Clark.[52] The idea had a substantive political base in that local branches of the Indian Workers' Association had been established in Smethwick and West Bromwich, and Prem hoped that in due course an Indian centre would be established for the city. Such developments had little impact on the operation of the Council's housing policy, though the Council did participate in a conference of 14 West Midlands authorities organised by Dr Prem in October 1955.

The policy of general non-interference in the whole issue of immigration in the late 1950s provided further scope for mobilisation of the anti-immigrant lobby. This campaign, however, produced only a weak response from such leaders as Prem who, as the President of the Birmingham Indian Association, urged that the immigrants were 'all members of the same community' and praised the city's avoidance of racial disturbance. The message was couched in terms of a rhetoric which urged 'the people of the Commonwealth' to 'join together and show the same spirit' in order 'to build the foundation of one world – one community of human beings'.[53] This was the language of the middle 1940s, stimulated by wartime idealism and Wendell Wilkie's *One World* ; it was unlikely to have much of an influence with the majority of Birmingham's white population.

Despite warnings from Labour politicians in the city, such as Dennis Howell, that a 'terrific anti-racial campaign' was about to be mounted,[54] the interesting thing about developments up to the 1964 general election is the relative localisation of anti-immigrant pressure, which by no means occurred in all areas of black immigrant settlement. In Sparkbrook the campaign of the Conservative candidate, Leslie Seymour, exemplified the more general appeal to material welfare and affluence, to which housing and immigration took second place. As a former resident of Sparkbrook, Seymour epitomised the middle-class suburban aspirations of the white Birmingham working and lower middle class as he commuted into the constituency from his new home in Sutton Coldfield. The populist theme was a feature of his campaign as he stressed the need for 40,000 houses 'for our own people'.[55]

The growing focus upon the immigration issue occurred when there were few black political figures to challenge the dominant assumptions of "white" Birmingham politics. The more overtly racist campaign of Peter Griffiths in Smethwick in the 1964 election epitomised a right-wing political trend against which there were few countervailing forces.[56] The main Westindian political organisation, the West Indian Standing Conference (WISC) was organised from London, and its federal structure tended to ensure a weak political presence in the city.[57] Its Chairman in Birmingham, Cedric Taylor, often focused upon small-scale issues such as the exclusion of blacks from public houses. His hope for a piecemeal improvement in this situation provided few grounds for thinking that a larger-scale campaign including housing would be mounted.[58] This problem of local political organisation became compounded as the 1960s progressed with the failure of the Campaign Against Racial Discrimination (CARD) in 1967 after the withdrawal of the WISC and the lack of success in mounting a British civil rights organisation.[59]

This general lack of strong black political leadership at the city level tended to exacerbate the segregationist pattern of settlement in which Asian and Westindian immigrants became heavily concentrated in the older housing of the middle ring wards. By 1961, for instance, over 80 per cent lived in the pre-1914 core of the city, with 50.2 per cent of the Westindians concentrated in the northern wards of Sandwell, Handsworth, Lozells, Soho and Rotton Park (where at that time only 19 per cent of the Asian population resided). Some 33.7 per cent of the Asians were concentrated in the southern wards of Market Hall, Balsall Heath, Moseley, Kings Heath, Sparkbrook, Sparkhill and Small Heath.[60] This localisation of the "immigrant problem" induced an attitude amongst Birmingham's councillors of containment and the avoidance of any active policy seeking to transform the situation beyond ensuring that there was no significant spread of multi-occupation in lodging houses beyond certain specified areas. The 1961 Housing Act gave local authorities powers of inspection and control, but not in the field of lodgings, despite a deputation from the Council to the Minister of Housing in November 1960. A resolution from the Council in July 1961 for further powers of registration ensured that the issues remained politically salient by the time the Labour government was elected in 1964. The Labour groups in the Birmingham Council, led by Alderman Harry Watton, were able to establish a fairly close partnership with the new Minister of Housing, Richard Crossman. Watton, indeed, seemed to Crossman 'the kind of Labour caucus leader that I like'[61] and a partnership was re-established between the Birmingham Council and the political centre in Whitehall which recalled the pre-war relationship forged by the Unionists under the Chamberlains.

The result of this new cooperation was the Birmingham Corporation Act of 1965 which enabled the Corporation to refuse registration of multi-occupied housing where the building or the area was deemed unsuitable. The issue highlights the thesis that local politics are dictated by consumption sectors with race being a key variable. Certainly, from the evidence collected of councillors' general views there was a strong feeling that the black immigrants were in some degree 'separate' and 'different', suggesting that policy should simply reflect the existing segregated situation. Thus one Conservative Alderman was reported by Newton as saying that 'They seem to be happy to live in the most distressing conditions, but there's no harm in that. They live with their own people. They live where they want. That's not a ghetto, it's a place where they live. This mixing up is wholly wrong.'[62]

For the most part the rhetoric in Birmingham city politics was divorced from an active ideology of segregationism as a tool of white supremacy, as in the case of South Africa or the Deep South.[63] It tended to be based rather on a folk wisdom or common sense outlook that was suspicious of attempts to politicise it; even Charles Collett was opposed to Oswald Mosley's attempt to use immigration in the city in 1956 to bolster the fortunes of his Union Movement.[64] Peter Griffiths, too, had an ambivalent and confused attitude to race, and his efforts to appease the racist anti-immigration lobby in the 1964 election had disastrous long-term results, for not only was he defeated in 1966, but he never secured any reputation in Conservative parliamentary circles sufficient to return him for another seat.[65] When the race issue did finally become politicised at the national level by the Wolverhampton MP, Enoch Powell, in 1968 it was in terms of repatriation rather than urban segregation.[66]

The importance of "segregation" in the case of the inner city situation in Birmingham is less overtly political than might be imagined. By the early 1960s a high degree of spatial separation of Westindian and Asian immigrants had occurred, repeating to a considerable degree a pattern that had been experienced earlier by the Irish. Birmingham City Council, reacting to white pressures to look after the interests of indigenous "Brummies", declined to be involved in any active policy to transform this pattern. From the 1950s it also pursued an increasingly ambitious policy of new housing and restoration of older stock to meet the demands of the indigenous working class. In general this was the politics of nativist exclusion practised at a time when the city was undergoing a major transformation in its status; from that of a second city with significant imperial trading and commercial links, to what it was hoped would be a hub for the technocratic transformation and modernisation of British society. This political pattern reflected not only a strong rejection of the immigrant "strangers" but also an affirmation of a provincial identity which was to have important implications for a wider British post-imperial withdrawal into an exclusivist nationalism.

For some observers on the left, this pattern appeared to be a major betrayal of all they had hoped for in both British liberal values and in the politics of the Labour Party. Some socialist intellectuals had envisaged the ideals of social welfare replacing those of empire by the end of the 1950s,[67] and this appeared, too, to be an important means of meeting the Conservatives' attempt to link affluence to opposition to black immigration in the early 1960s. However, the net result of this left/liberal conscience on empire and immigration was not a policy of planned immigration from the Westindies and South Asia[68] but rather increased restrictions in the 1965 White Paper *Immigration from the Commonwealth*. Thereafter a 'moral wreckage' appeared to ensue, in which the crux of the whole immigration issue lay in housing.[69] In this increasingly pessimistic climate on the left, one glimmer of light appeared to shine from the dark racialist cloud, namely the strong support given to increased public housing from the Cullingworth Committee in 1969. The report, as Hazel Flett has suggested, was shaped to a considerable degree by the Birmingham experience, and it suggested that a major campaign should be mounted to dispel immigrants' 'ignorance' of the council house system which, while 'difficult enough for the sophisticated' might well be 'totally incomprehensible and shrouded in mystery to a relative newcomer'.[70]

The paternalism implicit within the report was perhaps symptomatic of a wider welfarist sense of benevolent trusteeship in the post-imperial era. Whatever the case, it reinforced the adoption of a dispersal policy in Birmingham even before the report was published, irrespective of whether or not black immigrants wished to be moved from middle ring areas to participate in a more even pattern of settlement.

The policy eventually led to growing charges of racial discrimination as the council was accused of appeasing white opponents of ethnic concentration in areas of public housing and the policy was abandoned in 1975. The motives behind the policy appeared to have shifted from one of benign neglect in the late 1950s and early 1960s, towards a feeling that there was a 'tribalistic' desire by white working-class families to live separately from blacks in inner city areas.[71]

Segregationism had become a more complex and multifaceted process than before, and the desire was now one of trying to prevent large concentrations of black communities in the middle ring; almost the opposite strategy, in fact, of an 'apartheid policy' to which the Council is still accused of adhering by analysts like Rex.[72] The proportion of black tenants housed in the suburbs declined from 44 per cent in 1974, while the dispersal policy was in operation, to 30 per cent in 1976 after its abandonment, suggesting a conscious desire by at least certain sections of the inner city black population to resist suburbanisation at this time.[73] The limitations of a conscious segregationist policy and the fact that it has clearly only worked with some active collaboration by a proportion of the inner city black population suggests that the focus of current research on the inner cities should shift to the patterns of choice adopted by communities in particular urban situations.

NOTES

1. Paul B Rich, *Race and Empire in British Politics*, CUP, Cambridge, 1986.
2. D Ward, "The Progressives and the Urban Question: British and American responses to the inner city slums, 1880-1920", *Transactions of the Institute of British Geographers*, NS9 1984, pp. 229-314.
3. C Van Woodward, *The Strange Career of Jim Crow*, OUP, New York, 1974; H N Rabinowitz, *Race Relations in the Urban South, 1865-1900*, University of Illinois Press, Chicago and London, 1980.
4. CAB 129/40, Memorandum by the Colonial Secretary on Coloured People from the British Colonies, 18 May 1950.
5. Rich, *op. cit.*.
6. Sheila Patterson, "Immigrants and minority groups in British society" in S Abbott (ed), *The Prevention of Racial Discrimination in Britain*, OUP, London, 1972, pp. 31-2.
7. John Rex, *Race Relations in Sociological Theory*, Weidenfeld and Nicolson, London, 1970, p. 108.
8. John Rex and Robert Moore, *Race, Community and Conflict*, OUP, Oxford for the IRR, 1967, pp. 273-4.
9. *Ibid.*, p. 276; John Rex, "The Concept of Housing Class and the Sociology of Race Relations", *Race*, 12 (1971), pp. 293-301.
10. J G Davies, "Race, Community and No Conflict", *New Society*, 9 July 1970.
11. M Plant, "The Attitudes of Coloured Immigrants in two areas of Birmingham to the concept of dispersal", *Race*, 12 (1971), pp. 323-28.
12. Badr Dahya, "The nature of Pakistani ethnicity in industrial cities in Britain" in A Cohen (ed), *Urban Ethnicity*, Tavistock, London, 1974, pp. 77-118.
13. R Ballard and C Ballard, "The Sikhs: The development of South Asian settlement in Britain" in J L Watson (ed), *Between Two Cultures*, Blackwell, Oxford, 1977; V Robinson, "The Development of South Asian Settlement in Britain and the Myth of Return" in C Peach and S Smith (eds), *Ethnic Segregation in Cities*, Croom Helm, London, 1981, pp. 149-69.
14. A Richmond, "Housing and Racial Attitudes in Bristol", *Race*, 12 (1970), pp. 49-58.
15. A Richmond, *Migration and Race Relations in an English City*, OUP, London, 1973, pp. 62, 127.
16. *Ibid.*, p. 125.
17. Valerie Karn, "A Note on 'Race, Community and Conflict: A Study of Sparkbrook' ", *Race*, 9 (1967), pp.100-14.
18. John Rex and Robert Moore, "A Rejoinder to Miss Karn", *Race*, 9 (1967), pp.104-7.
19. Davies, *op. cit.*
20. *Race, Community and Conflict*, pp. 1-2.
21. *Ibid.*, p. 19.
22. John Rex, *Race, Colonialism and the City*, Routledge and Kegan Paul, London and Boston, 1973, pp. 88-9.
23. Hazel McFerson, "Racial Tradition and Comparative Political Analysis: notes towards a theoretical framework", *Ethnic and Racial Studies*, 2 (1979), p. 491.
24. Colin Holmes, "Nativism and violence", *Race Today*, 3 (1971), pp. 99-100.
25. Peter Abrams, *Historical Sociology*, Open Books, Shepton Mallet, 1982.
26. R J Holton, *Cities, Capitalism and Civilisation*, Allen and Unwin, London, 1986.
27. G Henry Warrren, *England is a Village*, Eyre and Spottiswoode, London, 1941.
28. M J Wise and P Thorpe, *The Growth of Birmingham, 1800-1950* in The British Association, *Birmingham and its Regional Settings*, The British Association, Birmingham, 1950, pp. 213-28.
29. "The Politics of Birmingham", *The Economist*, 7 February 1970; A Sutcliffe and R Smith, *Birmingham, 1939-1970*, OUP, London, 1974, pp. 79-83.
30. Sutcliffe and Smith, *op. cit*, pp. 123-4.
31. *Ibid.*, pp. 232-33.
32. Rich, *op. cit.*

33. Martin Weiner, *English Culture and the Decline of the Industrial Spirit*, CUP, Cambridge, 1980.
34. Jonathan Mendilow, "Merrie England and the Brave New World: Two Myths of the idea of empire", *History of European Ideas*, 6 (1985), pp. 41-58. See also introduction and chapter one.
35. J B Priestley, *English Journey*, Heinemann, London, 1934, p. 78.
36. *Ibid.*, p. 86.
37. S P B Mais, *The English Scene Today*, Salisbury Square, London, 1948, p. 166.
38. *Race, Community and Conflict*, pp. 66, 75.
39. Priestley, *op. cit.*, p. 86.
40. H Manzoni, "Redevelopment of Blighted Areas in Birmingham", *Journal of the Town Planning Institute*, 16 (1955), p. 16.
41. Tony Newton, *Second City Politics: Democratic Processes and Decision-Making in Birmingham*, The Clarendon Press, Oxford, 1976, p. 89.
42. P Dunleavy, "The Urban Basis of Political Alignment: Social Class, Domestic Property Ownership, and State Intervention in Consumption Purposes", *British Journal of Political Science*, 9 (1979), p. 422.
43. *Race, Community and Conflict*, p. 193.
44. M Blanch, "Imperialism, Nationalism and Organised Youth" in J Clarke *et al.*, *Working Class Culture*, Hutchinson for the CCCS, London, 1979.
45. S Joshi and R Carter, "The Role of Labour in the Creation of Racist Britain", *Race and Class*, 25, 1984, pp. 53-77; Paul B Rich, "The Politics of 'Surplus Colonial Labour': Black Immigration to Britain and Governmental Responses, 1940-1962" in Colin Brock (ed), *The Caribbean in Europe*, Frank Cass, London, 1986, pp. 36-61.
46. *Birmingham Evening Mail*, 5 January 1960.
47. *The Daily Express*, 19 and 20 January 1955; Sutcliffe and Smith, *op. cit.*, p. 369.
48. Paul Foot, *Immigration and Race in British Politics*, Penguin Books, Harmondsworth, 1965, pp. 196-9; Sutcliffe and Smith, *op. cit.*, p.369.
49. Donley T Studlar, "Social Context and Attitudes toward Coloured Immigrants", *British Journal of Sociology*, 28 (1977), p. 179.
50. Sutcliffe and Smith, *op. cit.*, p 373.
51. E R Braithwaite, "The 'Coloured Immigrants' in Britain", *Contemporary Review* 181, February 1967; G K Lewis, "Protest Among the Immigrants", *The Political Quarterly*, 40 (1969), pp. 426-35. Most West Indian migrants in Birmingham who were interviewed in the mid-1950s only expected to stay in the Uk for about five years. Simon Taylor, *A Land of Dreams*, London and New York, Routledge, 1993, p. 111.
52. Dani Prem, *The Parliamentary Leper*, The Metric Press, Aligahr, 1965; Sutcliffe and Smith *op. cit.*, pp. 364-5.
53. *The Birmingham Post*, 27 January 1960.
54. *The Birmingham Post*, 8 May 1961.
55. A Shuttleworth, "Sparkbrook" in N Deakin (ed), *Colour and The British Electorate*, Pall Mall Press, London, 1965, p. 60.
56. Foot, *op. cit.*, pp. 28-9; M Hartley-Brewer, "Smethwick" in Deakin *op. cit.*, pp. 77-105.
57. G K Lewis, op. cit., p. 429.
58. *Birmingham Evening Mail*, 5 May 1964.
59. B Heinemann, *The Politics of Powerlessness*, OUP and IRR, Oxford and London, 1972.
60. P N Jones, *The Segregation of Immigrant Communities in the City of Birmingham*, University of Hull Press, Hull, 1967, pp.7-8; Taylor, *op sit.* p. 145.
61. Richard Crossman, *The Diaries of a Cabinet Minister, Vol. 1, Minister of Housing 1964-66*, Hamish Hamilton and Jonathan Cape, London, 1975, p. 399.
62. Newton, *op. cit.*, p. 210.
63. John Cell, *The Highest Stage of White Supremacy: The Origins of Segregation in South Africa and the United States*, CUP, Cambridge, 1982.
64. Sutcliffe and Smith, *op. cit.*, p. 373.

65. Paul B Rich, "Conservative Ideology and Race in Modern British Politics" in Zig Layton Henry and Paul B Rich (eds), *Race, Government and Politics in Britain*, The Macmillan Press, London and Basingstoke, 1986, pp. 45-72.

66. J Western, "Social Engineering through spatial manipulation: apartheid in South African cities" in C Clark, D Ley and C Peach (eds), *Geography and Ethnic Pluralism*, Allen and Unwin, London, 1984, pp. 113-40; Robin Cohen, *Endgame in South Africa?*, James Currey, Paris and London, UNESCO Press, 1986, pp. 15-37.

67. John Strachey, *The End of Empire*, Gollancz, London, 1959, p. 229.

68. John Rex, "The Race Relations Catastrophe" in J Burgess *et al., Matters of Principle: Labour's Last Chance*, Penguin Books, Harmondsworth, 1968, p. 70.

69. *Ibid.,* pp. 72, 82.

70. Central Housing Advisory Committee, *Report of the Housing Management Sub-Committee, Council Housing: Purposes, Procedures and Priorities* (The Cullingworth Report), HMSO, London, 1969, p. 17, para 383; Hazel Flett, "The Politics of Dispersal in Birmingham", RUER Working Paper, University of Aston, 1981, p. 15.

71. Flett, *op. cit.,*pp. 44-47.

72. "Professor Highlights Inner City Apartheid", *Birmingham Post,* 23 January 1985.

73. Flett, *op. cit.,* p. 44.

Chapter Nine

T H Green, Lord Scarman and the Issue of Ethnic Minority Rights in English Liberal Thought

The disturbances in a number of British towns and cities since the early 1980s and the resulting debate stemming from *The Scarman Report* have received surprisingly little attention from scholars of political theory. This perhaps reflects the manner in which issues surrounding race and ethnicity in Britain have been deflected into the sociological subdiscipline of "race relations", in which academic research on racial disadvantage in such areas as housing, employment, education and access to welfare provision has become allied to a broad band of social and community workers and local government officers. From this race relations debate there has emerged a general consensus on the essential nature of the issues and their sociological determinants without any necessary directives on actual social policy.[1] One effect of the race relations paradigm has been a general disconnection in British social science between the study of institutions and social structures on the one hand, and social and political thought on the other. For political studies, this has also reflected a further fissure between the study of political institutions, at both the state and local level, and debates in political theory and jurisprudence.[2]

The emergent research on the significance of ethnic minorities in terms of political parties and local and national elections has, therefore, failed to address itself to more general issues of the political legitimacy of ethnic minority group rights and the concepts of political pluralism which have been associated with racial divisions in the colonial and post-colonial context.[3] The emergence of race and ethnicity as an important issue in British politics can be seen as a challenge to the adaptability of mainstream English liberal thought and its capacity to cope with claims of minority group rights over and above the more conventional claims of the individual. The English liberal tradition has, in the course of the twentieth century, made a remarkable series of adaptations to the demands of a mass electorate, collective economic management and the liberal corporatism of both trade unions and employers. This was due in part to its being underpinned by a cohesive notion of British, and more particularly English, national homogeneity which accommodated to a considerable degree to the extension of state power. Thus, while Britain, like other capitalist societies, has exhibited what the German philosopher Habermas has termed a 'legitimation crisis' induced by continuous extension of state intervention in pursuit of equity and justice, the resulting erosion of nonstate and private support for state power has been tempered by a strong sense of national affiliation.[4]

There has been a strong emphasis within English political thought in the twentieth century on notions of "national character". This reinforced the Idealist claim to social cohesion but also reflected an essentially provincial philosophical achievement, certainly in comparison with the movements in social and political thought in Central Europe in the late nineteenth and early twentieth centuries.[5] Idealism remained at best only a potential social theory through which to interpret pre-First World War British society within the bounds of the bourgeois nation-state.[6] It remains a challenge to the proponents of the liberal tradition to reaffirm their political legitimacy in a more diverse and socially plural society in which the traditional sanctions of religion and class deference have been considerably diminished.

This chapter will discuss this tradition of liberal values in terms of the thought of one of the last great Victorian political philosophers to address the question of political obligation, Thomas Hill Green. Green's conception of a positive role for state power serves as a model for later elaborations of the liberal ideal in the twentieth century, which will be briefly discussed in the second part of this chapter, and indeed for its considerable vulgarisation in a period of growing concern with nonstate structures and the diminution in the autonomy of politics. It can be used in some respects as a yardstick for the assessment of the political content of the debate surrounding *The Scarman Report* in 1981, which is the substance of the last part of the chapter. As a liberal jurist, Scarman has been concerned to renegotiate the terms of liberal discourse on both ethnic minority rights and the constitution in general. He has sought to legitimate state institutions whilst at the same time promoting policies directed at alleviating both racial disadvantage and political disaffection amongst black youth in Britain's inner cities. Though there are clearly many differences in the separate worlds and thought of Green and

Scarman, there are also important similarities. Both have been concerned with state legitimation at times of social and class tension and political stress, and it is this theme which is this chapter's major concern.

T H Green and the Sources of Political Obligation

T H Green (1836-1882) wrote at the time of fairly rapid political change surrounding the 1867 Reform Act and the 1870 Education Act. His posthumous writings *Prolegomena to Ethics* and *Lectures on the Principles of Political Obligation* went on to have a considerable impact on the new generation of concerned liberal clergymen, civil servants and politicians from the 1890s to the start of the First World War. Thereafter his political message seemed increasingly out of tune with the new era of growing state economic intervention and welfare provision. Some of his students turned Idealism away from the "New Liberalism" of advancing welfare provision and democratic rights and towards a more positive conception of state power linked to citizenship in the nation-state. Nevertheless, his ethical Kantianism left its mark on English intellectual life in a number of ways. One prominent example was A D Lindsay, Master of Green's old college of Balliol, Oxford, who presided from 1924 to 1946 and had amongst his students Roy Jenkins, Edward Heath and Denis Healey.[7]

The liberal Idealism that Green articulated represented a secularised Anglicanism that updated the Victorian middle-class conscience and helped direct Oxford into a broad church philosophy of duty.[8] This reconstruction of British liberalism involved the employment of Kantian moral idealism in order to convert individual self-seeking into a wider general good.[9] This was by no means a complete break with the older Benthamite utilitarian tradition based on the materialist notion of the greatest good for the greatest number, for Green continued to believe in a capitalist free market economy, free trade and the promotion of only limited state reforms. In effect, he sought to reconcile British capitalist economic doctrines with German ethical philosophy.[10] Green saw the essential weakness of the utilitarian philosophy as lying in its central ethical imperative that the vocation of man was merely to seek pleasure and avoid pain, with the ultimate sanction being the fear of the consequences if he did not. While he shared the utilitarian disdain for justifying political rights on the grounds of prior natural rights, Green saw the utilitarian doctrine as failing to provide any positive guide to the ethical basis of political action. Employing Kantian ethics, he sought to rest political action on the conception of an ideal end, for

Without this conception the recognition of a power as a right would be impossible. A power on the part of anyone is so recognised by others, as one which should be exercised, when these others regard it as in some way a means to that ideal good of themselves which they alike conceive: and

the possessor of the power comes to regard it as a right through
consciousness of its being thus recognised as contributory to a good in
which he too is interested.[11]

Furthermore, 'only through the possession of rights can the power of the
individual freely to make a common good his own have reality given to it.'
These rights were thus 'what may be called the negative realisation of
this power'.[12] This linked the individual's own ethical striving to a wider
common good and, on this basis, Green went on to construct a theory of a
political obligation to which the work of Habermas bears some important
similarities. This theory stemmed from a rejection by Green of Austin's
doctrine of sovereignty based on the idea of a determinate person or
persons who had the right in the last resort to impose laws and enforce
their observance. Obedience to the sovereign, argued Green, was only
obtained through fear of the consequences of disobeying and it was
necessary to look for ethical ends beyond those of the 'analytical jurists'.[13]
The point about 'habitual obedience' to the state lay in the fact that it
was 'a power residing in the common will and reason of men,
i.e. in the will and reason of men as determined by social
relations, as interested in each other, as acting together
for common ends.' It was accordingly 'a power which this
universal rational will exercises over the inclinations of the individual,
and which only needs exceptionally to be backed by coercive force.'[14]
(emphasis mine) Ultimately, will and not force was the basis of the state.

How could such a 'universal rational will' be construed? It did not lie
for the most part in the intervention in social relationships of the law, for
beyond a certain point Green saw laws as producing social disruption as
the more tacit *corpus juris* became destabilised. Moreover, it did not lie
in some new version of a social contract theory, for Green rejected the
notion of rights in a state of nature prior to the advent of civil society.
Such rights implied a system of 'natural justice' which he saw as a
contradiction in terms since rights could only be obtained through the
fulfilment of ethical ends in society.[15] Ultimately, Green envisaged an
ideal model of bargaining between individuals and the agreement to
consent to a 'common good' on the assumption that the members of the
society were rational beings:

> *...what is certain is, that a habit of subjection founded upon fear*
> *could not be a basis of political or free society; for to this it is*
> *necessary, not indeed that everyone subject to the laws should take*
> *part in voting them, still less that he should consent to their*
> *application to himself, but that it should represent an idea of*
> *common good,* **which each member of the society can make his**
> **own so far as he is rational,** *i.e capable of the conception of a*
> *common good, however much particular passions may lead him to*

*ignore it and thus necessitate the use of force to prevent him from
doing that which, so far as influenced by the conception of a common
good, he would willingly abstain from.*[16] *(emphasis mine)*

There is an important resemblance here to Habermas' attempt to
construct a new *Sittlichkeit* on the basis of an ethical theory dependent
on the notion of undistorted communication between rational parties to a
discursive consensus. In this effort Habermas, who was strongly
influenced by the critical theory of the Frankfurt school, sought to move
beyond the generalisable norms of bourgeois ethical theory which, as we
have seen in the case of Green, could be 'exceptionally' backed by the
coercive forces of state power. Habermas imagined rather a model of a
communication community *(Kommunikationsgemeinschaft)* of
participants who test the claims of norms and arrive at the rational
conviction that they are inherently 'right', so moving to a cognitive
conception of ethical right freed from the constraints of force:

Insofar as norms express generalizable interests, they are based on a
rational consensus *(or they would find such a consensus if
practical discourse could take place). Insofar as norms do not
regulate generalizable interests, they are based on force* **(Gewalt)**; *in
the latter context we use the term normative power* **(Macht)**.[17]

In liberal bourgeois societies Habermas saw only pseudo compromises
being arrived at on the question of norms, which were thus ideological in
so far as they were backed by force. The point was to develop a social
theory that was critical of ideology and based on a 'model of the
suppression of generalizable interests and which compares normative
structures existing at a given time with the hypothetical state of a
system of norms formed, *ceteris paribus*, discursively.'[18] Exactly how
such a non-ideological theory of norms could be arrived at remains
problematic and an area for more detailed analysis by philosophers in
the analytic tradition.[19] However, it can be argued that, in the final
analysis, Habermas' actual mode of reasoning is not substantially
different from that of Green in that he imagines some model of
consensual bargaining by people who are assumed to act rationally. The
difference lies in the emphasis put on the possibility of critical reasoning
free from contemporaneous ideological constraints which for Green,
writing in the latter part of the nineteenth century, was not a
fundamental issue. Green did not see the ideal of the 'common good' held
by the ordinary citizen of a 'civilised society' in terms of the state only. It
might well be held in the more local or parochial terms of 'a clear
understanding of certain interests and rights common to himself with his
neighbours, if only such as consist in getting his wages paid at the end of
the week, in getting his money's worth at the shop, in the inviolability of

his own person and that of his wife.' If the citizen did not have such an 'instinctive recognition' of the common good he became one of the 'dangerous classes, virtually outlawed by himself'.[20]

Green's limited model of state legitimation or 'political obligation' was derived from his own involvement in politics; he was an Oxford city councillor at a time of an embryonic mass political awareness following the franchise and educational reforms of the 1860s and 1870s.[21] This led him to formulate only a partially politicised conception of citizenship in the modern state, a fact which would have long-term ramifications on British political thought. The life of citizenship in a modern state based on representative institutions, he thought, would probably not be able to have the same 'civil vitality' as that of the ancient civilisations based on direct democracy, or of Rousseau's ideal of a small state under the sovereignty of the general will. This would probably be, Green concluded, 'a temporary loss that we have to bear as the price of having recognised the claim to citizenship as the claim of all men.'[22]

At one level, there was a basic problem in Green's formulation of the citizenship concept in that it did leave an opening for an inherently illiberal conception of the state which made claims on the whole of the citizen's political allegiances. Since rights were not seen as being derived from a state of nature outside society, it became difficult for a citizen to claim rights against the state. Green was careful to limit this doctrine as far as possible, arguing that:

> *The general principle that the citizen must never act otherwise than as a citizen, does not carry with it an obligation under all conditions to conform to the law of his state, since those laws may be inconsistent with the true end of the state as the sustainer and harmoniser of social relations. The assertion, however, by the citizen of any right which the state does not recognise must be founded on a reference to an acknowledged social good.[25]*

Green's conception of citizenship was one of the most important notions he bequeathed to his followers. In the twentieth century it has become a basic political concept in the discourse of the welfare state and expanding political democracy, allied to a biological organicism derived from Darwinism.[23] Essentially, it gave a political meaning to the idea of equality which progressively expanded from the social and political realms to that of the economic. It provided a moral basis for a political consensus in Britain by the middle years of the century and in turn the truce between the rival political ideologies of advancing state socialism and *laissez faire* capitalism.[24]

In the twentieth century, furthermore, a number of reformers have sought to develop this citizenship notion as far as possible in a more liberal direction, laying, by the late 1930s, the foundations for an ideology of social democratic reform.[26] The exact mode of this discourse is for intellectual history to discover, but it is clear from the writings of L T Hobhouse, the first Martin White Professor of Sociology at the LSE and a follower of T H Green, that the liberal conception of citizenship was sociologically plural in order to ensure individual rights against the state and so free liberalism from the Idealist conception of the state forcing man to be free. Hobhouse wrote in *The Elements of Social Justice* in 1922:

> *Any constituent element that is necessary to the life of the community may be said to have its rights. Thus any corporate personality – a family, a municipality, a company, a trade union is a possible subject of rights. We may even say that functions, or at any rate, the representatives of functions have their rights. Thus religion, patriotism, education, insofar as they contribute to the common good, have a function to perform and a certain claim on society to maintain the conditions under which those functions are best fulfilled.*[27]

The attempt by Hobhouse to redefine liberal rights in industrial society was tied to an evolutionist sociology that did little field work and had only a limited impact on English social thought in the interwar period. This sociology had no general theory of the social process to challenge the dominant intellectual tradition of positivism and so failed to develop liberalism in any significant manner beyond John Stuart Mills' mid-Victorian conception of individual rights and duties.[28] It was thus unable to explain the dominance of patriotism in British political thought beyond its more general contribution to the 'common good'.

A key dimension of Green's conception of the state's role in the promotion of the common good was the emphasis on a culturally homogeneous patriotism. This Green conceived in an active rather than a passive sense for an 'active interest in the service of the state' could not arise if the individual's relation to it was as a 'passive recipient of protection in the exercise of his rights of person and property'.[29] The notion of public duty led Green beyond a simple defence of the state as the defender of capitalism and private property, despite the fact that he did not find much fault in them. The fundamental point was that the development of a conception of true citizenship meant the espousal of a principle of self-sacrifice that moved beyond the mere self-interest championed by the utilitarians.[30] Such an active notion of public service was anchored in a conception of 'patriotism in the better sense' in which the fatherland became a 'natural object'. This was only possible when the state became 'the object only so far as it is an organisation of a people to whom the individual feels himself bound by ties analogous to those which bind him to his family, ties derived from a common dwelling place with its associations, from common memories, traditions and customs, and from the common ways of feeling and thinking which a common language and still more a common literature embodies.' This notion of an homogeneous people was epitomised for Green by the modern state.[31]

Green linked the secularised Anglican notion of an active state and public duty to the similarly secularised Victorian conception of the British national community rooted in kinship and territorial affinities.[32] It was a creed which was never fully challenged in later British liberal thought and it indicated the divergent paths of British liberal thought and that of the United States. In the latter case the impact of mass immigration from Southern and Eastern Europe in the late nineteenth and early twentieth centuries caused a considerable lurch towards cultural and ethnic pluralism amongst a number of liberal thinkers, especially those linked to the settlement movement such as Jane Addam's Hull House in Chicago.[33] Despite the links forged by progressive reformers in Britain and the United States in the early twentieth century, for the most part the philanthropic and settlement tradition in Britain remained more culturally exclusive than that of the United States. By the early 1930s, in the case of the Liverpool Settlement, it moved to a position of actively supporting immigration restriction.[34] Political thought in Britain often tended to reflect this national exclusiveness as Idealists in the twentieth century such as Bernard Bosanquet and D G Ritchie drifted away from the liberal championing of individual rights towards asserting collectivist state intervention in pursuit of the pre-eminent needs of the social organism and eugenic racial fitness.[35]

By the end of the First World War, a bifurcation began to emerge in the liberal tradition as some pluralists, such as Harold Laski, began to move towards a libertarian socialism.[36] Other Idealists articulated a less liberal position on citizenship and one of Green's pupils, W H Hadow, saw the state as a collective personality. Just as the English statute book attributed a personality to corporate bodies, Hadow argued, so could the same claim be made for the state itself which needed to be understood in terms of its own unique 'national characters'. This could not be defined in terms of 'a mere mechanical combination of separate ingredients' for it was 'organic if we can imagine an organism each member of which retains its individual vitality and yet is profoundly affected by its associations with others'.[37] It was clear, furthermore, that the individuals who made up this social organism were products of a distinct racial history for 'each of us is, in part, an epitome of his race: a stone of the rock whence we are hewn, a clod of the pit where we are digged. Not only our bodily substance but our impulses, our emotions, our propensities have been moulded by the growth and are stimulated by the contact of the environment in which we live.'[38] This conception of 'national character' had a considerable popularity amongst political philosophers in the 1920s. In 1927 Ernest Barker drew the logical conclusion, as far as immigration policy was concerned, when he argued that, though 'right laws and sound morals form the strongest safeguard of every national state', nevertheless 'a sound racial basis is also necessary'. Futhermore:

> *A nation may be enriched by the varied contribution of foreign immigration; but if the stream of immigration grows unchecked into the volume of a great river, a nation may lose the integrity of the solid core which is the basis of its tradition. And the nation which loses its tradition has lost its very self.*[39]

Despite Green's attempts to reassert the positive rights of the individual against the power of the state, his followers were by no means so careful. In one sense, the long-term tendency for much liberal political philosophy, divorced from the concerns of jurisprudence, was to assert the pre-eminence of the social organism and national community in the legitimation of state power. This impulse within political philosophy was reinforced by the failure of jurists to respond to the claims by the pluralists of the school of Maitland, Fiddis and Gierke for the rights of groups and collectivists, and their tendency to respond only to pressure from commercial groups.[40] Furthermore, the rise of a more centralist social democracy in the Labour Party in the 1930s nullified the hopes of the pluralist school. The experience of the wartime coalition reinforced a faith in state power to achieve social welfare objectives at the same time as it was allied to a strong sense of British national cohesion.[41] While there were universalist claims underpinning the social democratic liberalism of the post-war British welfare state, it would be a misnomer to describe it as such in isolation from a self-conscious political provincialism which by the 1960s had developed into a nativist assertion of English national identity.

The defeat of the pluralist school and the divorce of liberalism and Idealism in British political thought left political philosophy unprepared for the issues that have emerged since black New Commonwealth immigration in the 1950s and 1960s. It is not altogether surprising that one of the most important liberal thinkers to address the issue of ethnic minorities in the British body politic was Chief Justice Lord Scarman, reflecting both the saliency of black claims for equal rights before the law as well as the more general issue of civil rights in British politics which has emerged since the Commission headed by Scarman on the disorder in Red Lion Square in 1974.[42] Accordingly, Scarman's thought on ethnic minorities proves an interesting contrast to the mainstream liberal tradition represented by T H Green.

Scarman and the Reassessment of the Liberal Ideal

Despite his modest claim to be merely 'someone educated, in a very established way, in the mainstream of very orthodox English Law',[43] Scarman has been a powerful voice, since the middle 1960s, for the modernisation and codification of English law. Initially this concern did not stretch as far as a reconstitution of individual rights and freedoms. Following the 1965 Law Commissions Act, Scarman directed his attention to the establishment of legal codes in order to systematise statutory law, which he saw as inevitably extending itself into the area of common law. This attitude reflected the faith in the 1960s, especially following the election of the Labour government of 1964, in guided state social engineering. Scarman saw these changes only as modifications of the relationship between legal codes and judge-made law and they did not involve the destruction of the latter but rather coexistence with it.[44]

This somewhat benign faith in a codified law, which could be developed and modernised 'by a planned legislative process which will rely not on the legal profession alone but on the skills and value of the whole community',[45] became tarnished in the 1970s following a growing crisis of confidence in the legitimacy of state power and its use of the law. As Scarman pointed out in his 1974 Hamlyn lectures, "English Law – the New Dimension", when times are normal and fear is not stalking the land, English law sturdily protects the freedom of the individual and respects the human personality. But when times are abnormally alive with fear and prejudice, the common law is at a disadvantage: it cannot resist the will, however frightened and prejudiced it may be, of Parliament.[46] Scarman was writing at a time of both a challenge to English law to adapt itself to a wider set of European legal codes in the aftermath of Britain's entry into the Common Market in 1971, and the rise of industrial conflict under the government of Edward Heath, culminating in the miners' strike of 1973-74, the three day week and the election defeat in February 1974.

Scarman argued forcibly for a new constitutional settlement, to replace that of 1689, which would include both a bill of rights and a supreme court to protect the constitution from Parliament.[47] These ideas by no means met with unanimous approval, even from within the mainstream of British political debate. As Ralph Dahrendorf has commented, the demand for a new constitutional settlement was 'less a need that can be argued for in general terms than a system of the end of constitutional politics, and beyond that, a symptom of the end of an underlying and undisputed agreement about certain assumptions on which this society is based'.[48] While this might be seen as the response of a somewhat nostalgic German Anglophile, the politicians' response, especially from the right, was to see the demand for a new constitution as merely reflecting the absence of strong governmental will. Thus Timothy Raison, presaging the climate of Thatcherite politics at the end of the decade, concluded that there was a need to 'revitalise our political institutions and end that loss of nerve which is our greatest political weakness at the moment'.[49]

As part of his reassessment of the English liberal tradition, Scarman also began to look at the question of ethnic minority rights. In a lecture to the Minority Rights Group in 1977, he perceived Britain as essentially a 'plural society', though this, he considered, had a meaning intrinsically different from the post-colonial context of many Third World states since this pluralism did not entail any possibility of creating separate ethnic group states. For Scarman, the pluralism entailed by the emergence of ethnic group identities amongst black immigrants had to be welded to the underlying homogeneity of British national institutions and culture. As the 'newest of plural societies',[50] Britain's response should have been, in the absence of a bill of rights on the American pattern, to 'have made more use of legislation and less use of judges'.[51]

Scarman saw the governmental response to ethnic minority demands for civil rights as reflecting a more general problem of state legitimacy as increasing use was made of statutory law to intervene in a field hitherto the domain of common law and the law of tort. The problem was that, once the state started to intervene in the area of ethnic group rights, this raised questions both of the principles upon which this intervention should be based as well as the relationship of these group rights to more conventional individual ones. Hitherto, these questions had been shelved, for the British 'reaction' was 'typical – pragmatic, empirical. We have not yet thought out a solution of principle. We have simply acted to meet urgent difficulties, preferring to use administrative and legislative methods wherever possible.' Ultimately, statutory legislation could not carry the same degree of legitimacy as action under constitutional principle, for the Supreme Court and the Bill of Rights in the United States carried far more public esteem than the quangos established in Britain, such as the Equal Opportunities Commission and the Commission for Racial Equality, to enforce legislation against sexual and racial discrimination.[52] The legitimacy of these institutions was important, for Scarman did recognise that, in order to build a 'civilised plural society', it would be necessary, for a period, to enforce positive discrimination in favour of disadvantaged groups, though 'any permanent loading of the law in favour of a particular group of persons may put the unity of society at risk'.[53]

Scarman concluded that the only direction forward for ethnic minorities lay in a bill of rights which would effectively establish the basis for a renegotiation of a liberal consensus, or what Green would term the 'common good'. However, even before the 1980-81 disturbances, Scarman had begun to recognise that the legitimation of state power in the context of a plural society could not, in the last resort, rest upon the individual's 'habitual obedience to authority', for positive group rights had to be asserted through the legal process, a notion that Green had rejected. For Scarman, such inverse discrimination was essential for both the continuing stability of a society based on liberal principles and the necessary 'balancing process which has to be undertaken when and where there is social and economic inequality. But the law must continue to emphasise the ultimate value of the individual.'[54] Though perhaps uncertain where this process of inverse discrimination would lead, Scarman was hopeful by the late 1970s that the law could be made to achieve positive goals of attacking racial discrimination and so, to a considerable degree, defuse a potentially violent situation such as had occurred in the United States.

The Scarman Report

The widespread disturbances of 1980-81 did come as a shock to Scarman, whose *Report* reflected a strong determination to buttress the power of the police at the same time as trying to meet many of the grievances of the black population in such localities as Brixton and St Paul's in Bristol. His exaggerated description of the Brixton disturbances and of the police as standing 'between our society and a total collapse of law and order in the streets of an important capital' has been seen as reflecting his failure to understand the issues at a basic level.[55] However, the *Report* was significant for the manner in which it recognised that the disturbances had politicised the issue of ethnic minorities. For the most part there was an avoidance of the discourse of race relations sociology and Scarman perhaps sensed that the mainstream race relations debate had failed to focus upon the question raised some years previously by Dilip Hiro of political obligation or on the manner in which the legitimacy of state institutions could be secured vis-à-vis the ethnic communities.[56] The disturbances made this a central issue in terms of securing the political loyalty of communities such as the black population in Brixton and the rebuilding of relationships between them and the local police. As he conceded at the outset, 'rightly or wrongly, young black people do not feel politically secure, any more than they feel economically or socially secure.'[57]

Scarman still assumed a basic imperative for black political obligation to the state, but did not proceed as far as Green's concession that citizens' rights could be held against the state provided such rights could be justified in terms of 'an acknowledged social good'.[58] Green had, for the most part, seen this as implying a duty to obey the law, since 'the public interest' had a greater concern with obedience to the law 'than in the exercise of those powers by individuals or classes which the objectionable laws unfairly withhold'. Only in extreme cases, such as slavery, would the rights of the individual override these 'objectionable laws'. Then violation of the law would not only be in the interests of the violators but in accordance with 'the general sense of right on which the general observance of law depends being represented by it, there is no danger of its making a breach in the law-abiding habits of the people'.[59]

However, Scarman felt that no matter what the position of the black minorities in British society, there could be no condolence of breaking the law; indeed, society's very survival was at stake:

All those who in the course of the disorders in Brixton and elsewhere engaged in violence against the police were guilty of grave criminal offences, which society, if it is to survive, cannot condone. Sympathy for, and understanding of, the plight of young black people, which I would expect to find in Britain now that the facts are widely known, are a good reason for political, social and economic aid, but they are no reason for releasing young black people from the responsibilities for public order which they share with the rest of us – and with the police.[60]

The wider public interest, as Green would put it, in the maintenance of the law thus outweighed the minority interests of the black people who attacked the police. Furthermore, by stressing the 'sympathy...and understanding' for 'the plight' of young black people from the rest of British society, Scarman refuted black claims for rights against the state in terms of a wider public good. The *Report* specifically denied that there were structures of institutional racism against which black people had to contend, though it did concede that 'discriminatory and hostile behaviour on racial grounds' was exhibited in a number of fields, including employment. However, this did not mean that British institutions were racist:

If by that is meant that it is a society which knowingly, as a matter of policy, discriminates against black people, I reject the allegation. If, however, the suggestion being made is that practices may be adopted by public bodies as well as private individuals which are unwittingly discriminatory against black people, then this is an allegation which deserves serious consideration, and, where proved, swift remedy.[61]

There was, accordingly, no rationale for black people to break the law on the same grounds that Green had justified slaves breaking the law, that is, according to a 'general sense of right'. Britain was not institutionally racist and there was in existence, Scarman believed, a level of public understanding of the black 'plight' which resembled Green's conception of public duty in the fulfilment of the ideal of citizenship.

Significantly, in Scarman's argument the notion of a common citizenship is missing and the thrust of the *Report* raises the issue of whether the older notion of equal citizenship rights is being superseded by a more restricted notion of communal rights and relationships. Green's conception of citizenship and its linkage to the 'common good' was based on the ideal of the individual's rights and duties. These may not always have been seen in terms of the state, for the individual may only have been concerned with specifically local rights for himself and his family as against those of his neighbours, but they were still distinctly individual ones. Scarman, however, saw the issues raised by the disturbances in terms of 'black people' and 'the black community', issues which often became defined in terms of their explicit characteristics of 'insecurity' and 'anxieties and frustrations' by people who 'live on the street'.[62]

Anne Beezer and Martin Barker have shown that Scarman employs the "community" notion in a variety of different senses, ranging from the "community" at the national level, a range of geographical meanings in terms of particular inner city communities, to more restricted ethnic minority communities based on distinct cultural and religious traditions such as "the Asian community" of Southall.[63] Taken to its logical extreme, Beezer and Barker have concluded, the Scarman discourse can be rooted in a 'new racism' that seeks to justify the professionalism of police power in terms of maintaining order over communities now seen as 'closed, homogeneous totalities, founded on an unreasoned sense of belonging'.[64] By the same token, British nationalism is also justified in the same exclusive sense of a 'community', founded not simply on 'traditions' but on 'a very hard and positive centre'. Such a changing discourse may thus herald the end of the older liberal citizenship concept in an era of declining political consensus and an attack by the government on many aspects of the post-war welfare state and local government.[65]

Beezer and Barker's analysis imposes on Scarman, however, a degree of ideological cohesiveness which is not revealed by a scrutiny of the text. There is no consistent employment of the "communal" notion in either the manner of Enoch Powell's speeches or those of the small group of right-wing Conservative MPs such as John Stokes and Ivor Stanbrook.[66] The "community" in Brixton is not defined in terms of an ethnically exclusive communalism, for Scarman also noted 'the vigour and liveliness of its multi-racial society'.[67] The *Report's* conclusions, too, are considerably open-ended. A general recommendation is made 'to involve not just black people, but all the community, both nationally and locally, in a better directed response to these problems. It is essential that people are encouraged to secure a stake in, feel a pride in, and have a sense of responsibility for their own area.'[68] This is to some considerable degree different from the exclusive communalism involving a definition of the British nation that has been articulated by some figures on the right.

The Scarman Report should be seen as in part a defensive measure, geared to restating traditional liberal political values at a time when there has been a resurgence of political thought seeking to legitimate state power through national ideals. John Casey, for instance, has urged the creation of a new moral *Sittlichkeit* in terms of an historic English patriotism. Echoing arguments from the 1920s, he has seen the 'historic community' of England as antipathetic to the liberal multiracial ideal. The 'sudden and recent entry' of black immigrants leads to a separate community based on race and colour, giving them 'a sense of identity and interests different (in their eyes) from that of the majority'. Such a separate community is 'structurally likely to be at odds with English civilisation' and the central imperatives behind English patriotism of 'continuity of institutions, shared experience, language, customs, kinship'.[69] A policy of repatriation is thus necessary to protect the tradition of English nationhood which, like Ernest Barker in 1927, Casey sees as threatened through uncontrolled immigration.[70]

While these arguments, expressed in *The Salisbury Review*, have so far had little direct effect on the actual course of government policy, they do represent a coherent attempt to shift the climate of political thought on the right into a nationalist direction. Anthony Flew, however, has recently argued in the same journal for an assimilationist ideal similar to liberal discourse in the early stages of immigration in the 1950s.[71] Scarman has warned that this political argument on the right would lead to a tough law and order campaign, linking crime with unemployed, and especially black, youth, and would ultimately result in a new Riot Act.[72] His more low-key approach, suggesting a new code of police conduct ensuring that the police are 'the servants of the community', was part of a wider social engineering vision, involving the redesigning of local inner city communities in which 'the law and order implications of environmental and social planning' were taken into account at an early stage. These more locally-based recommendations Scarman saw as a means of avoiding a centralised process of state control of law and order.[73]

Since the publication of the *Report*, Scarman has continued to emphasise the positive role of the law both in promoting individual and collective rights as well as resisting the power of the state, though this has sometimes been couched in coded language. While major constitutional changes involving a written constitution and a bill of rights are not on the current political agenda, Scarman has concentrated on the less ambitious theme of the judicial review of executive action through which positive rights could be developed for minorities. Whereas Green's political emphasis was on the rights of the individual secured against the Austinian notion of untrammelled state sovereignty, Scarman has chosen to concentrate on the legal dimensions. This is in part a consequence of his legal perspective as a High Court judge, but it is also a product of the contemporary political fragility of the liberal pluralist model. Whilst Green could reflect a more general Victorian confidence in securing for the individual greater political rights vis-à-vis the state within a framework of ethical obedience to the structures of governmental authority, the same cannot be said for the post-war models of political pluralism. They have exhibited a tendency to fragmentation and division in the states in which they have been tried. For Scarman, therefore, the general 'toleration' in which minorities are secured positive rights is partly directed towards ensuring that ethnicity as such does not become a salient unit of political mobilisation:

If that goodwill is there and if we develop the toleration that I have been indicating, it may never be necessary for the new minorities themselves to form political parties, they can join other political parties, of which other ethnic groups are members and act politically in the homogeneous way which we have understood in our country for a very long time.[74]

This emphasis on the law itself leads by a roundabout way back to the issue of a major constitutional transformation, since the challenge of securing rights through the legal process means that:

The judges today face a challenge greater than any faced by English judges since the seventeenth century. The judges of the House of Stewart failed to master the divine right of the Kings and the result of that was civil war. Let us hope that the judges of the House of Windsor can impose restraints upon majority action at all levels to relieve poverty, disadvantage, hopelessness and despair. Unless this is done, our plural society will fall apart. If it **is** *done, then our plural society will be the best of all societies, one and many at the same time.*[75]

While this bears some resemblance to the pluralist tradition in English political thought in recognising the authority of the state to regulate group activities, Scarman has placed less emphasis than the earlier pluralists on the rights of groups to regulate their own internal activities because of the law and order dimension of inner city planning and community development.[76] At the level of cultural and religious differences, Scarman has not consistently supported the rights of groups to resist pressures towards uniformity and has cited the case of the House of Lords reversing a decision of the Court of Appeal against the right of a Sikh boy to wear a turban at school. The Lords' decision, under the 1976 Race Relations Act, Scarman considered an 'interesting illustration of how one individual's freedom of choice was limited in order that a member of a minority group could exercise a positive right recognised by the law', thus indicating that positive rights can 'degenerate into a system of burdensome privileges'.[77] It is clear that Scarman's pluralism is a guarded and cautious one which, while seeking to check the powers and pressures of the majority community in Britain by moving beyond the old *laissez faire* approach through common law, is nevertheless keen to defuse ethnic minority pressures towards political mobilisation on communal grounds. Though generally favourable to an unhampered cultural expression by ethnic minority groups, Scarman is concerned that these should not conflict with the traditional rights of individuals secured under the mainstream liberal interpretation of the law.

Over a century separates the writings of T H Green and Lord Scarman, during which time the philosophical domination of informed political debate in Britain has sharply declined. As an example of a philosopher turned politician, who D G Ritchie saw as 'apt to take certain phrases more seriously than other men',[78] Green was a significant figure in the reformulation of functions of the Victorian state and the rights and duties which accompanied equal citizenship and the promotion of a 'common good'. The clarification of the state functions and the manner in which political obligation can be secured left a lasting legacy on the tradition of British thought; a tradition which, in the twentieth century, has tended to live off the capital of its Victorian forbears whilst being seduced periodically by the glittering but ephemeral charms of the younger discipline of sociology. One item in the somewhat tattered wardrobe of this political tradition has remained generally unchanged, however, namely the emphasis on cultural homogeneity and patriotism. Despite some moves towards a more pluralist theory of corporate rights, the defeat of guild socialism after the First World War and the rise of Fabianism and administrative centralism behind the social democratic consensus of the 1930s and 1940s left these issues unchallenged. In one respect, Green's hope that there would be a general evolutionary development in rights in relationship to successive forms of community, from family to clan to nation, have by no means been realised.[79]

Political theory has, furthermore, been left ill-equipped to cope with demands for the definition of new political rights and duties in the more ethnically diverse society of recent years. Substantial evidence for this emerged in the debate surrounding *The Scarman Report*. As the focus of discussion has shifted away from equal citizenship rights within a culturally homogeneous society towards a more pluralistic conception of minority group rights, there has arisen an emphasis upon the power of the courts and the decision of judges. This has arisen both from a more general crisis of state legitimacy and the failure of specific bodies established to deal with racial discrimination, such as the Commission for Racial Equality, to have the same legitimacy as the courts of law. Scarman has sought to break from the assumptions of national homogeneity that have underpinned the liberal conception of political rights against the state stretching back to least to Green, though it is by no means clear that there has yet emerged an alternative tradition of liberal political legitimacy. This can in part be explained by the tradition of pluralism in British political thought, which has generally emphasised the rights of groups to separate cultural fulfilment, whilst the American pluralist tradition has recognised the rights of groups to pressurise government to perform some substantive good.[80] The development of English liberal thought on ethnic minority group rights is thus bound up with the wider issue of a new constitutional settlement and a bill of rights guaranteeing the rights both of individuals and minorities. When these reforms have been achieved the liberal tradition may then be strong enough to assert the positive rights of ethnic groups against the state in a manner similar to the Greenian assertion of positive individual rights linked to a 'common good'.

NOTES

1. Mike Phillips, "Danger! Astrologers at work: a critical note on the orthodoxy of race relations research", *Community Development Journal*, 18, 3 (1983), pp. 265-9.
2. L S Lustgarten, "Liberty in a Culturally Plural Society" in A Phillips Griffiths (ed), *Of Liberty*, CUP, Cambridge, 1983, p. 91. See also Trevor Smith, "The British Science of British Politics", PSA Conference Paper, University of Manchester, 16-18 April 1985, p. 5.
3. See, for example, Zig Layton Henry, *The Politics of Race in Britain*, Allen and Unwin, London, 1984, and John Benyon (ed), *Scarman and After*, Pergamon Press, Oxford, 1984.
4. Jurgen Habermas, *Legitimation Crisis*, Heinemann, London, 1979, p. 48.
5. H Stuart Hughes, *Consciousness and Society*, Paladin, London, 1974.
6. Stefan Collini, "Sociology and Idealism in Britain, 1880-1920", *European Journal of Sociology*, 19, 1978, pp. 3-50. Stefan Collini, Donald Winch and John Burrow, *That Noble Science of Politics*, CUP, London, 1983, pp. 3-21. For a plea for a return to a more restricted neo-Victorian politics see Arianna Stassinopoulos, *The Other Revolution*, Michael Joseph, London, 1978.
7. Craig Jenks, "T H Green, the Oxford Philosophy of Duty and the English Middle Class", *British Journal of Sociology*, 28, 4 (December 1977), p. 495.
8. *Ibid.*, Melvin Richter, *The Politics of Conscience: T H Green and his Age*, Weidenfeld and Nicolson, London, 1964.
9. D G Ritchie, "The Political Philosophy of the Late Thomas Hill Green", *The Contemporary Review*, 51, June 1887, pp. 841-51, reproduced in *The Principles of State Interference*, George Allen and Co., London, 1891, pp. 127-51.
10. Richter, *op. cit.*, p. 271.
11. Thomas Hill Green, *Lectures on the Principles of Political Obligation*, Longmans Green and Co., London, 1911, p. 44.
12. *Ibid.*, p. 45.
13. *Ibid.*, p. 98.
14. *Ibid.*, p. 103.
15. *Ibid.*, p. 48.
16. *Ibid.*, p. 126.
17. Habermas, *op. cit.*, p. 111.
18. *Ibid.*, p. 113.
19. Raymond Plant, "Jurgen Habermas and the idea of Legitimation Crisis", unpublished paper, University of Southampton, 1982.
20. Green, *op. cit.*, p. 129.
21. Richter, *op. cit.*, pp. 346-8 and *passim*.
22. Green, *op. cit.*, p. 127.
23. Michael Freeden, "Biological and Evolutionary Roots of the New Liberalism in England", *Political Theory*, 4, 4 (November 1976), pp. 471-90.
24. T H Marshall, "Citizenship and Social Class" in *Citizenship and Social Class and Other Essays*, CUP, Cambridge, 1950, pp. 1-85. Keith Middlemas, *Politics in Industrial Society*, André Deutsch, London, 1979.
25. Robert Pearson and Geraint Williams, *Political Thought and Public Policy*, Longman, London and New York, 1984, pp. 147-8; Green, *op. cit.*, p. 148.
26. Pearson and Williams, *op. cit.*, p. 148.
27. L T Hobhouse, *The Elements of Social Justice*, Allen and Unwin, London, 1922, p. 41. See also Peter Weiler, "The New Liberalism of L. T. Hobhouse", *Victorian Studies*, December 1972, pp. 141-61.
28. Weiler, *op. cit*: Noel Annan, *The Curious Strength of Positivism in English Political Thought*, OUP, London, 1959; Reba N Soffer, "Why Do Disciplines Fail? The Strange Case of British Sociology", *English Historical Review*, CCCLXXXV (October 1982), pp. 767-802.
29. Green, *op. cit.*, p. 130.

30. Richter, *op. cit.*, pp. 354-5.

31. Green, *op. cit.*, pp. 130.

32. For the religious basis of the western nationalist conception see the essay by Benedict Anderson, *Imagined Communities*, Verso, London, 1983.

33. Milton M Gordan, *Assimilation in American Life: The Role of Race, Religion and National Groups*, OUP, New York, 1964, esp. pp. 133-59; F H Matthews, "The Revolt Against Americanism", *The Canadian Review of American Studies*, I.I (Spring 1970), pp. 4-31. For British links with American Progressivism see Melvyn Stokes, "American Progressives and the European Left", *American Studies*, 17, 1 (April 1983), pp. 5-28.

34. Paul B Rich, "Philanthropic Racism: The Liverpool University Settlement, the Anti-Slavery Society and the issue of 'half caste' children, 1919-1951", *Immigrants and Minorities*, 3, 1 (March 1984), pp. 69-88.

35. John Morrow, "Liberalism and British Idealistic Political Philosophy: A Reassessment", *History of Political Thought*, 5, 1 (Spring 1984), pp. 91-108; Stefan Collini, "Hobhouse, Bosanquet and the State: Philosophical Idealism and Political Argument in England, 1880-1918," *Past and Present*, 72 (1976), pp. 86-111.

36. W H Greenleaf, "Laski and British Socialism", *History of Political Thought*, 11, 3 (Winter 1981), pp. 573-91.

37. W H Hadow, *Citizenship*, Clarendon Press, Oxford, 1923, p. 118.

38. *Ibid.*, p. 91.

39. Ernest Barker, *National Character*, Methuen, London, 1927, p. 47.

40. Lustgarten, *op. cit.*, p. 96. See also David Nicholls, *The Pluralist State*, Macmillan, London, 1975.

41. Middlemas, *op. cit.*, pp. 214-43; David Howell, *British Social Democracy*, Croom Helm, London, 1976, esp. pp. 85-106. For the intellectual roots behind the nationalism of the Second World War see Geoff Hurd, *National Fictions: World War Two in British Films and Television*, London, BFI, 1984.

42. Lord Scarman, *Report on The Red Lion Square Disorder of 15 June 1974*, Cmnd 5919, HMSO, London, 1975.

43. Sir Leslie Scarman, "Opening Remarks" in *English Law and Social Policy: A Symposium based on Sir Leslie Scarman's 1974 Hamlyn Lectures*, Centre for Studies in Social Policy, London, 1975, p. 7.

44. Sir Leslie Scarman, *Codification and Judge Made Law*, University of Birmingham, 1966, p. 5; see also Sir Leslie Scarman, *A Code of English Law?*, University of Hull, 1966.

45. *Codification and Judge Made Law*, p. 17.

46. Sir Leslie Scarman, *English Law – The New Dimension*, Stewart and Son, London, 1974, p. 15.

47. *Ibid.*, pp. 81-2.

48. *English Law and Social Policy*, pp. 34-5.

49. *Ibid.*, p. 36.

50. Rt Hon Lord Scarman, *Minority Rights in a Plural Society*, Annual Lecture Minority Rights Group, Minority Rights Group, London, 1977, pp. 2, 5.

51. *Ibid.*, p. 5.

52. *Ibid.*, p. 6.

53. *Ibid.*, p. 7. For the race relations sociologist John Rex, this argument for positive discrimination was premature in a context of continuing 'systematic old fashioned negative discrimination' for 'so long as that exists, it is misleading and dangerous and damaging to minorities to engage in campaigns allegedly on their behalf calling for positive discrimination,' John Rex, *Race, Law and Politics*, Address to the British Sociological Association, 11 April 1979, p. 7. Scarman has argued, though, that basic civil rights under the law have already been achieved for black minorities in Britain, even in the absence of a civil rights struggle as occurred in the United States in the 1950s and early 1960s.

54. *Ibid.*, pp. 7-8.

55. Lord Scarman, *The Scarman Report: The Brixton Disorders, 10-12 April 1981*, 4, 98,

HMSO, London, 1981, and Penguin Books, Harmondsworth, 1982, cited in John Clare, "Eyewitnesses in Brixton" in Benyon, *op. cit.*, p. 47.

56. Dilip Hiro, *Black British, White British*, Penguin Books, Harmondsworth, 1973, pp. 322-3.
57. *The Scarman Report*, p. 35.
58. Green, *op. cit.*, p. 148.
59. *Ibid.*, pp. 150-1.
60. *The Scarman Report, p. 34.*
61. *Ibid.*, p. 28.
62. *Ibid.*, pp. 35-6.
63. Anne Beezer and Martin Barker, "An Inquiry into Lord Scarman on Brixton: Report on a Disorder", paper presented to the Conference on Anglo-Saxon Racial Attitudes, c 1870-1970, Westhill College, Birmingham, September 1982, pp. 7-8.
64. *Ibid.*, p. 19. See also Martin Barker, *The New Racism*, Junction Books, London, 1981; David Edgar, "Bitter Harvest", *New Socialist*, September/October 1983, p.22.
65. *Ibid.*, p. 18.
66. For an analysis of this Conservative ideology see Paul B Rich, "Conservative Ideology and Race in Modern British Politics" in Zig Layton Henry and Paul B Rich (eds), *Race, Government and Politics in Britain*, The Macmillan Press, London and Basingstoke, 1986, pp. 45-72.
67. *The Scarman Report*, p. 34.
68. *Ibid.*, p. 175.
69. John Casey, "One Nation: the Politics of Race", *The Salisbury Review*, I, Autumn 1981, p. 26.
70. *Ibid.*, p. 25.
71. Peter Riddell, *The Thatcher Government*, Martin Robertson, Oxford, 1983, pp. 54-5. Anthony Flew, "The Race Relations Industry", *The Salisbury Review*, Winter 1984, p. 25.
72. Lord Scarman, "Postscript" in Benyon, *op. cit.*, p. 260.
73. *The Scarman Report*, p. 160.
74. Lord Scarman, *Toleration and the Law*, University of York, 1983, p. 12.
75. *Ibid.*, p. 13.
76. Lustgarten, *op. cit.*, p. 94.
77. *Toleration and the Law*, p. 9.
78. Ritchie, *op. cit.*
79. John Rodman, "What is Living and What is Dead in the Political Philosophy of T H Green?", *Western Political Quarterly*, 26, 3 (September 1973), p. 583.
80. Nicholls, *op. cit.*, p. 118.

INDEX

About Hansib Publishing

Hansib Publishing Limited is Britain's largest independent publisher specialising in issues concerning the Caribbean, African and Asian communities.

Founded in 1971, with *Westindian Digest*, a monthly magazine, Hansib has expanded to become an internationally reputed, Third World oriented publisher of books, periodicals and newspapers with over fifty titles that cover subjects as diverse as literature, history, travel, the arts, sport, children's books and socio-political reference books. Its weekly newspapers, *Caribbean Times (incorporating African Times)* and *Asian Times*, are amongst Britain's most authoritative and campaigning publications. While radical in their views, they are highly respected and their combined readership forms a powerful platform for the visible minority communties in Britain.

National and international in its scope and publishing activities, Hansib's books and publications are useful for the general reader, the student, the researcher and expert alike. Hansib strives to make available information that would otherwise remain inaccessible to the widest possible reading public.

Other titles by Hansib Publishing

Political/Historical

RASTA AND RESISTANCE - From Marcus Garvey to Walter Rodney. By Dr Horace Campbell. Tracing the cultural, political and spiritual sources of this movement of resistance, highlighting the quest for change among an oppressed people. Paperback £8.95

THE GREAT MARCUS GARVEY. By Liz Mackie. The biography of one of the great black leaders of the twentieth century, a powerful influence on the development of black pride and black power in America and the Caribbean, and on Pan-Africanism in general. Paperback £4.95

OUR STORY - A Handbook of African History and Contemporary Issues. Edited by Akyaaba Addai-Sebbo and Ansel Wong. A collection of speeches delivered in London by distinguished Pan-African scholars and activists on the themes of African history, Africa's contribution to world science and civilisation and the way forward. Paperback £7.95

AFRICAN HISTORY - an Illustrated Handbook. By Earl Sweeting and Lez Edmond. An ideal pamphlet for young people who wish to know about Africa's ancient heritage and its immense contributions to world civilisation. Paperback £1.50

SPEECHES BY ERROL BARROW. Edited by Yussuff Haniff. A collection of speeches made by the late Barbadian Prime Minister, showing Barrow as a true Caribbean man, fighting for the region's independent identity. This book is noe recommended reading in most Barbadian schools. Hardback £10.95

HOGARTH, WALPOLE AND COMMERCIAL BRITAIN. By Dr David Dabydeen. Dr Dabydeen's first book on William Hogarth was widely acclaimed as a pioneering work on English art and social history. This book, his second on this subject, is an analysis of Hogarth's radical political critique of corruption in works like A Harlot's Progress and A Rake's Progress. Hardback £15.95

FORBIDDEN FREEDOM - The Story of British Guiana. By Dr. Cheddi Jagan. A classic document of anti-colonialist and anti-imperialist struggle from one of the veteran freedom leaders of the Third World. Paperback £6.00

A NEW SYSTEM OF SLAVERY - The Export of Indian Labour Overseas 1830-1920. By Hugh Tinker. The first comprehensive historical survey of a hitherto neglected and only partially known migration- the export of Indians to supply the labour needed in producing plantation crops all over the world. Paperback £11.99

INDIA IN THE CARIBBEAN. Edited by Dr David Dabydeen and Dr Brinsley Samaroo. A collection of essays, poems and prose by leading Indo-Caribbean scholars and writers, on East Indian history and culture in the Caribbean. Paperback £8.95. Hardback £11.95

BENEVOLENT NEUTRALITY - Indian Government Policy and Labour Migration to British Guiana 1854-1884. By Dr Basdeo Mangru. A detailed, scholarly essay on Indian migration, which, for the first time, studies the Indian background of the indentured labourers and explains the economic, political and cultural factors which encouraged migration. Hardback £12.95

PASSION AND EXILE. By Frank Birbalsingh. A wide ranging collection of essays that offer an illuminating commentary on the literary and social history of the English speaking Caribbean. Paperback £7.95

A LIGHT IN THE DARK TUNNEL. By Ashton Gibson with Charles Lewis. Described as "an invaluable contribution to race relations", this book responds to the urgency felt by professionals, doctors, social workers and probation officers to understand the needs of the Westindian community and their children. Paperback £4.95

THE STATE OF BLACK BRITAIN. By Dr Aaron Haynes. This book is a major statement on the effects of public policy on black people in Britain and is an important reference source for practitioners, professionals and students seeking an understanding of the realities of the implications of various policies for black families. Paperback £3.75. Hardback £5.95

THE UNEQUAL STRUGGLE. By Ashton Gibson with Jocelyn Barrow. A book aimed at examining the reasons behind the poor performers of Westindian children in British schools. Paperback £6.95

RACISM AWARENESS TRAINING - A Critique. Based on a conference organised by the former London Strategic Policy Unit, (LSPU) this book takes a critical look at the policy of Racism Awareness Training (RAT) which has been imported from the United States as a supposed panacea for racism, prejudice and discrimination. Paperback £2.50

THE IDEOLOGY OF RACISM. By Samuel Kennedy Yeboah. A comprehensive and well-researched study of the history of peoples from the African diaspora, listing outstanding achievements in the fields of arts, science and technology. Paperback £8.95

Biographaphic

BARRISTER FOR THE DEFENCE. By Rudy Narayan. This book is not so much intended to be critical of the standards of advocacy at the English Bar as to seek to improve the quality of advocacy in the criminal courts. Paperback £6.95

INSEPARABLE HUMANITY. Inseparable Humanity is an anthology of reflections by one of the world's leading thinkers, Shridath S Ramphal - the former Commonwealth Secretary-General. Hardback £14.95

FROM WHERE i STAND. By Roy Sawh. A moving autobiography from one of Britain's leading black spokesmen and a notable orator at Speaker's Corner, Hyde Park. This book is unique in being the first Indo-Caribbean autobiography published in Britain. Paperback £5.95

Fiction

KING OF THE CARNIVAL AND OTHER STORIES. By Willi Chen. A unique collection of short stories from the Caribbean, capturing the violence, trickery, pathos and racial comedy of Trinidadian society. Paperback £5.95

THE OPEN PRISON. A novel by Angus Richmond. The story of Angela, a sensitive and disturbed child, growing up on the estate of her white guardian in British Guiana, is slowly and painfully awakened to a society in turmoil, in which both black and white are struggling to reassert their roles during the First World War. Paperback £4.95

Reference/Critique

A READER'S GUIDE TO WEST INDIAN AND BLACK BRITISH LITERATURE. By Dr David Dabydeen and Dr Nana Wilson-Tagoe. An invaluable aid to teachers seeking to expand and deepen the literature curriculum. Specially prepared for the G.C.S.E. curriculum, the book is a lucid introduction to Westindian and Black British literature. Paperback £6.95

THE WEB OF TRADITION: USES OF ALLUSION IN V.S. NAIPAUL'S FICTION. By Dr John Thieme. An exciting study of one of the Caribbean's major and most controversial novelists, V.S. Naipaul, who has won several of the world's literary prizes including the Booker Prize. Paperback £6.95

THIRD WORLD IMPACT - 8th Edition. Edited by Arif Ali. The only fully comprehensive work of reference regarding the presence of the visible minorities in all spheres of British life. It includes an invaluable reference section with the biographies of well over 1,000 prominent members of the minority communities. Hardback £15.95

ETHNIC MINORITIES DIRECTORY. The Ethnic Minorities (EM) Directory lists over 20,000 Caribbean, African and Asian business and social organisations in Britain and is to date the only directory of its kind available. Paperback £40.00

Music

THE REGGAE FILES. By Gordon C. A collection of interviews with reggae superstars from Jamaica and Britain who speak about the influence of Jamaican politics, Rastafarian ideas and the black British experience on the creation of their music. Paperback £6.95

Travel

ANTIGUA & BARBUDA - A Little Bit of Paradise (2nd revised edition). This edition explores in a highly informative and sensitively illustrated way, the history of these idyllic islands form the emergence of the Siboney (stone people) 4,000 years ago to the present day democracy, enjoying one of the highest standards of living in the Caribbean. Hardback £25.00

DOMINICA - Nature Island Island of the Caribbean. This 320 page book, richly illustrated in full colour, captures the little known beauty of this Caribbean country and offers a brief account of its sometimes turbulent history and rich culture. Hardback £19.95

Sport

INDO-WESTINDIAN CRICKET. By Professor Frank Birbalsingh and Clem Shiwcharan. Two brilliant essays on Westindian cricket by two of the region's leading cultural historians. They highlight the sheer genius of cricketers like Kanhai, Kallicharan and Ramadhin, discussing technique and craftsmanship and also the political and cultural contexts in which their game is located. Hardback £7.95

100 GREAT WESTINDIAN TEST CRICKETERS. By Bridgette Lawrence with Reg Scarlett. Through the eyes of the leading players of the last 60 years, Bridgette Lawrence traces the rise of Westindian Test cricket from its beginnings at Lord's in 1928 to the triumphs of the last two decades. Hardback £14.95

DIAMOND JUBILEE OF WESTINDIAN CRICKET 1928-1988. A magazine produced to celebrate 60 years of Westindian cricket, this contains a history of the Westindian cricket team from 1928 with articles on the Captains, the Master Batsmen, the great All-Rounders and other important subjects. Paperback £2.00

Poetry

COOLIE ODYSSEY. By David Dabydeen. This book, Dabydeen's second collection of poetry, probes the experience of diaspora, the journeying from India to the Caribbean then to Britain, dwelling on the dream of romance, the impotence of racial encounter and the metamorphosis of language. Paperback £3.95

GRASSROOTS IN VERSE. An extensive collection of poetry and verse submitted by the readers of Caribbean Times, Asian Times and African Times. Lively, humorous, provocative and thoughtful - feelings experienced by young and old alike. Paperback £6.95

General

THE BOOK OF COMMON SENSE. Compiled by Neil Prendergast. A collection of proverbs and quotations, old and new, bringing to the reader sections on humour, wisdom, life, love marriage, etc. and drawing on the writings of 'many wise people'. Paperback 6.95

ALL ENQUIRIES TO: HANSIB PUBLISHING LIMITED, TOWER HOUSE, 141-149 FONTHILL ROAD, LONDON N4 3HF. TEL: 071-281 1191, FAX: 071:263 9656.